KASHMIR
IN THE
SHADOW OF WAR

KASHMIR
IN THE
SHADOW OF WAR

Regional Rivalries in a
Nuclear Age

Robert G. Wirsing

M.E. Sharpe
Armonk, New York
London, England

Library of Congress Cataloging-in-Publication Data

Wirsing, Robert.
    Kashmir in the shadow of war: regional rivalries in a nuclear age / Robert G. Wirsing.
       p. cm.
    Includes bibliographical references and index.
    ISBN 0-7656-1089-2 (hc. : alk. paper) ISBN 0-7656-1090-6 (pbk. : alk. paper)
      1. Jammu and Kashmir (India)—Politics and government. 2. Nuclear warfare.
3. Nuclear weapons—India. 4. Nuclear weapons—Pakistan. 5. Pakistan—Foreign
relations—India. 6. Indian—Foreign relations—Pakistan. I. Title.

DS485.K27 W58 2002
954'.605—dc21

                                          2002030926

Printed in the United States of America

The paper used in this publication meets the minimum requirements of
American National Standard for Information Sciences
Permanence of Paper for Printed Library Materials,
ANSI Z 39.48-1984.

BM (c) 10 9 8 7 6 5 4 3 2
BM (p) 10 9 8 7 6 5 4 3

Preface

The writing of this book, from initial conception to finishing touches, sprawled over six years. The foundations were laid in 1996 in the course of field-research visits to India and Pakistan. These visits were supported by timely and generous grants from the United States Institute of Peace, the American Institute of Pakistan Studies, and the Walker Institute of International Studies at the University of South Carolina. To these organizations (and not least for the patience exhibited!), I am profoundly grateful.

Work on the book began to take more definite form over the next several years, aided to no small extent by my collaboration in that period with the Kashmir Study Group. Under the auspices of this group, I first joined other members in conducting team interviews in India and Pakistan of scores of Indians, Pakistanis, and Kashmiris. Later I participated in team-written assessments of our findings. I was no stranger to either thinking or writing about the Kashmir dispute, but the experience of doing these things collectively—as a member of a team of fully accomplished area experts with their own finely tuned perspectives on the problem—was especially valuable to the development of this book. For making my collaboration with the group as intellectually rewarding as it turned out to be (and also for their tolerance of my refusal, still visible in the pages of this book, to concede on every point), I thank the group's members and especially its founder, Farooq Kathwari.

It hardly requires pointing out that the South Asian region did not remain still while I worked on my book. First came the nuclear tests of May 1998, then (all in 1999) the Lahore Summit between Prime Minister Atal Bihari Vajpayee of India and Prime Minister Nawaz Sharif of Pakistan, the mini-war at Kargil, the Washington Summit between President Bill Clinton and Prime Minister Nawaz Sharif, and the military coup in Pakistan that toppled Sharif. The year 2000 brought its own blizzard of developments, a couple of abortive attempts at a ceasefire in Kashmir among them. The Agra Summit in July 2001 briefly aroused hopes that a new era was dawning in India-Pakistan relations. Whatever remained of those hopes was utterly dashed to pieces, however, by the traumatic events of 2001—the toppling of the Taliban regime in Afghanistan, the terrorist attack on the Indian parliament building, and the subsequent massive mobilization of Indian and Pakistani forces on their common border—that followed in the region in the wake of September 11, 2001. To put it mildly, these constant upheavals all forced adjustments not only in the argument I was making but also in my writing schedule. Readers will have to judge for themselves, of course, but the elongated and somewhat tortured history of the book's writing forced me to reconsider its design and purpose more than once, and thus may have been a blessing in disguise.

For their reading of one or more chapters of the book (and for remarkably helpful comments), I want to give special thanks to Rodney W. Jones and Martijn van Beek. A number of anonymous reviewers of the entire manuscript also deserve thanks for their thoughtful observations and suggestions. Philip Schwartzberg of Meridian Mapping proved wonderfully adept, as always, in preparing maps of religious and linguistic distribution in Jammu and Kashmir State. I want to express appreciation to Irina Burns, my editor at M.E. Sharpe, Inc., and to her gifted associates who, with meticulous care and admirable skill, magically transformed a manuscript into a book.

To the many Indians, Pakistanis, and Kashmiris who have unselfishly and trustingly shared with me their knowledge of the Kashmir dispute in all its ramifications, I express here my everlasting gratitude. They will want to take issue, naturally, with some of my conclusions, but they may rest assured that I rarely drew a conclusion without reflecting, often at great length, on what they told me.

Former colleagues and students at the University of South Carolina deserve warm thanks for many years of stimulating discussion and debate of the issues dealt with in the book. For sustaining a wonderfully congenial, intellectually challenging, and supportive working environment, I express equally warm thanks to Lt. General (retd.) H.C. Stackpole, president of the Asia-Pacific Center for Security Studies in Honolulu, as well as to the faculty and staff of the center where I have had the good fortune to work since July 2000.

The judgments expressed in this book are of course entirely my own and should not be attributed to the Asia-Pacific Center for Security Studies, the Department of Defense, or the United States Government.

Finally, for loving support and intellectual companionship that has grown deeper with every passing year, I wish to give warmest thanks of all to my wife, Nancy.

I dedicate this book to my parents, Albert J. and Marie A. Wirsing, whose memory I cherish.

Honolulu, Hawaii, July 2002
R.G.W.

To the memory of my parents

Table of Contents

KASHMIR
IN THE
SHADOW OF WAR

Introduction

The question of what to make of the extraordinarily fluid political-military situation in Asia today has bedeviled policymakers in numerous world capitals with increasing persistence since the demise of the Cold War. Did the Soviet Union's precipitous decline at the end of the twentieth century presage the blossoming of a unipolar world at the onset of the twenty-first in which the United States would exercise for an indefinite time unrivaled hegemonic power? Or was the Soviet Union's collapse less an occasion for American triumphalism than a deceptive distraction from the more elemental truth that a momentous shift in global power was under way, that new centers of power were rising with inexorable force in Asia, and that, when the shift was concluded, we would likely be living in a much more Asia-centric and multipolar world? If such a world were actually developing, who would be the main contenders in it? Which of them would be allies? And which of them enemies? Especially in China's case, where the country's huge size and mounting economic and military capabilities naturally command the widest possible audience and make the answers to these questions far from academic, the assessment of its political ambitions and future potential increasingly topped foreign office agendas (giving birth to legions of China-watchers reminiscent of the now vanished breed of Kremlinologists that once monitored the minutia of the Soviet Union's Communist overlords). But in India's case, too—albeit with a reduced sense of urgency—many foreign office agendas were beginning to give more attention than had been customary to its leaders' ambitions and to the country's ability to support them. India was rising, many agreed, and it was now also a country to be reckoned with.

Reckoning with India inescapably entailed reckoning also with Pakistan. Like India, it was a large state, bound soon to be the world's fifth most populous country. It shared a lengthy border with India, much of it contested. Having fought three wars with India since the two of them gained independence from Britain in 1947 and having converted itself, at great social cost, into a formidable military power—one possessing nuclear weapons—Pakistan couldn't simply be written off. Neither, however, was reckoning with Pakistan likely to be free of reservations. Few Asian states, in fact, had begun the twenty-first century with a shakier economy. And few had begun it more heavily burdened with an international reputation—whether or not deserved—for political and diplomatic failure. Even its friends chafed at some of its actions. After all, its military leaders had overthrown a duly elected civilian prime minister, locked him up in prison, and then, in what seemed to most a mockery of justice, tried and convicted him of an assortment of crimes; for over six years, they had backed a notoriously maverick Taliban regime in Afghanistan that struck just about everyone as medieval and not a few, in the aftermath of the devastating terrorist suicide assaults on the World Trade Center and the Pentagon, as also evil; they were committed to a nuclear weaponization program that, like India's, paid scant heed to global nonproliferation norms; and they seemed unable or unwilling to curb what India relentlessly insisted were acts of terrorism in Indian Kashmir. Indeed, Pakistan's drop over the past decade or so from favored Cold War client to near-pariah status in the American strategic accounts book had been just as swift and nearly as calamitous for its leaders' aspirations as had been the crumbling of the Soviet Union's superpower standing. There were even some observers—fewer now, very likely, than existed before Pakistan's painful decision in September 2001 to back Washington's global coalition against terrorism—urging that Pakistan be classed with the likes of North Korea, Iran, Iraq, and Libya as a "rogue" state. Many voices could be heard urging at the same time that India replace Pakistan as America's strategic ally in the belly of Asia.

Sooner or later in the process of assessing the likely strategic future of either India or Pakistan, one inevitably confronted the problem of Kashmir. It was the site of two of the three wars fought between India and Pakistan (or three of the four wars if one chooses to class the 1999 Kargil conflict as a war). The region has the dubious distinction of being heralded nowadays a "nuclear flashpoint" and one of the most dangerous spots on earth—a distinction that very few observers would contest in the face of the sudden and massive mobilization of Indian and Pakistani air, sea, and land forces that was ordered in the waning days of 2001 and that continues at the time of this writing. Kashmir draws attention, however, not only because of its obviously menacing characteristics but also because its persistence for well over fifty years as an unresolved issue clouds the world's reckonings—and tarnishes the prestige—of both India and Pakistan. For India, Kashmir is a palpable and embarrassing manifestation of its own huge political shortcomings. It is an open wound, so to speak, whose continued festering inevitably puts in question not only India's democratic but its secular credentials. When it comes to Pakistan, Kashmir is obviously a dangerous and expensive venture, but it is also a colossal diplomatic burden. Keeping the world receptive to Pakistan's historic claim to Kashmir in all the many forums in which Pakistan pursues its bilateral and multilateral agendas has clearly taxed the imaginations, resources, and perseverance of Pakistan's diplomatic envoys more than any of them would be likely to admit. Keeping the world from judging Pakistan's present activities in Kashmir in terms other than those preferred by the Pakistanis themselves has been even more taxing.

This book offers an interpretation of the political-military circumstances prevailing in South Asia since the Indians and Pakistanis conducted back-to-back tests of nuclear explosives in May 1998. The book's focus is relatively narrow—the Kashmir dispute between India and Pakistan; but its purpose—to assist with the reckonings now in progress in regard to South Asia's strategic future—is considerably broader. It is intended to speak to South Asians, upon whose material well-being Kashmir has already had an enormous impact. A no less important audience, however, is in the West, especially in the United States, where strategic decisions now being made in regard to the South Asian region are bound to have momentous and long-term consequences. Finishing touches to the book were made in May 2002, at a moment when the subcontinent seemed on the brink of another India-Pakistan war. Only months earlier Afghanistan's Taliban regime had suffered a crushing military defeat. A few months before that the landmark meeting between Pakistani President Pervez Musharraf and Indian Prime Minister Atal Bihari Vajpayee had taken place at Agra. This was a time when the world's attention was riveted on South Asia, drawn there especially by events in Afghanistan, the site of a massive international manhunt for Osama bin Laden, the reputed mastermind of global terrorism. Emotions were at a fever pitch, and there was an almost frantic reassessment of South Asia policies underway in almost all the major world capitals. The unresolved dispute over Kashmir, a land caught once again in the crosshairs of India-Pakistan rivalry, was a dominant theme in many of these reassessments.

In the writing of this book, I was mindful of the urgent need for impartiality. Kashmir is not a subject that Indian, Pakistani, or Kashmiri writers ordinarily approach with equanimity. Against a background suddenly supercharged with the threat of horrific terrorism and mobilization for war, objective analysis of Kashmir seemed likely to grow even more infrequent. A foreign author on this subject thus has added responsibility, I believe, to examine it dispassionately and through more than a single national lens. I was acutely conscious at the same time, however, of the no less imperative requirement for candor. This book has a point of view, one that I have acquired in over three decades of study of the region. By no stretch of the imagination does it take a neutral position on the key issues associated with the Kashmir dispute. On the contrary, the book is structured as a multifaceted argument. And its argument, which I will shortly synopsize below, is unquestionably out of step with much—indeed, I think with most—that has been written on the topic of Kashmir in recent years. It is also out of step with many of what I take to have been the main premises of U.S. policy toward the South Asian region in recent years. In other words (and with the best of intentions), by being out of step with mainstream views I meant to step (lightly) on many toes.

Each of the book's four substantive chapters focuses on a bloc of issues pertaining to a major dimension of the Kashmir dispute. Chapter 1 takes up the mammoth problem of regional rivalry between India and Pakistan over Kashmir in the novel context (for this region) of overt nuclear weaponization. It surveys the roller-coaster record of India-Pakistan relations since the nuclear tests of May 1998, seeking to extract from this record clues to the probable course in the immediate future of the nuclearized bilateral relationship between the two countries. In this context, the discussion dwells at some length on the motives that underlay Pakistan's Kargil venture in spring 1999 as well as on the implications for the India-Pakistan relationship of subsequent peace initiatives. It also addresses the profoundly important question of the potential impact on this relationship of the counter terrorist war launched in October 2001 by the United States on the Taliban regime in neighboring Afghanistan. Chapter 2 deals with the problem of global intervention in regard to Kashmir in the wake of the nuclear tests. It assesses world reaction to the South Asian region's self-declared nuclear status, focusing in particular on Washington's response to the eruption of fighting over Kargil. The discussion considers the implications of India's remarkable rise in global esteem (and Pakistan's equally remarkable—albeit now reversed—decline). Close scrutiny is given the evolution in this period of Washington's South Asia policy and to its seeming "tilt" in India's direction. The implications of the events of 11 September for this tilt and the subsequent revival of the U.S.-Pakistan strategic alliance are dealt with. Chapter 3 focuses on the knotty but immensely important problem of religious identity as it relates to Kashmir. Its three-fold focus is on (1) religion in Kashmiri cultural identity, (2) religion in Kashmiri separatism, and (3) religion in the state strategies of India and Pakistan toward Kashmir. The contentious matter of linkage between religious identity and terrorism in the context of Kashmir is also considered. Finally, Chapter 4 takes up the problem of conflict resolution, focusing in particular on an assessment of autonomy's probable utility for bringing peace to long-troubled Kashmir. I have been motivated with respect to each chapter by my belief that there is a need to rethink the issues discussed in them, whether the issue happens to be, for instance, the linkage that exists between Kashmir and nuclear deterrence, the virtue in Washington's bid to "decouple" India and Pakistan in its South Asia policies, or the practicality of autonomist solutions when it comes to resolving Kashmir.

The discussion takes advantage of my repeated visits to the region (most recently in May 2002) and of countless discussions I have had over the years with key figures involved with Kashmir in both India and Pakistan. It unhesitatingly criticizes, fairly I hope, the interpretations and arguments put in print by others—professional analysts, scholars, and journalists—on the same topics dealt with in this book. The object was not to demean them but to make as crystal clear as I could my own chosen path through what has become a veritable thicket of arguments. It will be for the reader to decide whether or not I have succeeded at this.

I set forth now in abbreviated form the essentials of the book's argument. I note in advance that there is some risk in this. Reducing the argument to a series of flat, barely qualified statements—stripping away, as it were, the usual buffering, softening, and guarded qualification that goes with extended discussion—may give it an abrupt, blunt, or even simplistic appearance. I take the risk, however, in the interest of clarity and candor. The argument goes like this:

The Problem of Regional Rivalry

• For the most part, the "Kashmir dispute" is not about Kashmir. It is at least not *mainly* about Kashmir. The phrase long ago mutated into an inclusive metaphor or "cover story" for the multifaceted interstate power struggle between India and Pakistan.

• Put in a slightly different way, the Kashmir dispute is as much a symptom as a cause of India-Pakistan rivalry. The rivalry is not Kashmir-dependent. This is disheartening since it means that "the Kashmir dispute" is extremely complicated. It is about far more than a contested piece of territory.

• The Kashmir dispute's "nuclearization"—the product of the region's seemingly inexorable movement up the ladder of nuclear weapons development—is one of the more recent additions to the dispute's composite character. Notwithstanding arguments to the contrary, nuclearization hasn't brought the dispute any nearer to settlement. Neither has it reduced the prospect of war, conventional or nuclear, between India and Pakistan. On the contrary, even if it hasn't actually increased the *prospect* of war, it has unquestionably increased the *dangers* inherent in war. Simply stated, the putative benefits of nuclear deterrence supply no reliable antidote to the Kashmir dispute.

• In principle, the "global war on terrorism" launched in September 2001 in the wake of the terrorist attack on the United States contained some potential for moderating the India-Pakistan rivalry in Kashmir. After all, both these states joined the antiterrorist coalition; and both of them—Pakistan most directly perhaps—contributed materially to the coalition's success in Afghanistan. There was thus the semblance, at least, of a major common cause to unite them. In fact, the unity was transparently shallow. Indians and Pakistanis, when it comes to Kashmir, cling to quite different understandings of the terrorist threat. These understandings spring from local, not global, circumstances. They reflect the two countries' radically antagonistic definitions of the Kashmir issue. Those definitions, as already noted, are not limited to terrorism. Now it is true that Pakistan's leaders, under enormous pressure from Washington and faced with the massive mobilization of Indian armed forces on its eastern border, themselves acknowledged the existence of a terrorist threat in Kashmir; and they accompanied that acknowledgment with unprecedented steps taken at the close of 2001 and in early 2002 to begin scaling back their support of the militants—in particular those motivated by an Islamist rather than Kashmiri agenda—fighting in Kashmir. That support, the Indians had insisted all along (and are insisting more vehemently than ever, as I write this), was tantamount to sponsorship of terrorism—the same phenomenon the Pakistanis were claiming to oppose in Afghanistan. In spite of the pressure, Islamabad was most unlikely, however, to cave in entirely to New Delhi's interpretation. For Pakistanis to lend credit to a definition of terrorist as *all* fighters in Kashmir—outside militants along with indigenous Kashmiris themselves—would obviously undermine, if not entirely destroy, Pakistan's longstanding claim to Kashmir. Thus, the eventual impact on relations between India and Pakistan of the global war on terrorism could not be readily foreseen. Chances for a breakthrough in the existing stalemate were undoubtedly present; but so were deep-rooted hostility and distrust. Apart from Kashmir, there were plenty of other issues—a relentless nuclear arms race, for one thing, and sharp differences of perspective over the composition and strategic outlook of a post-Taliban regime in Afghanistan, for another—to fuel tensions between them. As the year 2002 progressed, the bilateral India-Pakistan relationship was, in fact, brimming with both hostility and peril. The "precarious equilibrium" these two rivals had maintained to this point in their history was showing signs of coming undone.

The Problem of Global Intervention

• Major global powers have been conspicuously reluctant in recent decades to become seriously engaged in the tasks of peacemaking between India and Pakistan. Even their punitive measures (the antiproliferation sanctions) have been puny.

• To the extent the major global powers have shown any long-range interest in South Asia, it has in recent years increasingly taken the form of an embrace of India. They pursued an intemperate "India First" policy, however, only at the huge risk of worsened India-Pakistan relations.

• The war against the Taliban has brought a massive increase in international involvement in the region. It has also brought with it a stunning, albeit possibly transient, restoration of Pakistan to its erstwhile role in America's strategic frontline. Coming in the midst of a steady warming in Indo-American relations, this change in Pakistan's fortunes from pariah to prized ally has compelled Washington to engage in an exceptionally ticklish regional balancing act. Its success in this, as has been made strikingly manifest in the near-war conditions that presently prevail in South Asia, is far from assured.

• One immediate consequence of this balancing effort is the requirement that Washington discard its ill-advised plan, made explicit after Kargil, to "decouple" India and Pakistan for purposes of U.S. policymaking in the region. Never a practical option in the face of the interlinked pattern of subcontinental security issues, decoupling in the current environment had to be understood as being also terribly reckless.

• Calling for discard, too, are international appeals to India and Pakistan to resolve the Kashmir problem *themselves* via bilateral dialogue. With international involvement in the region now massive and likely to persist indefinitely, such appeals are pointless, even irresponsible. They fell on deaf ears before 11 September; they ignore profound shifts in the regional balance of power now in progress.

• Unwelcome as the idea may be in foreign capitals, major international (especially U.S.) involvement in the search for a more stable and secure relationship between India and Pakistan is both urgent and inescapable.

The Problem of Religious Identity

• The multiple and conflicting religious identities of Indians, Pakistanis, and Kashmiris are deeply and unavoidably implicated in the Kashmir dispute. The Kashmir dispute's roots simply cannot be described entirely or even mainly in secular terms. Like it or not, the Kashmir dispute is, in no small part, a dispute over religion.

• Religious extremism (a.k.a. fundamentalism) is only one element, however, and not necessarily the largest or most important element, of religion's role in the Kashmir dispute.

• Religious identity figures prominently in the state strategies of both India and Pakistan as well as in those of their Kashmir-level proxies.

• Terrorism is commonplace in Kashmir. Unavoidably, it now represents one element—an important element—in what goes by the name of the "Kashmir dispute." Some of the terrorism is state-sponsored (by India as well as by Pakistan); some of it is not. The alleged forging of links in recent years between Osama bin Laden's Al Qaeda organization and guerrilla groups operating in Jammu and Kashmir should not be airily dismissed. Neither, however, should one ignore New Delhi's relentless exploitation and magnification of these links. It is a profound misrepresentation of the situation, in fact, to describe Kashmir as being simply or even mainly a terrorist matter. Indeed, the Kashmir dispute is not at bottom a *terrorist* issue, even less an *Islamic* (or, for that matter, *Hindu)* terrorist issue.

• Religious identity will persist indefinitely not only as an integral component of Kashmir's political chemistry but also as a powerful tool for political mobilization and opinion formation in regard to it.

The Problem of Conflict Resolution

• Autonomy, like its conceptual parent self-determination, has ideological appeal but very limited immediate political utility when it comes to resolving the Kashmir dispute.

• In the political environment of the Kashmir dispute, autonomist solutions are virtually bound to fall victim to political expediency and distrust. They "succeed" only in the abstract. They cannot materialize on the ground in Kashmir in anything like an ideal form.

• Insofar as the Kashmir separatist issue is concerned, there is, in fact, no practical and *peaceful* solution at all in sight. Thus, Kashmir's final status must be indefinitely postponed.

• Conflict resolution has to shift its sights from the separatist issue to the negotiation of reduced tension in the political-military rivalry between India and Pakistan. This is an urgent necessity *and* a practical possibility. It also happens to promise major benefits, long and short term, to all sides, including the separatists.

• To succeed, the negotiation of reduced tension has to be internationally mediated, robustly institutionalized, long term, and motivated largely by positive incentives for all sides. In this, the United States must play a major role.

• In short, the "solution" to Kashmir has to be sought, ironically, in its indefinite postponement *and* simultaneous internationalization.

1

The Problem of
Regional Rivalry
The "Nuclearization" of the Kashmir Dispute

In spring 1998, India and Pakistan jettisoned the officially preferred status of "nuclear ambiguity" and "recessed" (or "nonweaponized") deterrence and became overt nuclear weapon states. India led the way with a stunning series of underground nuclear tests—the first since its 1974 "peaceful nuclear explosion"—that took the world largely by surprise. On 11 May, Prime Minister Atal Bihari Vajpayee announced that India had successfully conducted three tests (of a fission, a low yield, and a thermonuclear device) at its Pokharan range in Rajasthan. Another announcement followed, on 13 May, of an additional two tests—both reported to be in the sub-kiloton range. Pakistan's response to India's action was both swift and predictable. Saying that Pakistan had "to restore the strategic balance" with India,[1] Pakistan's Prime Minister Nawaz Sharif announced on 28 May that Pakistan had conducted five nuclear tests of its own—like India's, said to be of varying magnitudes—at its Chagai test range near the Iranian border in Baluchistan. A sixth Pakistani test followed on 30 May.

The tests provoked a hail of condemnation.[2] Some fourteen countries, led by the United States, imposed economic sanctions of one sort or another on both India and Pakistan. Most of the world's great military and economic powers joined in issuing urgent appeals to the Indian and Pakistani governments to head off a nuclear arms race and to avoid further damage to the world's painstakingly erected nuclear nonproliferation regime. Meeting in Geneva on 4 June, the foreign ministers of the five permanent members of the United Nations Security Council (the

United States, Britain, Russia, France, and China—the so-called P-5) issued a joint communiqué condemning the tests and calling on India and Pakistan to stop all further testing and to "refrain from the weaponization or deployment of nuclear weapons, from the testing or deployment of missiles capable of delivering nuclear weapons and from any further production of fissile material for nuclear weapons." The communiqué also called on them to adhere to the Comprehensive Nuclear Test Ban Treaty "immediately and unconditionally,"[3] Two days later, on 6 June, the fifteen members of the Security Council, meeting in New York, voted unanimously for a similar set of demands[4] and on 12 June, the world's leading industrialized nations—the so-called Group of Eight (the P-5 less China, joined by Germany, Japan, Canada, and Italy)— added yet another list of appeals to the diplomatic barrage.[5]

Dramatically highlighted in these appeals, along with the nuclear threat, were the subcontinent's longstanding Kashmir territorial dispute and the increased urgency of finding a solution to it. On the eve of the P-5 meeting in Geneva, U.S. Secretary of State Madeleine K. Albright reportedly acknowledged in a news conference that resolving the Kashmir dispute was fundamental to calming tensions in the South Asian region.[6] The P-5 statement itself formally expressed global concerns in this regard. Its fifth paragraph commented as follows:

> The ministers concluded that efforts to resolve disputes between India and Pakistan must be pursued with determination. The ministers affirm their readiness to assist India and Pakistan, in a manner acceptable to both sides, in promoting reconciliation and cooperation. The ministers pledged that they will actively encourage India and Pakistan to find mutually acceptable solutions, through direct dialogue, that address the root causes of the tension, including Kashmir, and to try to build confidence rather than seek confrontation. In that connection, the ministers urged both parties to avoid threatening military movements, cross-border violations or other provocative acts.[7]

In the months immediately following the tests, there were few encouraging signs that either India or Pakistan was prepared to take such counsel to heart. Their governments' public reactions seemed in large part, in fact, to reaffirm the timeworn positions on Kashmir that had given the dispute its well-established reputation for intractability. While both sides indicated their general willingness to resume bilateral discussions that had been suspended the preceding year (in September 1997) following three rounds, each hesitant step forward in the direction of resumption faced almost immediate repudiation by one or the other side. The Indian government made it crystal clear that its willingness to undertake what it called a "comprehensive, constructive and sustained" dialogue with Pakistan on all outstanding issues went hand-in-hand with its total rejection of any third party involvement in their resolution.[8] The Pakistan government, in turn, made it just as clear in its responses that it viewed the nuclear-inspired revival of global interest in Kashmir as a tailor-made opportunity not to renew the search with India for common ground in regard to Kashmir but to press forward with an agenda for internationalizing the dispute that was bound to meet with India's rejection. "We feel, after all, Kashmir is the core issue," the government's Information Minister Mushahid Hussain was reported to have observed in reacting to Western apprehension over the region's nuclear crisis. "[For the international community to ignore it] would be like staging *Hamlet* without the Prince of Denmark. It is Kashmir that has been the cause of war."[9] Particularly discouraging, in light of the seeming absence of any give in the two governments' formal positions on Kashmir, was the sharp escalation in cross-border skirmishing, including prolonged artillery duels in late summer that resulted in unusually heavy civilian casualties, along the Line of Control (LOC).[10]

By the end of August 1998, however, India-Pakistan relations began showing signs of yielding to the global political fallout of the nuclear weapons tests. On 29 August, the foreign secretaries of India and Pakistan, meeting at a Non-Aligned Movement summit gathering in Durban, South Africa, appeared to achieve some progress in regard to the modalities for resuming the stalled bilateral talks, and when the two prime ministers (Vajpayee and Sharif) met at the opening of the UN General Assembly session in New York on 23 September, they announced an agreement to proceed directly to bilateral talks. Their agreement set in motion a diplomatic warming trend that astonished observers. For the first time in many years, the possibility of achieving an India-Pakistan reconciliation seemed suddenly within reach. The idea of a settlement over Kashmir, after fifty-one years of unending conflict, itself seemed suddenly a matter for serious contemplation. The onset of heightened nuclear tension between India and Pakistan, it occurred to many, could be significantly offset by lowered tension between them over Kashmir.

The alacrity with which mere contemplation of regional reconciliation was converted to the seeming substance of it, and then for that promising substance to be unceremoniously bumped to the side with no less alacrity by a shooting war on the LOC, was dizzying to behold. In an emotional and unprecedented meeting at Lahore in February 1999, the prime ministers of India and Pakistan had first embraced one another and then together presided over a blitz of agreements that appeared to most observers to push the two governments decisively in the direction of normalization of relations. How indecisive the push was shortly became, in fact, embarrassingly plain. In the first week of May, two Indian Army units patrolling in remote mountainous areas in the Kargil sector of the LOC discovered that hundreds of well-armed "intruders," whom the Indians claimed had crossed the LOC into Indian territory from Pakistan, had gotten there ahead of the Indians and dug bunkers for themselves on the upper slopes of still-wintry peaks. The Indian Army rushed troops to the area, and the Indian Air Force, making the first such use of air power since the outbreak of the Kashmir insurgency a decade earlier, launched air attacks on the infiltrators' positions on 26 May. These actions bespoke, in the thunderous language of modern ordnance, the vanished fortunes of bilateral dialogue. Since they occurred roughly on the first anniversary of the preceding year's nuclear tests, they naturally provoked worried and worldwide reflection on their potential for escalation to the nuclear level.

This "nuclearization" of the Kashmir dispute—its coupling with the region's rising nuclear danger and piggybacked elevation in importance on regional and global diplomatic agendas as a consequence of the nuclear-tests crisis—is the focus of this chapter. The discussion examines the gradual nuclear repackaging of this territorial dispute since May 1998 from two points of view—first, from the standpoint of regional diplomacy (starting with the revival in autumn 1998 of the India-Pakistan dialogue, through the cease-fire initiatives that got underway in summer 2000, on to the Agra Summit that took place in mid-July 2001, and concluding with the precipitous downturn in India-Pakistan relations amid the radically changed circumstances following the 11 September terrorist attack on targets in the United States),[11] and second, from that of armed conflict between India and Pakistan (especially the outbreak in spring 1999 of major military hostilities between the two sides in the Kargil sector of the LOC). The discussion's objective is also twofold: first, to identify the particular ways in which nuclearization has materially affected regional rivalry over Kashmir, and second, to attempt to clarify why nuclearization, in spite of its earlier promise, has proven itself thus far a disappointing catalyst for the Kashmir dispute's bilateral resolution. Our consideration of nuclearization's impact on the *global* diplomacy of Kashmir is postponed until Chapter 2.

Naturally, the immediacy of the developments under discussion compels prudence in speculating about their likely longer-term political fallout—specifically, about whether they may or may not serve eventually to ignite a more earnest and sustained regional search for a solution to Kashmir. Enough is apparent already, however, to suggest fairly strongly that whatever momentum in that direction might have been gained as a consequence of the nuclear events in May 1998 is almost bound to prove insufficient *by itself* to move the subcontinent much beyond its present diplomatic stalemate over Kashmir. The obstacles to that are simply too great to be so easily swept aside. It is the argument of this chapter that there is no recognizable silver lining in the nuclearization of the Kashmir dispute and that regional diplomacy, in the face of the persistent severe military and political rivalry between India and Pakistan, is most unlikely to produce one.

Regional Diplomacy—The Revival of India-Pakistan Talks

The first substantial indicator of a potential thaw in India-Pakistan relations had come in June 1997, nearly a year before the May 1998 nuclear tests, in a joint statement that concluded a meeting in Islamabad of the two countries' foreign secretaries. In the statement, they announced agreement on a sustained and comprehensive dialogue on all major issues between them. Eight issues were explicitly identified: peace and security, including confidence-building measures (CBMs); Jammu and Kashmir; Siachen Glacier; Wullar Barrage/Tulbul Navigation Project; Sir Creek; terrorism and drug-trafficking; economic and commercial cooperation; and promotion of friendly exchanges in various fields. The agreement included a commitment "to set up a mechanism, including working groups at appropriate levels, to address all these issues in an integrated manner."[12] Some of the issues were to be dealt with at the foreign-secretary level, the others in the expert working groups. India's willingness to *include* Kashmir on the list of issues, and Pakistan's to agree to discuss Kashmir *alongside* other bilateral matters, were remarkable departures from long-established habits of diplomatic intransigence.

Operationalizing the wished-for "mechanism"—the precise operational format that was to contain such wide-ranging discussions—proved a great deal more difficult, however, than had vocalizing the wish at Islamabad. Disagreement broke out almost immediately, in fact, over what had really been agreed to, the Indians insistent that the Kashmir issue should continue to be dealt with exclusively in foreign secretary-level discussions focused generally on peace and security, the Pakistanis, not wanting the unexpected blessing of Kashmir's inclusion among the "major issues" to slip between their diplomatic fingers, just as insistent that discussion of Kashmir deserved separate lodging in its own permanent working group.[13]

Composite Dialogue: The "Two Plus Six" Formula

The matter of the mechanism was not finally and formally settled until the two prime ministers, meeting at the United Nations in September the following year in the nuclear-charged atmosphere following the May tests, announced agreement on a compromise "two plus six" formula for the talks. This formula provided for treating the two obviously more sensitive and important issues—peace and security, and Jammu and Kashmir—separately from the working groups and at the foreign-secretary level (obvious concessions to India), but first in the series and at Islamabad (concessions to Pakistan). The other six issues were to be taken up sometime later, by several working groups, meeting sequentially in New Delhi. (See Table 1.1 on pages 20–23).

This elaborately structured dialogue process—what its creators called a "composite and integrated" process—was launched with a good deal of fanfare in mid-October 1998. When it came to an end a month later, there was little palpable achievement to boast of: In what were generally described as rather brief and perfunctory meetings, neither side appeared to stray far from established positions on the issues and no major agreements—except to resume the talks early the next year—were reached.

One seemingly trivial agreement was reached during these discussions. First mooted at the prime ministers' meeting in September, it covered restoration of regular bus service—suspended for 51 years—between Lahore, Pakistan, and New Delhi. Details in regard to it were hastily ironed out before the end of the year and a "dry run" from Lahore to New Delhi was staged, in a public atmosphere charged with considerable emotion, in January. Hard on its heels came the stunning announcement by the Indian prime minister in early February 1999, responding to the invitation of his Pakistani counterpart, of his intention to travel to Lahore on the inaugural run of the bus service from India.[14] Some questioned the sincerity of his motives, but the boldness and novelty of the idea stirred up enormous excitement on both sides of the international boundary. Hailed both within the region and abroad as a landmark event pregnant with both substantive and symbolic historical significance, it seemed to open up undreamed of possibilities in India-Pakistan relations.[15]

"Bus Diplomacy" and the Lahore Declaration

At the symbolic level, the impact of Vajpayee's 24-hour visit to Lahore can hardly be overstated. This was only the third time an Indian prime minister had set foot on Pakistani soil since independence, and when the luxury tour bus that had carried him the twenty-eight miles from the city of Amritsar rolled past the Wagah border check-post in the afternoon of 20 February, Vajpayee became the first Indian prime minister ever to make a surface crossing of the border. Stepping down from the bus, Vajpayee toasted the event in his brief arrival statement as "a defining moment in South Asian history."[16] The description seemed apt. After all, here warmly embracing the Pakistani prime minister was not merely the elected head of the Indian government but a longtime member of the militantly Hindu revivalist Rashtriya Swayamsewak Sangh (National Volunteer Corps) as well as the leader of a Hindu nationalist political party, the Bharatiya Janata Party (BJP), that had been on record for decades as the sworn enemy of Pakistan. Few of those present could have missed the irony or been unmoved by it. The members of the handpicked Indian delegation that accompanied Vajpayee, according to a veteran Indian journalist, "were uncontrollably exuberant and emotive."[17] No less intense must have been the feelings of Pakistanis the following day when Vajpayee, in a singularly profound gesture of India's acceptance of the partition of 1947 (and, thus, of the legitimacy of the Pakistan state), paid a visit to the Minar-i-Pakistan, a national monument marking the site where in 1940 the Muslim League issued its first formal appeal for the creation of a separate national homeland for the Muslims of British colonial India.[18]

Substantive results of the Lahore summit, while obviously overshadowed by the stunning symbolic gestures put on display there, were also impressive. Three formal documents emerged: the Lahore Declaration,

Table 1.1

Direct Bilateral Talks Between India and Pakistan, on or Including Kashmir, 1947–2002

Date	Auspices/location	Level	Outcome
1 November–8 December 1947	Joint Defence Council Lahore, New Delhi	Governors-general and prime ministers	No agreement reached. Abandoned in favor of UN intercession.
25–27 July 1953	Karachi	Prime ministers	Preliminary discussions only.
17–20 August 1953	New Delhi	Prime ministers	Expert committees approved, plebiscite endorsed. No agreement reached in follow-up correspondence.
14–18 May 1955	New Delhi	Prime ministers	No agreement reached. Further talks called for.
19–23 September 1960	World Bank Karachi	Prime ministers	Indus Waters Treaty signed. No progress on Kashmir.
27–29 December 1962 16–19 January 1963 8–10 February 1963 12–14 March 1963 21–25 April 1963 14–16 May 1963	Rawalpindi, New Delhi, Karachi, Calcutta, Karachi, New Delhi	Ministers (railways and foreign)	Joint Communiqué issued at end of sixth round reported no agreement.
1–2 March 1966	Rawalpindi	Foreign ministers	Terminated upon failure to agree on Kashmir's inclusion in formal agenda.
28 June–2 July 1972	Simla	Prime ministers	Kashmir excluded from formal agenda. New cease-fire line (LOC) agreed. Commitment to final settlement of Kashmir included in peace treaty.

Date	Location	Level	Outcome
2–3 January 1994	Islamabad	Foreign secretaries	Seventh round in series commenced in 1990. Kashmir implicitly included on agenda. No progress reported. No further meetings scheduled.
28–31 March 1997	New Delhi	Foreign secretaries	First round in fresh series. "All issues" on agenda. Further meetings planned.
9 April 1997	NAM conference New Delhi	Foreign ministers	Commitment to bilateral talks reaffirmed.
12–14 May 1997	SAARC summit meeting Male (Maldives)	Prime ministers	Commitment made to resume foreign-secretary level talks. Plan announced to constitute joint "working groups."
19–23 June 1997	Islamabad	Foreign secretaries	Second round in series. Agreement announced to form eight "working groups" to consider major issues between them, including Kashmir.
15–18 September 1997	New Delhi	Foreign secretaries	Third round in series. No agreement on any issue except to hold another round of talks.
23 September 1997	UN General Assembly New York	Prime ministers	Commitment made to take action to end border skirmishes in Kashmir.
29 July 1998	SAARC summit meeting Colombo, Sri Lanka	Prime ministers	Failed to agree on restarting negotiations.

(continued)

Table 1.1 (continued)

Date	Auspices/location	Level	Outcome
29 August 1998	NAM summit meeting Durban, South Africa	Foreign secretaries	Agreement reached on modalities for resuming stalled talks.
23 September 1998	UN General Assembly New York	Prime ministers	Agreement reached to "operationalize the mechanism to address all items in the agreed agenda of June 23, 1997, in a purposeful and composite manner in October and November." Agree on 6+2 integrated format for discussions: peace and security, and Kashmir at foreign-secretaries level at Islamabad; remaining 6 in New Delhi in November.
15–18 October 1998	Islamabad	Foreign secretaries	No substantive progress reported either on peace and security, including CBMs, or on Jammu and Kashmir. Agreement to resume talks in February.
5–14 November 1998: 5 November 6 November 9 November	New Delhi	Water and power secretaries Defence secretaries Surveyor generals	Reviewed Wullar Barrage (Tulbul Project), Siachen Glacier, Sir Creek, economic and commercial ties, terrorism and drug trafficking, and promotion of friendly exchanges. No substantive agreements reached. Talks to be continued.
10 November 13 November 14 November		Commerce secretaries Home secretaries Culture secretaries	
20–21 February 1999	Lahore	Prime ministers Foreign ministers Foreign secretaries	Lahore Declaration signed committing both sides to "the resolution of all outstanding issues, including the issue of Jammu and Kashmir."

Date	Location / Participants	Description
		Promised to avoid interference in one another's internal affairs. Agreed to intensify composite and integrated dialogue process. Also agreed on a number of CBMs in nuclear and conventional arms fields. Memorandum of Understanding (MoU) signed and joint statement issued committing two sides to additional CBMs in nuclear and other fields. Commitment to resume composite dialogue in March.
19 March 1999	SAARC Council of Foreign Ministers meeting Nuwara Eliya, Sri Lanka	Foreign ministers	Joint statement issued reaffirming urgency of implementing preceding month's agreements—Lahore Declaration, MoU, and joint statement—and reporting that the two ministers "agreed that the composite and integrated dialogue process must be intensified." Time frame charted for official-level negotiations. Next round of "composite integrated dialogue process" at foreign-secretary level scheduled in New Delhi and Islamabad over six-week period starting in May. Foreign ministers would meet again following this round. Group of experts for implementing CBMs contained in the Memorandum of Understanding to meet during next two months. Ministers of state meeting also set to be held in April.
14–16 July 2001	Agra	Prime minister and president	Talks focused largely on Kashmir concluded after two days of intensive discussions without agreement on wording of a declaration or joint statement. Invitation to visit Pakistan before end of year accepted by Indian prime minister. Later declined.

spelling out the principles of a common post-nuclear-tests vision of India-Pakistan bilateral relations, signed by the two prime ministers; a Memorandum of Understanding, enumerating specific nuclear confidence-building measures they had agreed upon, signed by their foreign secretaries; and, summarizing the visit's accomplishments, a joint statement.[19] In concrete terms, these documents committed the two sides to little more than further dialogue. But the commitments themselves signified dramatically heightened recognition of the changed (nuclearized) security calculus that now prevailed between India and Pakistan and of the need for significant enlargement of security cooperation between them. The Lahore Declaration identifies avoidance of war between the two countries as "in the supreme national interest of both sides"; and the Memorandum of Understanding, tacitly acknowledging this, covers a broad range of issues (e.g., nuclear doctrine, advance notification of ballistic missile flight tests, prevention of incidents at sea, upgrading of hot lines) that are entirely military in nature. As a perceptive Indian observer commented, the Memorandum of Understanding could just as well have been titled a "military memorandum of understanding."[20]

Notable were the several explicit references in these documents to the urgency of resolving the Kashmir issue. The two governments, in the first operative paragraph of the Lahore Declaration, expressed their agreement to "intensify their efforts to resolve all issues, including the issue of Jammu and Kashmir." Carefully worded to remain consistent with India's longstanding refusal to acknowledge Kashmir as a *disputed territory*, these references, by inscribing Kashmir indelibly—and prominently—on the official bilateral agenda, were, nevertheless, a clear concession to Pakistan.

On the surface, at least, these verbal concessions to Pakistan appeared to be outweighed by the Kashmir dispute's implicit downgrading in the formal agreements. Long heralded by Pakistanis as the "core issue" in India-Pakistan relations (the issue in the absence of whose resolution progress on nothing else was obtainable), Kashmir was visibly displaced at Lahore by a bundle of undeniably critical military and strategic issues catapulted out in front by the May 1998 nuclear tests. Kashmir was still on the diplomatic stage, of course, but not at *center* stage. Naturally, Pakistani leaders, in the immediate post-Lahore period, offered public reassurances that there had been no secret understanding with India or any compromise of Pakistan's "principled position" on Kashmir. "The memorandum of understanding," the Pakistani foreign minister was quoted as telling the Senate, "also establishes a clear linkage between an environment of regional peace and security and a resolution of the Kashmir issue."[21] But the "linkage" he spoke of was entirely undefined, and nowhere in these agreements was the *precedence* of Kashmir's resolution stipulated. On the contrary, the Lahore Declaration and its companion agreements lent themselves to the interpretation that the Kashmir dispute had been quietly moved to the back burner.

Back-Channel Diplomacy and the "Chenab Plan"

Far from having been swept off the diplomatic agenda at Lahore, the Kashmir dispute, more precisely the matter of its *resolution*, acquired over the next several months a centrality in India-Pakistan relations— at least in their informal or "back-channel" version—that had not been witnessed in many years and that yielded before it was over one of that dispute's most intriguing, one might even say bizarre, diplomatic episodes. I refer to the nine rounds (two in New Delhi, seven in Islamabad) of secret discussions about Kashmir that were held between officially designated representatives of the Indian and Pakistani governments between 3 March and 27 June 1999. Mr. Niaz A. Naik—a retired diplomat, former Foreign Secretary of Pakistan, and the Pakistan government's emissary in all but the first of these talks—narrated his account of them to the author in an interview in Islamabad on 18 January 2001. According to Naik, the talks were conducted in earnest, bound to a fixed timetable, and aimed specifically and explicitly at a compromise settlement of the Kashmir dispute. Naik's version of the talks is the only detailed account that I have available to me. An Indian version would certainly differ, perhaps substantially. Nevertheless, I believe that Naik's comments even by themselves shed valuable light on an extraordinary episode in India-Pakistan relations. I reproduce here my record of the interview.*

---

*My account of the interview is reported here with the consent of Mr. Naik. He did not review my written account, however, and thus is responsible neither for the accuracy of the details nor for the interpretation given of them. My account is based entirely on my handwritten notes. They were copious, however, and often verbatim. To assure clarity and readability, I have taken some liberties in reconstructing the text of the interview (including some abbreviation to eliminate unnecessary detail). I believe it is faithful to Naik's narrative. I am not aware of any publicly available official Indian account of these talks.

The two prime ministers—Atal Bihari Vajpayee of India and Nawaz Sharif of Pakistan—had agreed in a private meeting between them during the Lahore Summit of February 1999 that they would work together to bring about forward movement on Kashmir before the end of the century. By this they meant within the ten months remaining in the year 1999. The two leaders were agreed that nothing positive could be achieved in the glare of publicity that inevitably surrounded formal meetings of the two countries' senior officials. Only in single-agenda, *back-channel* talks, in other words, could one expect progress toward a solution to the Kashmir problem. The two leaders also agreed that only *one* person, someone who enjoyed the full confidence of the prime minister, should represent each side in such talks, at least in their initial phase.

Very early in March, less than two weeks after returning to New Delhi from Lahore, Vajpayee telephoned Nawaz with the query—Are you ready to begin? Nawaz replied that he was. On the Indian side, Vajpayee chose R. K. Mishra, a newspaper tycoon and business entrepreneur with close ties to the country's ruling political elite, as his emissary. Mishra had acquired a reputation for being both a skilled politician and seasoned negotiator. To represent the Pakistan side, Nawaz chose Anwar Zahid, the younger brother of Akram Zaki, a distinguished Pakistani diplomat. A date for the meeting was quickly decided. Only days later (on 3–4 March), Mishra met secretly with Zahid in Islamabad to work out the modalities for further talks. Suddenly stricken with a severe illness, however, Zahid died on 11 March. That misfortune did not interrupt the planned dialogue. Vajpayee telephoned his Pakistani counterpart that same day, offering both his condolences and the reassurance that he wanted to proceed with the dialogue.

Nawaz telephoned me on 17 March and offered me the job of emissary, which I accepted. Nawaz instructed me that I was to take guidance strictly and directly from him [the Prime Minister] and not from the Foreign Office. On 20 March, with the project back on track, Mishra again journeyed to Islamabad for the second round of discussions, this time with me. That meeting was followed soon thereafter by another, this time in New Delhi, that extended over five days beginning on 27 March. I spent the entire five days sequestered in my hotel room, avoiding contact with anyone who might recognize me. Not even Pakistan's High Commissioner to India had been informed of my presence in New Delhi.

My understanding of the mandate driving this third round of talks was that the two emissaries were to look to the future to find a solution to Kashmir. With that in mind, Mishra and I set out initially to construct future-looking building blocks to guide further discussions. We held both morning and afternoon sessions. Fairly quickly, we managed to agree upon three basic elements to guide our deliberations. These were:

- Both sides should move beyond publicly stated positions on Kashmir;
- A solution to Kashmir must take into account the interests of India, Pakistan, and the Kashmiri people; and
- The solution to Kashmir must be just, fair, and feasible (able to be implemented, in other words).

At this point, after conferring with Vajpayee, Mishra informed me that the Indian prime minister wished to make two changes to these elements. One was simply to add the words "above all" before "the Kashmiri people" in the second guideline. The other, more important, was to add a fourth basic element. This was:

- The agreed solution to Kashmir must be final and not partial.

This provision, as I understood it, implied that certain proposals that had been made from time to time about Kashmir—like the proposal that there should be installed in Kashmir a United Nations Trusteeship, and only after some years had passed that there should then be a popular referendum on the matter—were ruled out. Mishra emphasized to me that the Indian prime minister was adamant that the talks be aimed at a settlement to be reached *within this century* (i.e., within the next ten months).

For the next two days in this round of talks, we applied these four guidelines systematically to nine or so options for Kashmir that had been compiled a few years earlier by participants in the so-called Neemrana talks—a Track II or nongovernmental channel that had been operating for some years between India and Pakistan.*

Mishra began the discussion with the suggestion that the best option would be to agree to recognize the Line of Control (LOC) as a permanent international border between India and Pakistan. I objected, explaining that this option was New Delhi's *present* position and that it did not represent movement "beyond publicly stated positions on Kashmir." At that, Mishra raised the alternative of *autonomy* for Kash-

---

*The talks took their name from the town of Neemrana in Rajasthan, where the talks were held.

mir. I again protested, saying that autonomy wouldn't do either, since the Kashmiris would consider it unfair and would reject it. When the option of *independence* for Kashmir came up for discussion, Mishra strongly resisted, saying that the Indian people were entirely opposed to it and that the Chinese disliked it too. We then examined the idea of *regional plebiscites*, first mooted by Sir Owen-Dixon in the early 1950s. Mishra was wary of it, suggesting that it had "communal" colors and that it was neither feasible nor acceptable to India. A number of other proposals were likewise examined and rejected. When all nine of the Neemrana options had been evaluated, it was apparent to me as well as to Mishra that for one reason or another none of them was really useful.

At this point in the deliberations, Mishra took time to consult with Vajpayee. Mishra then reported to me that the Indian prime minister had urged that Mishra and he come up with something new and innovative. During an evening discussion on 30 March [the fourth day of dialogue], I offered a compromise solution. It was to *partition* the Indian portion of Jammu and Kashmir: the Valley of Kashmir [about 10 percent of the territory of the pre-1947 princely state] would be given to Pakistan, the rest to India. The division, I explained to Mishra, had to be made along easily identifiable geographic features. I suggested that the Chenab River was possibly a suitable natural dividing line. Mishra confessed that he was uncertain of Kashmir's geography and needed more specific details. I agreed that the idea needed more study. Mishra asked if I had a map of Kashmir. I did not. We then purchased a tourist map of northern India from the hotel lobby. At this point in the discussion, however, with the Chenab option on the table, we broke off the meeting. It was late afternoon on 31 March. Up to this point, I had had no contact with Nawaz Sharif.

At 10:00 the next morning [1 April], I met with Vajpayee. He stressed the need to keep up the momentum of the talks. He suggested that Mishra and I should meet again, this time in Islamabad, on 9 April. In the meantime, Vajpayee suggested, I should prepare detailed maps of Kashmir clarifying my proposal. This made it apparent that the Chenab option [the division of the state between the two sides] must have been discussed. It also meant that the Indian side was seriously interested in the Chenab option.

At this same meeting, Vajpayee also brought up the Kashmir Study Group proposal on Kashmir.* Specifically, the prime minister asked me:

---

*The proposal referred to here by Naik is the so-called Livingston Plan that had been circulated in India and Pakistan following a meeting called by Farooq Kathwari, a prominent Kashmiri-American businessman, at his Livingston, New York, estate in late 1998. This plan is considered in detail in Chapter 4.

"What was Pakistan's position on it?" I responded that I couldn't say, but that it was under study in Pakistan. There had been no interagency coordination in regard to it.

Vajpayee also asked me at this meeting to convey a personal message to Prime Minister Nawaz Sharif. It was that in the last nine or ten years, whenever infiltration had started up on the Pakistan side in the summer, shelling across the LOC had soon followed. "Please," he said, "see that this pattern is not repeated again this summer, as much as possible."

I returned to Islamabad on 1 April. At 8:30 the next morning [2 April], I met with Nawaz Sharif and fully briefed him on the meeting. The first question he asked me was: "Did you contact the Pakistan Army?" I said that I hadn't. Nawaz then informed me that two days earlier [on 27 or 28 March], he [Nawaz] had been given a military briefing on Kashmir at Joint Staff Headquarters in Rawalpindi. In the course of the briefing, the matter of negotiating a division of Indian-held Kashmir at the Chenab River line had come up. It was noted that Prime Minister Bhutto had made a similar suggestion during the Kashmir negotiations held with India in the early 1960s. At this point in the discussion, Nawaz telephoned Lt. General Ziauddin, Director General of ISI [Inter-Services Intelligence Directorate]* and requested that I be given the same briefing. He also told Ziauddin that I would give him a briefing on my talks with Mishra in New Delhi. Nawaz also mentioned to Ziauddin that I required detailed maps of Kashmir. At this point, I went straight to ISI headquarters and gave Ziauddin and six or seven brigadiers a complete briefing on the New Delhi meeting. I was given detailed maps of Kashmir.

At 8:00 the same evening [2 April], I met with Lt. General Pervez Musharraf, Chief of Army Staff. Lt. General Ziauddin was also present. The meeting lasted two hours. I supplied a detailed briefing of the discussions in New Delhi. Musharraf said to me: "We think it's a good starting point, but a combination of the Kashmir Study Group's Livingston Plan and the Chenab Plan could open the door to a solution."

On 12 April, a few days later than had been initially scheduled, Mishra came again to Islamabad. This time, however, he appeared to be a little perturbed. Vajpayee had told him that Indian intelligence was reporting that the usual springtime infiltration of militants across the LOC was already under way. Nawaz Sharif told Mishra in my presence that he would use his influence to correct the situation.

---

*Lt. General Ziauddin was among the confederates of Nawaz Sharif who were jailed by Pakistan's military rulers for their roles in the October 1999 coup.

On 21 April, Mishra returned to Islamabad for yet another round of talks. He stated that India was now in possession of much more information about militants' infiltration across the LOC. He made no specific mention of the Kargil sector, however. At this, Nawaz promised to take concrete steps to rectify the problem.

The 5th of May was the date on which the first skirmishing between Indian and Pakistani forces took place in the Kargil sector. It happens that Mishra returned to Islamabad on this date for another round of talks. On this occasion he requested that I convey a message from Vajpayee to Nawaz. It was that the Indian prime minister wished to affirm that he trusted Nawaz Sharif's word. He wanted to know, however, whether Nawaz knew in advance of Kargil.

Mishra returned to Islamabad again on 17 May. He told me that Vajpayee was under fire from hawkish elements in India. The Indian prime minister was still awaiting clarification of the situation from Nawaz. At this 17 May meeting [the seventh since they had begun in early March], Mishra expressed the desire to see Prime Minister Nawaz Sharif alone, unaccompanied by me. His wish was granted. He met with Nawaz alone while I waited outside the prime minister's office. There was a little tension in the air. After about ten minutes, Mishra stepped out of the prime minister's office to go to the washroom. In his absence, Nawaz asked me (in Punjabi): "What's wrong with him? He is asking me whether on 20 February [the date of the Lahore Summit] I knew of the Kargil plan." Nawaz did not give Mishra a reply to this question, at least not in my presence. Using ambiguous language, he told Mishra that he would look into the matter.

From that time [17 May] until 25 June, there were no further meetings between Mishra and me. When Mishra finally came again to Islamabad on 25 June [the same day on which General Anthony C. Zinni, Commander-in-Chief of U.S. Central Command arrived in Islamabad for discussions], he was greatly disturbed. Mishra observed to me that India and Pakistan [in Mishra's words] were "one inch away from war." He said: Tell Nawaz this. Once he received the message, Nawaz prepared a written message for Vajpayee, which was given to Mishra. This message held four points. These were:

- Both prime ministers should reiterate their commitment to the Lahore process;
- Both India and Pakistan should take concrete steps to restore the sanctity of the Line of Control;
- The Indian side should stop the shelling and aerial bombing in the Kargil sector in order to restore an atmosphere conducive to peace; and

- Both prime ministers should renew efforts to complete the process started at Lahore [in February 1999], to include resolution of all issues between them, including Jammu and Kashmir.

With this message in hand, Mishra left for New Delhi on the 4:30 afternoon flight.

The following day [26 June] at 9:00 A.M. I received a telephone call from R. K. Mishra, who said that the Indian prime minister wished me to come immediately to Delhi to consider the four points of Nawaz's message. I phoned Nawaz, who instructed me to contact the foreign secretary [Shamshad Ahmad] with the news. Shamshad suggested that they try to strengthen it, meaning to give substance to the four points. I resisted the suggestion, saying that any modifications should be conveyed strictly in verbal form so as not to put chances for the resumption of dialogue in any jeopardy.

In the evening of the same day [26 June], I flew to Delhi, where for the first time I met with both R. K. Mishra and the prime minister's national security advisor, Brajesh Mishra. Regarding the four points, I was told that the Indians found them acceptable but that they wanted one additional point included. It was: "Pakistan has agreed to withdraw from the Kargil heights." I said no; this was impractical. Both sides would have to be included. I added that the word "withdrawal" couldn't be used in any event because of its negative connotations. The discussion went on for three hours. Brajesh Mishra was very difficult to deal with. Finally, he said: "OK, you can try your position out on Prime Minister Vajpayee directly."

The next morning [27 June], I met with Vajpayee at his residence. He opened the conversation with the question: "How did the journey we began at Lahore end in Kargil?" He went on to say that Pakistan should announce the withdrawal of its forces from Kargil and all would be OK. I stressed that *both* sides would have to commit themselves to withdrawal. Vajpayee repeated the urgent necessity for Pakistan's withdrawal. He suggested that the directors-general of military operations of each side's army should together work out a plan for the mutual withdrawal of forces. I responded that the matter of withdrawal was extremely sensitive politically and that only the two prime ministers could defuse it. Vajpayee noted that Nawaz was scheduled to fly to China the same evening [27 June]. The meeting was then terminated. While I waited, Vajpayee met privately for about fifteen minutes with the two Mishras, Brajesh and R. K. Then R. K. Mishra drove me back to my hotel. On the way, he commented to me: "We've persuaded Vajpayee that Nawaz Sharif ought to route his flight to Beijing over New Delhi. Vajpayee wants Nawaz to make a stop in Delhi and meet with him for three or four hours. To facilitate such a scheme, Nawaz's plane had to fly at least a little through Indian airspace. While in Indian airspace, as was customary, he could send a message of peace and goodwill to the Indian prime minister, who would then reply with an invitation to Nawaz to make a brief technical stop in Delhi." Mishra instructed me: "When you brief Prime Minister Nawaz Sharif in this regard, urge him to send an advance copy of his intended goodwill message to Delhi to expedite matters." Mishra also advised that I should myself return to New Delhi from Pakistan on 28 June so that I would be present to aid in preparing a press statement on the prime ministers' meeting. These arrangements were agreed. The time of 10:15 P.M. on 27 June was fixed for the exchange of messages to occur. I then immediately returned to Pakistan.

Back in Islamabad, I briefed Nawaz, who was pleased with the news. The goodwill message was promptly drafted and faxed to New Delhi. In addition, a draft press statement was drawn up. Nawaz was scheduled to leave for Beijing at 8 P.M. from Chaklala Air Force Base at Rawalpindi. Both Nawaz and I then left for Lahore.

At about 7:35 P.M. on 27 June, R. K. Mishra, following several abortive efforts to reach me, telephoned me with the information that in the meantime "a bombshell" had been dropped on New Delhi: The Press Trust of India [PTI] news service had leaked full details of the back-channel dialogue on Kashmir that Mishra and I had been conducting. Included were the details of my 27 June visit to Delhi. The PTI report claimed that Vajpayee had issued a warning to me that Pakistan *must* withdraw its forces from Kargil or "New Delhi would take appropriate action."

When Nawaz reached Lahore, he was still hoping that a breakthrough agreement with Delhi was imminent. However, 7:45 P.M. came without any message from Delhi to confirm either receipt of Nawaz's draft message or that the exchange of messages set for 10:15 P.M. was still on course. Nawaz's departure for China, scheduled for 8 P.M., was put on hold. At 9:50 P.M., with Nawaz's departure still on hold, a fax arrived from New Delhi with a message along the lines of the "warning" mentioned in the PTI report—in other words, Pakistan must immediately withdraw the intruders or suffer the consequences. In the message there was mention neither of a goodwill message nor of a meeting of the two prime ministers in Delhi. At 10:15 P.M., in my presence, Nawaz telephoned Vajpayee. He was set to leave for China at 10:30 P.M. Vajpayee told Nawaz that I had "completely misunderstood" what had been said in New Delhi. "No such arrangement [as an exchange of messages] had been agreed." Nawaz responded by saying that I was no child, that I was a seasoned diplomat, and that I could not have misunderstood what was said. That ended the conversation. Nawaz then instructed me to contact R. K. Mishra and seek to clarify the situation. I telephoned Mishra but did not immediately reach him. At 10:35 P.M., with Nawaz having already left for China, Mishra telephoned. He asked to speak with Nawaz, but instead was put in contact with Tariq Fatemi at the Foreign Office. Fatemi advised him that the prime minister had already departed but that, before departing, had said that he would meet with Mishra any-place of Mishra's choosing. Nawaz had also said that he should be kept informed of any developments in this regard while he was in Beijing. This ended the episode: Never again since the night of 27 June 1999 had R. K. Mishra been in touch with me.

Just how close the Indians and Pakistanis had actually come to agree-ment over the cessation of hostilities at Kargil before the talks collapsed remains conjectural. Indeed, a sizable row developed in the wake of Kargil— among both Pakistanis and Indians, and between Pakistan and India—not only over the precise content of the talks but, more heatedly, over just why they failed and who or what it was that bore responsibility for failure.

According to some observers, including the senior and respected Indian columnist A. G. Noorani, these talks came very close, in fact, to producing an agreed pullout of Pakistani forces. Noorani argued at the time in a provocative account in *Frontline* magazine that Kargil's eventual internationalized outcome, since it featured the United States in a key intermediary role and thus violated New Delhi's longstanding commitment to bilateralism in its dealings with Islamabad, was far less of a diplomatic triumph for New Delhi than the government was claiming. Pieced together from scattered British, Indian, and Pakistani news reports and, in particular, from Naik's own limited public disclo-sure of his role in the talks to the British Broadcasting Corporation on 29 June, Noorani's account claims that Naik did indeed return from his talks with Indian leaders in New Delhi on 27 June bearing a draft agreement on de-escalation that included a provision calling for an expeditious solution to the Kashmir dispute within a specified time frame.[22] The fact that the Pakistanis were greeted with a blunt demand for a unilateral pullout from Kargil instead of with the expected invita-tion for an ad hoc prime ministerial summit Noorani attributes to suc-cessful lobbying by the Indian establishment's hawkish element. Leaking the aborted plan to the press finished it for good. Bilateral efforts at reaching a solution collapsed. Then came Nawaz Sharif's desperate dash to Washington in search of a solution to the crisis (considered in Chapter 2).

The scrapping over back-channel diplomacy did not end there. Months later, on 14 September, Pakistan's most widely circulated daily, the Urdu-medium *Jang*, ran an article attributing to Niaz Naik remarks on the back-channel discussions that not only heightened dramatically their possible significance in India-Pakistan relations but that pointed an oblique finger of responsibility for their eventual failure at the Pakistan army. Naik, according to the *Jang* reporter, had revealed in informal remarks at a public gathering in Karachi that the Kargil crisis had shattered a secret and extremely promising dialogue process between the Indian and Pakistani governments that had been launched almost immediately after the Lahore summit and that had as its objective a far-reaching agreement over Kashmir. The process had included, besides routine telephone exchanges between the two prime ministers, nearly a dozen rounds of back-channel meetings. The reporter wrote that Naik made the explicit claim that this process would have yielded a major agreement on Kashmir by September or October. Naik was also said to have claimed that Pakistan's military planners, unaware of the government's protracted back-channel initiative, went ahead with Kargil without communicating to the prime minister that there was more involved in it than a routine annual military exercise. Once the fighting broke out at Kargil, Naik allegedly claimed, Vajpayee's National Security Advisor, Brajesh Mishra, telephoned him urging that he (Naik) intervene to help defuse the situation.[23]

In a carefully drafted press release at the time, Naik vehemently denied having made the alleged remarks.[24] His denial met with overwhelming skepticism in both the Indian and Pakistani media, where the most commonly expressed view was that Naik had been urged to make his disclosures in order to shift to the army the whole of the burden of responsibility for the increasingly unpopular decision to pull out of Kargil.[25] The Pakistan army denounced Naik's alleged statements, and the Indian government, meanwhile, denied having entered into any such agreement. The affair is widely believed to have added fuel to the simmering distrust between the army and Nawaz Sharif that ended finally in the October 1999 coup. In his discussion of these developments with me in January 2001, Naik had this to say:

> I had been invited to address a meeting in Karachi of the Pakistan-China Friendship Association. Not being from Karachi, I was unable to recognize who were the press representatives present at the meeting. There were five

or six present, including a reporter from the *Jang* group. Following my talk, this reporter put a series of questions to me about Kargil, to which in every instance I replied that I was not in a position to respond. I simply kept quiet. Later on, back in my hotel room, I received a late night phone call from one Mr. Liaquat Jatoi. Jatoi informed me that his "interview" with me was to be published the following day in the Urdu-medium *Jang* [Pakistan's largest circulation daily] and that he was calling to give me the opportunity to check his account for accuracy. I protested that I hadn't given any interview. The article appeared the following day. Jatoi had simply converted his *questions* into my *answers*. I found myself in hot water. Back in Islamabad, I went to the Foreign Office where a strong rejoinder was drafted. The chief of army staff [General Pervez Musharraf] indicated that he was satisfied with it. I have no proof but I believe that the *Jang* reporter had been "planted" in the Karachi audience by a member of Nawaz Sharif's cabinet, who sought to shield the prime minister from blame for the diplomatic debacle by shifting it to the army. The army could then be charged with scuttling the Lahore process.

Naik's narrative of the back-channel diplomacy that went on between India and Pakistan in the months following the Lahore Summit leaves ample room for the two sides to draw their own conclusions about it. Pakistanis may well be inclined to interpret New Delhi's seeming last-minute change of heart as a characteristic act of deceit and betrayal—a "double cross" that reaffirms the persistent perfidy in their neighbor's appeals for peace. Indians, in turn, will not find it difficult to discover in these events ample evidence that Pakistan's civilian leaders are simply not in command of their country's foreign policy—not enough of it, in any event, to make India's serious investment in risky bilateral diplomatic initiatives a worthwhile undertaking. What neutral observers are likely to extract from the narrative, I suspect, are two equally compelling lessons: One, that given suitable circumstances the elected leaders of India and Pakistan are quite capable of engaging one another in dispassionate, imaginative, and constructive dialogue about Kashmir; and two, that shielding such dialogue from regional and domestic political crossfire is for all practical purposes nearly impossible. As for Naik himself, the outcome of his encounter with back-channel diplomacy does not seem either to have dulled his enthusiasm for this species of diplomacy or to have permanently tainted his confidence in Pakistan's ability to negotiate successfully with its Indian neighbor. My question to him in regard to Prime Minister Atal Bihari Vajpayee's actual determination to pursue peace with Pakistan as well as a settlement of Kashmir drew from him the comment: "Vajpayee was [at the time of the back-channel initiative] and still is sincere."

We come now to examine in greater detail the principal *military* event of the post-nuclear-tests period—the clash at Kargil—that developed alongside, and eventually marginalized, the seemingly promising back-channel diplomacy we have just reviewed.

Nuclear Brinksmanship on the Line of Control

Scarcely more than two months following the Lahore summit, Indian and Pakistani forces found themselves immersed in a pitched battle for control of mountain heights along a roughly 200-kilometer (120-mile) stretch of the approximately 775-kilometer (465-mile) LOC in northern Kashmir.* An advance Pakistan-backed force numbering between 700 and 1,000 troops, which Islamabad insisted were Kashmiri freedom-fighters (or *mujahideen*) but which New Delhi maintained were almost wholly drawn from Pakistan's Northern Light Infantry (NLI) units under the Force Commander Northern Areas (FCNA), had crossed the LOC at several points between the towns of Drass and Batalik, and infiltrated these heights unobserved during the winter months.** In some areas, they penetrated as far as 11 kilometers (6.6 miles) into Indian-administered territory. The focal point for much of the fighting was the peaks and ridges rising westward of the Indian-controlled district headquarters town of Kargil, which sits astride Indian National Highway 1A at a point where it comes perilously close to the LOC. A crucial warm-weather road link between Srinagar and Leh, the highway was at that time the only existing major surface supply route serving Indian forces deployed further north in defense of India's claim to the Siachen Glacier.*** Indian military convoys moving along this route, suddenly within easy range of directed Pakistani artillery fire, found their passage forcefully interdicted. Following successful (and American-assisted) negotiation

---

*The length of the LOC is given variously as being from 720 to 800 kilometers.

**In the face of horrendously difficult winter conditions, advance reconnaissance teams seem to have first crossed the LOC into Indian-claimed terrain in February. The main body of troops took up positions in April. They at that time began construction of bunkerlike fortifications made from available rocks and boulders. They were detected on 3 May.

***Roughly one oversized division in strength at the time of the Kargil fighting, these forces currently stand at two divisions.

by Indian and Pakistani military teams of what was described as "disengagement," India reported on 26 July that Pakistan-backed forces had been entirely withdrawn.[26] After more than two months of fighting, Pakistan conceded the loss of 267 of its regular soldiers;[27] India, which had concentrated upwards of two divisions in the area, 410.[28] Unofficial estimates of casualties were typically much higher.*

Baffling to many observers in the wake of the fighting over Kargil were the precise reasons it had broken out in the first place. The Pakistani side hid behind official disclaimers of any government responsibility for the intrusions. It was, declared Pakistani spokesmen repeatedly to deeply skeptical audiences, a Kashmiri freedom-fighter show practically all the way. The Indian side, in its turn, fought back with a barrage of colorful invective attributing responsibility wholly to the Pakistanis and describing their behavior as "Janus-faced," "barbarous," and a "betrayal of trust." An editorial in the ordinarily restrained *Times of India* spoke of Pakistan's "savage mercenaries" and branded Pakistan's hastily renewed appeals for serious talks on Kashmir a "jackal's trap."[29]

Cutting through the diatribe and inflated rhetoric unleashed by the fighting, one finds a more complicated bundle of ingredients making up the Kargil episode than either instantly meet the eye or are contained in official versions of what transpired. Reviewing these ingredients may shed additional light on the fundamentally refractory character of the India-Pakistan rivalry. It may also give us some insight into the actual effects on that rivalry of the region's undisguised crossing of the nuclear Rubicon.

Roots of Kargil

The Kargil episode presents us with a number of puzzles. Among them is the *timing* of Pakistan's military operation, which obviously came at an awkward moment, at least from the diplomatic perspective, in the middle of a negotiating process in which more than a few onlookers found at least some promise. If the idea for an intrusion onto the Indian side of the LOC in the Kargil sector had been gestating in the minds of Pakistani policymakers for two years or more, as some suggested, and if, as has been widely claimed, serious physical preparations for it had begun at least by the preceding October (well in advance of the Lahore

---

*Unofficial estimates generally ran to well over a thousand on each side.

meeting in February in other words), what is one to make of the logic of Pakistan's Kashmir policy? What was the point of the hoopla surrounding bus diplomacy? Was all of that merely a cosmetic wrapping concealing a sinister Machiavellian design, as many Indians have claimed?

A second puzzle relates to the *authorization* for the operation—to who commissioned it, in other words. Was it conceivable, as some claimed, that Prime Minister Nawaz Sharif had been a victim of cozenage—deceived by Pakistani generals whose game plan for Kashmir differed in important particulars from that of the country's civilian leadership? Is the real meaning of Kargil to be wrested, accordingly, from Pakistan's tortured legacy as "the state of martial rule"—from a decision-making structure still mired, in other words, in the autocratic habits of its praetorian past?

A third, and by far the most baffling, puzzle surrounds the operation's *objective*—what its organizers expected to gain by it. Was it a payback operation replying to India's seizure of the Siachen Glacier in April 1984? Did the organizers' ambition, fed by the prospect of cutting off Indian troops on the Siachen from the rest of Kashmir by interdicting traffic on the main supply route, extend as far as the actual recovery of the glacier? Or was the operation designed simply to acquire for Pakistan at a strategically important spot on the LOC what Indian forces already possessed in abundance in that vicinity—namely, advantageous high ground that would lend needed strength to Pakistan's otherwise vulnerable military position? Was the operation a monstrous fiasco, as most observers (including many Pakistanis) concluded, since it ended with the withdrawal of Pakistani forces? Or was it at least a qualified success, as Pakistani officials maintained, given that its goal, they insisted, was in large measure political—to compel global attention to the Kashmir dispute, to force its internationalization, in other words—rather than one of capturing new territory?

Solving these puzzles in any conclusive way will require the revelation of far more reliable details than have so far been disclosed.[30] A preliminary probe of them, in particular of the circumstances surrounding them, is possible, however, on the basis of information currently available.

I begin, however, with a comment on my general understanding of the Kargil episode. If I've judged it rightly, Kargil did add a new and substantial chapter to the Kashmir dispute. Three reasons for this come to mind. First, it undoubtedly put a new twist on the dispute's military history, including Pakistan's apparent bid, its first since 1965, to wrest an important slice of territory from India's grasp. Second, it at least temporarily altered the dispute's global diplomatic context, for the most part—since Islamabad more often than not was held responsible for it—in ways injurious to Pakistan. Third, it also raised to unprecedented levels the volume and intensity of chauvinist nationalism in regard to Kashmir, in India no less than in Pakistan. In its fundamentals, however, I believe that Kargil did not represent a sharp break with the pattern of regional rivalry, whether conceived in military or political terms, that India and Pakistan have maintained for decades. On the contrary, it is the continuity of this pattern, one of nearly unremitting hostility and failed diplomacy, which Kargil largely reconfirmed, that is its most striking and important feature. Kargil marked neither the end of an era, nor the start of a new one. Instead, it was emblematic of a malaise in India-Pakistan relations that threatens, in the absence of serious and concerted efforts to put these relations on a more productive footing, to darken their passage well into the twenty-first century.

Now, there is no reason to quibble with the obvious fact that the Kargil operation, viewed from almost any angle, was ill timed. Not only did it wreak havoc with the plans for normalization of relations set in motion at Lahore, it inevitably also dealt a blow to the personal credibility—hence, to the future diplomatic effectiveness—of Prime Minister Nawaz Sharif. Given the frequency of international, especially American, warnings in the post-tests period about the nuclear dangers inherent in the volatile Kashmir dispute, the time was clearly unripe for premeditated exhibition of one's heedlessness in the face of those dangers. To very few would Kargil qualify as a sensible strategy for building up international confidence in the sobriety and perspicacity of Pakistani leaders, much less in the soundness of Pakistan's Kashmir policy. Kargil was also ill timed, we might add, for the eminently practical reason that Pakistan's annual budget had virtually no slack remaining for additional defense expenditures.[31] Why, then, was the Kargil operation given a go-ahead? Two almost certain reasons immediately present themselves.

One is that few key members of Pakistan's foreign policy elite ever entertained high expectations of the dialogue process set in motion at Lahore. Hence, the "promise" of Lahore, touted by the international community, never carried much credibility in Pakistan. The "sacrifice" of this promise at Kargil, it follows, would not have counted heavily against the operation's launching. True, media commentary in Pakistan at the time of the Lahore summit, even in those corners of the press ritually hostile to India, was largely supportive of the process; but skepticism about its underlying motivations—the suspicion that it was driven more by international pressures than by any significant change in the calculations of national interest by the South Asian parties to the talks themselves, coupled with the Pakistanis' deeply ingrained habit of pessimism in regard to any Kashmir-related proposal initiated by New Delhi—severely limited the surfacing of a significant public constituency deeply and irrevocably committed to negotiations.[32] Not having heralded a "new dawn" breaking over South Asia, as had many Indian observers at the time of the Lahore summit,[33] Pakistan's leadership knew it could embark upon the Kargil venture with very little risk of *domestic* political backlash. On the contrary, since Kashmir had stood for decades in Pakistan as an expedient device for rallying popular support, Kargil—in the calculations of policymakers burdened with a galaxy of insoluble economic and political problems—might well have seemed a politically tempting move.

A second reason is that Kargil was also, and to no small extent, a *militarily* tempting move. For an army with few, if any, recent victories to boast of, and with an adversary whose capacity for steadily widening the existing immense arms imbalance between them leaves little room for doubt, the presence in the heights above Kargil of a very likely transient "window of opportunity" to offset the imbalance, even at some risk, would have been hard to resist. As a number of seasoned Indian defense analysts pointed out, the Kargil theater of operations had witnessed fierce fighting before—first in the 1947–48 conflict, then again in the 1965 war, and then also in the 1971 Indo-Pakistan war. Securing control of the high ground above Kargil, after all, had always stood high on the list of both Pakistani and Indian military priorities. "From 1948 to 1965," observed retired Lieutenant General V. R. Raghavan, the erstwhile Director General of Military Operations of the Indian army, "the Kargilis lived under the direct sight of Pakistanis, who rained artillery fire [on them] without any pretext every other day. . . . Aircraft would land [at Kargil] by running the gauntlet of fire. The Pakistani artillery fire made the road that brought supplies to Kargil and Leh unusable for long periods."[34] Indian forces cleared most of the hilltops around Kargil during the 1965 war, but, as part of the Tashkent Accord worked out in 1966, they were returned to Pakistan. Indian forces captured even more of the high ground around Kargil in the 1971 war, however, and it was not repatriated in the 1972 Simla Agreement. Some stretches of the Srinagar-Leh highway were still visible to Pakistanis from the positions they retained after 1971, Raghavan noted, but they were beyond effective artillery range. This had not stopped the Pakistanis from shelling across the LOC in this sector, Raghavan further pointed out, especially in recent years.[35] Civilians, by the way, were among the casualties of this shelling. In this regard, the ethnic composition of Kargil and the villages around it may have helped to mute complaints that Pakistanis were firing on Kashmiri Muslims, the very people they claimed to be seeking to liberate. It happens that the area is settled overwhelmingly by Shia Muslims, who have shown little eagerness to support the Pakistan-backed (and overwhelmingly Sunni Muslim) militants during the past decade. Their suffering and property damage attract little notice, it seems, either among the numerically dominant Sunni Muslims of Indian-held Kashmir or among the also dominant Sunni Muslims of Pakistan.[36]

Clearly of more than modest relevance to the matter of Pakistani motivations was Raghavan's observation in the *Frontline* account that the Kargil sector "is the only sector on the Line of Control (LoC) where Pakistani posts have an advantage of higher positions. Elsewhere on the LoC," he said, "they are at a disadvantage since the dominating heights are held by the Indian military." I have described elsewhere the devastating consequences for Pakistan of the unequal distribution of high ground between the two sides in some sectors of the LOC.[37] Among them were instances of the Indian army firing, with the attendant high costs, on civilian as well as military targets in Azad Kashmir. Accordingly, Pakistani frustration over India's ability to inflict damage on the Pakistan side virtually at will in some sectors has been festering for many years. The frustration has not been eased any by the Pakistan army's utter inability to dislodge the Indians from the Siachen Glacier, a no-man's land seized without warning (and in seeming violation of the 1972 Simla Accord) by the Indians in April 1984, where Indian troops also happen to occupy the high ground. It has very likely been compounded, one might add, by the inescapable realization that Pakistan's military options in Kashmir are gradually, and perhaps permanently, dwindling.

The scale of the Pakistani intrusion at Kargil in 1999, as well as of the fighting that resulted from it, obviously far exceeded in magnitude the skirmishing that has for long been the norm on the LOC. In this sense, there was nothing routine or ordinary about it. Nevertheless, while the Pakistani intrusion at Kargil in 1999 struck most outsiders (and not a few insiders) as an entirely rash and unprecedented action with no reasonable logic to support it, closer scrutiny suggests that Pakistan's action bore a strong family resemblance to established norms of military custom on the LOC—norms observed for over fifty years by *both* sides, I might add. The point is that jockeying for military advantage on the LOC has been a fairly large part of what both armies have long been engaged with in Kashmir on a routine basis. Gaining an edge over the other side in this contest has constituted no small portion of military tactics. Not to take advantage of occasional tactical blunders or intelligence lapses by the other side in regard to the LOC would strike strategists of both armies, and certainly those of the weaker side, as downright irresponsible. As one senior Indian army officer reportedly observed while the fighting around Kargil still raged, the Pakistan army, noticing the Indian army's evacuation of bunkers at high elevations in the Kargil sector during the bitter winter months, simply put into practice the "finders keepers" rule that both sides had long observed.[38]

If the above two circumstances are accepted as *necessary* ingredients of the decision to go ahead with the Kargil operation, they obviously fall well short of being *sufficient* grounds for it. The Kargil operation was, after all, a major decision, and it had major consequences. There are credible but unverified reports that something akin to it had already been proposed, and rejected, once or twice during Benazir Bhutto's tenure as prime minister,[39] and, more recently, at an earlier point in Nawaz Sharif's tenure, by the then Chief of Army Staff General Jehangir Karamat. In any event, no one in a position of authority in Pakistan could possibly have been unaware that the Kargil operation held implications demanding far more than unreflective application of the "finders keepers" rule. What, then, might stand as sufficient grounds for its implementation?

The authors of *From Surprise to Reckoning*, the report of the Kargil Review Committee commissioned by the Indian government to investigate multiple aspects of the Kargil episode, identify eight suggested motivations for Pakistan's undertaking of the Kargil intrusions. They classify them as follows:

Political-Strategic Motives

1. To internationalize Kashmir as a nuclear flashpoint requiring urgent third party intervention;
2. To alter the Line of Control (LOC) and disrupt its sanctity by capturing unheld areas in Kargil; and
3. To achieve a better bargaining position for a possible trade-off against the positions held by India in Siachen.

Military/Proxy War-Related Motives

4. To interdict the Srinagar-Leh road by disrupting vital supplies to Leh;
5. To outflank India's defenses from the South in the Turtok and Chalunka sectors through unheld areas, thus rendering its defenses untenable in Turtok and Siachen;
6. To give a fillip to militancy in Jammu and Kashmir by military action designated to weaken the counterinsurgency (CI) grid by drawing away troops from the Valley to Kargil. It would also give a boost to the morale of the militants in the Valley;
7. To activate militancy in the Kargil and Turtok sectors and open new routes of infiltration into the Valley; and
8. To play to the fundamentalist lobby and the Pakistani people by bold action in Kashmir, which continues to remain a highly emotional issue.[40]

To these motivations, the report's authors add eight "assumptions" that were likely to have underlaid the intrusions:

1. [Pakistan's] nuclear capability would forestall any major Indian move, particularly across the international border, involving use of India's larger conventional capabilities. [Pakistan] appears to have persuaded itself that nuclear deterrence had worked in its favor from the mid-1980s.
2. Confidence that the international community would intervene at an early stage, leaving [Pakistan] in possession of at least some of its gains across the LOC, thereby enabling it to bargain from a position of strength.
3. China would adopt a favorable posture in light of its perceived anti-Indian stand in the post–Pokhran II [nuclear tests] period.

4. A weak and unstable government in India would be incapable of a quick and firm response and would not be inclined to open a new front.
5. The Indian army would not be able to respond adequately due to its heavy CI [counterinsurgency] commitment in Jammu and Kashmir.
6. Due to an inadequacy of resources east of Zojila [Pass], India would not be able to react effectively against the intrusions before Zojila opened for traffic by end May/early June.
7. The Indian army would not be able to muster adequate forces with high altitude training and acclimatization to fight on the Kargil heights.
8. Rapidly returning normalcy in Jammu and Kashmir. needed to be thwarted in order to sustain [Pakistan's] "cause."[41]

The report's authors suggest that the *original* motivation for the Kargil intrusion may have been "the desire to avenge Siache", and they add to the other motivations—on the grounds that his background in Pakistan's Special Services Group (SSG) and expertise in mountain warfare predisposed him to favor the sort of unconventional operation witnessed at Kargil—the "strong indication that the assumption of office by General Musharraf as COAS was an important factor in Pakistan's decision to go ahead with this plan."[42] They otherwise do not endorse any one factor over the others.[43]

I believe that we can dismiss, without hesitation, the argument put out by Pakistani officials that the Kargil operation was decided upon not by Pakistanis but by Kashmir-based Kashmiri freedom-fighters.[44] The Government of India has produced a mountain of evidence—including the corpses of soldiers from the Pakistan army's Northern Light Infantry, personal diaries, and the intriguing transcript of an intercepted telephone conversation allegedly held between Pakistan's Chief of Army Staff General Pervez Musharraf and his Chief of General Staff Lieutenant General Mohammad Aziz[45]—to suggest otherwise. It strains credulity, furthermore, to think that Pakistan's ability peremptorily to order the withdrawal of these fighters in July was not intimately related to a preexistent army-dominated chain of command. Not a few Pakistanis themselves have publicly questioned whether it was "reasonable to believe that freedom–fighters can fight at 15,000 feet above sea level without Pakistani rations, clothing, logistics, ammunition and intelligence support."[46] Until irrefutable evidence to the contrary is made available, we have to assume that the Kargil operation, in most important respects, was a Pakistan army operation.

We can also reject outright the notion, a favorite of Indian propaganda organs at the time, that the Kargil operation was part of a "terrorist binge" embarked upon by an increasingly "talibanized" Pakistan. Such a notion was embodied in the comments of Indian Minister of External Affairs Jaswant Singh, who in a public lecture in late July branded Pakistan's action, with a touch of wry wit, "an overspill of the 'Afghanistan disorder syndrome' . . . a manifestation of this medieval malevolence spilling over from Afghanistan."[47] This theme, given lavish play throughout the Kargil conflict by Jaswant Singh and other Indian leaders, took advantage, of course, of the popular, and to some extent official, perception in Western countries that the threat of world Communism had been replaced by the turn of the century by the no less sinister threat of Islamic fundamentalism. Invoking the threat aligned India with the West on this deeply emotional issue, maligned Pakistan's reputation, and, of course, conveniently absolved India of practically any responsibility for the appalling state of India-Pakistan relations. As a mischievous weapon in the ongoing psychological warfare over Kashmir between India and Pakistan, the terrorist indictment had obvious utility: it drew upon an undeniable record of terrorist incidents in the Kashmir insurgency. As an explanation for the Kargil episode, however, it left much to be desired. Terrorism's alleged links with Kashmir surfaced again, of course, in the wake of the 11 September terrorist attacks on East Coast targets in the United States. Then, the apparent material connections between Afghanistan's Taliban leaders and Osama bin Laden's shadowy Al Qaeda terrorist network lent credibility to the notion of a spreading contagion of Islamic extremism or talibanization that had not been present before. We reexamine this theme, from different angles, in both Chapter 2 and Chapter 3.

Generally unconvincing, too, is the argument that the Kargil operation was deliberately intended mainly to provoke a massive Indian counterattack and thus, in the new nuclearized circumstances of the Kashmir conflict, to precipitate its "internationalization." Putting the spotlight on Kashmir, it is said, would increase the pressure on India to engage in serious negotiations with Pakistan in regard to Kashmir.[48] If one holds to this logic, the intruders' eventual withdrawal, once they had demonstrated their courage and prowess against Indian forces, was more or less acceptable. So long as the operation triggered international intervention, it could still be portrayed as a glorious victory—a Himalayan grand stand reminiscent, in some respects, of Masada, or at least of the Palestinian Intifada.[49] The unmistakable taint of alibi and of ex post facto rationalization—the desire to escape the ignominy of defeat—hovers over this argument. It assumes a level of wiliness and deft maneuvering in the prelude to the operation that is largely belied by the maladroit and undignified manner of its ending. It also presupposes the Pakistan army's willingness to absorb still another costly defeat on the strength of the belief that it would be compensated by timely and responsible intervention by the international community. For us to swallow this, we would have to assume a nearly suicidal propensity for gambling on the part of Pakistan's generals, for whom the international community's past record of involvement with Kashmir would have offered no reassurance at all in regard to the present. More likely, I think, is that the Pakistanis had convinced themselves they would be able not only to seize, but to hold on to, what they considered, rightly, a militarily valuable piece of Indian turf.

Not the least compelling of all the explanations offered for the operation's go-ahead was to be found, I think, in the fractured, cryptic, and largely unmeditated character of the decision-making process that had come to characterize Pakistan's institutionally weak quasi-democracy in recent decades. In this process, the danger of underestimating both the risks to oneself as well as the capabilities of the adversary tended to be greatly magnified. Costs and benefits were not adequately explored. There was not enough restraint on impulse and derring-do. We do not know precisely when Prime Minister Nawaz Sharif became aware of the planned intrusion. There are reports that he was fully briefed on it well in advance—according to some reports, even in advance of the Lahore Summit.[50] There has also been speculation, drawn in part from inferences based on the intercepted telephone conversation between Musharraf and Aziz mentioned earlier, that his awareness, at least of the full details, came fairly late in the game. Whether it came early or late, however, the fact is that, while it endured, he lent the operation his unequivocal and enthusiastic public support. The precise role that he, or the Defense Committee of the Cabinet, played in the shaping of the Kargil plan may be less important to our understanding of its genesis, in any event, than the existence of fundamental defects in Pakistan's governing structure that were revealed in the operation's unfolding. If the truth were told, there is little in Pakistan's political institutions deserving of the word accountability. The two leading parties, the ruling Pakistan Muslim League and the opposition People's Party of Pakistan, have for years, to put it lightly, engaged in a markedly ruthless struggle for power. The army and its assorted intelligence arms, in particular the Inter-Services Intelligence Directorate (ISI), have never ceased to vie with the civilian bureaucracies for control over government policy in the crucial domain of national security, including Kashmir. In the months preceding the operation, the Kargil question would have surfaced for policy consideration in an environment combining some of the anxieties of a garrison under siege with the turmoil of a three-ring circus—not one, in any event, conducive to calm, detached, and exhaustive examination of all the factors involved. The requirement for absolute secrecy, paramount in an operation of this kind, would inevitably have constricted further a process of consultation already severely attenuated in Pakistan's politically hazardous institutional environment. Even within the military, planning for the Kargil operation was probably known to very few. According to Dr. Maleeha Lodhi, at the time editor of *The News* and subsequently appointed for a second stint as Pakistan's ambassador to the United States, "the lack of wider consultation within the military on the decision to support such a [Kargil] plan left it unexposed to rigorous scrutiny; even corps commanders and other service chiefs were excluded from the original consultative process." She concluded that

> the most important lesson of the two-month crisis ensues from the disastrous consequences of unstructured governance. The Kargil affair has exposed systemic flaws in a decision-making process that is impulsive, chaotic, erratic and overly secretive . . . playing holy warriors this week and men of peace the next betrays an infirmity and insincerity of purpose that leaves the country leaderless and directionless.[51]

Of course, Pakistan is far from alone among South Asian states in the clobbering its decision-making takes occasionally from "systemic flaws." Witness India's not dissimilar decision in early 1984 to seize control of the Siachen Glacier. Description of that military operation (Operation Meghdoot) as a "mistake" by the Indian general—Lieutenant General M. L. Chibber—who commanded the forces that accomplished it, has been echoed many times since then, often in even more flatly derogatory language, by other senior Indian bureaucrats and army officers.[52]

What may distinguish the Siachen from the Kargil misadventure, however, is that while Pakistan can't afford one, India can.

With the above inventory of more or less persuasive reasons prompting Pakistan's go-ahead at Kargil, we have clearly not exhausted all the possibilities. Important to bear in mind, in this regard, is Rodney Jones's observation that Kargil "may have had more than one motive, perhaps a hierarchy of them, with different actors in the decision chain leaning more to one than another, based on their bureaucratic or political interests. These motives did not have to be convincing to outsiders (either in the West or in India) to be convincing to their authors within Pakistan, nor did they necessarily have to be proved certain of achieving their objectives to win approval within the narrow circle of decision-makers."[53] Especially important to keep in mind, I think, is the possibility that the Kargil episode developed in a way that no one in Pakistani decision-making circles had anticipated and that at least some key decisions were made, so to speak, on the fly. There is great likelihood, in fact, that Pakistani expectations of military gains from Kargil were quite modest, that the main motivation was simply to bring relief to Pakistan's exposed and beleaguered transport routes along the LOC by bringing India's own primary route within range of Pakistani artillery, and that Pakistani decision makers were caught significantly off guard by the effort's stunningly swift escalation into a major conflict. In this connection, it is noteworthy that while the Kargil Review Committee Report observes that the Pakistani "operation was extremely well planned and executed and that Pakistan was able to achieve total surprise," it also notes in the same paragraph that

> the intruders were perhaps discovered a little too soon and were unable either to reach or firmly establish themselves on the forward features before the Indian Army reacted. This is evident from the fact that many of the forward hill features occupied by the intruders had very limited quantities of ammunition, water and supplies when they were recaptured by the Indian forces.[54]

One way to interpret this is that the Pakistan army, not having expected to find as many vacated Indian military positions at Kargil and as little Indian resistance as it did, was simply not prepared for the magnitude of the operation's initial successes. In this sense, then, the Pakistanis may have been every bit as "surprised" by Kargil as were the Indians!

A more definite sorting out of Kargil's roots than we are able to accomplish in these pages may become possible with the passage of time. We set the matter aside now, turning our attention directly to Kargil's nuclear dimension.

Kargil and Nuclear Deterrence

The Kargil episode witnessed the heaviest fighting between India and Pakistan since the Bangladesh war of 1971. For the most part, however, fighting was localized. Mortar and artillery shelling went on at many points on the LOC, but the most severe fighting by ground troops—and all of the bombing and strafing by aircraft—was concentrated in the Kargil sector. There was some reported penetration by Indian aircraft of Pakistani airspace, but Indian forces, in spite of the obvious attraction of cutting the intruders' lines of supply, were clearly operating under a general prohibition against crossing the LOC. Thus, the fighting ended without having escalated into a full conventional war. Is one lesson of Kargil, therefore, that there are now new (and comforting) rules of nuclear deterrence operating in South Asia that put a lowered ceiling on permissible levels, types, and aims of conventional warfare? In other words, is a de facto doctrine of nuclear deterrence already functioning—and functioning in the interest of peace—in the region?

Both sides unquestionably indulged in fairly reckless rhetorical invocation of the nuclear threat while fighting raged at Kargil. According to one count, Indian and Pakistani "officials and ministers delivered indirect and direct nuclear threats to one another [during the Kargil crisis] no fewer than 13 times."[55] Senior Indian leaders, publicly committed to "no first use" of nuclear weapons, were a bit more guarded in their public comments. Pakistan's leaders, whose nuclear outlook has been conditioned by the brute fact of conventional force inferiority, issued unmistakable warnings in their turn that from the Pakistani perspective a preemptive first strike could not be ruled out. Pakistan's Foreign Secretary Shamshad Ahmad was reported at an early point in the crisis, for instance, to have observed bluntly to a group of Pakistani news reporters: "We will not hesitate to use any weapon in our arsenal to defend our territorial integrity."[56]

Did the threat of a nuclear exchange extend beyond rhetoric? A *Washington Post* article published soon after the Kargil crisis ended claimed that the South Asian region had, in fact, come uncomfortably close to a nuclear Armageddon. The Kargil conflict, it said, "came much closer to full-scale war than was publicly acknowledged at the time—and raised very real fears that one or both countries would resort to using variants of the nuclear devices each tested last year."[57] American spy satellites had picked up signs in Rajasthan, hundreds of miles to the south of Kargil along India's main border with Pakistan, that the Indians were loading tanks, artillery, and other "strike force" equipment onto flatbed railcars, presumably preparations for an invasion of their neighbor. Military leaves, the report claimed, had been canceled nationwide. Pakistan, it said, had also begun to ready its offensive units. The article quoted a senior Clinton administration official, speaking on condition of anonymity, who described the Kargil crisis as "'one of the most dangerous situations on the face of the earth. . . . It was very, very easy to imagine how this crisis . . . could have escalated out of control, including in a way that could have brought in nuclear weapons, without either party consciously deciding that it wanted to go to nuclear war.'" The Indian government promptly and predictably dismissed the report as ill conceived and unfounded.[58] Media commentary in both India and Pakistan was emphatic that preparations had been entirely precautionary and defensive in nature. The Clinton administration's doomsday forecasting, it was said, was a way of claiming greater success for President Clinton's personal intervention in the crisis than it deserved.[59]

The argument that India and Pakistan were near nuclear war during the Kargil crisis was strongly renewed, almost exactly three years later, in an article prepared by Bruce O. Riedel for the Center for the Advanced Study of India at the University of Pennsylvania. Riedel, the senior director for South Asia on the Clinton administration's National Security Council at the time of the Kargil episode, claimed in the article that by early July, American intelligence possessed "disturbing evidence that the Pakistanis were preparing their nuclear arsenals for possible deployment." Suddenly confronted with this evidence at his hastily called 4 July summit with President Clinton in Blair House, Pakistan's Prime Minister Nawaz Sharif, according to Riedel, "seemed taken aback."[60]

Conclusive evidence that either side was readying its nuclear weapons for use against its adversary during the Kargil episode (or, for that matter, that either side had by that time actually stockpiled militarily useable nuclear weapons) has not been publicly revealed. Pending such revelation, one must allow for the possibility that American public estimates at that time of the nuclear danger may have been speculative and exaggerated, perhaps overstating the extent of conventional (air and ground) force mobilization in the two countries, for instance, or caricaturing the leaders of these countries as naive or even trigger-happy when it came to nuclear weapons. It needs emphasis, however, that Kargil stands as the first major *conventional* armed conflict to be fought in the nuclear age between two *nuclear-weapon-capable* states—neighboring and bitterly adversarial states at that. Hence, notwithstanding the possibility that the West's rhetoric was unduly alarmist, perhaps even self-serving, the West's disquiet could hardly be faulted.

Debate over earlier crises in India-Pakistan relations—about how close they came to nuclear war—goes on unabated today; so it is hardly surprising that the same sorts of claims and counterclaims made in regard to those crises crop up again in the Kargil context. Does the debate about those earlier crises supply us with useful guidelines about the role nuclear deterrence may have played in the more recent one?

One of the last decade's more systematic treatises written on the issue of nuclear deterrence in South Asia was by Devin T. Hagerty.[61] His book, authored before the nuclear tests of May 1998, focused on the period in India-Pakistan relations between late 1986 and mid-1990. This period witnessed two Indo-Pakistani crises—the Brass Tacks crisis of 1986–87, which takes its name from a massive and prolonged military exercise bearing that name staged by India in Rajasthan near the Pakistani border, and the crisis that developed at the time of the outbreak of the Kashmir insurgency in 1990. Over the course of the Brass Tacks exercise, the Indians carried out what amounted to a partial mobilization of India's available ground forces to war-fighting levels. A force mobilization on that scale anywhere in the vicinity of Pakistan's borders naturally had to be viewed with real alarm in Pakistan, which responded predictably with defensive preparations of its own conventional forces that were in turn seen as potentially threatening by the Indians. Pakistan was not known at the time to have acquired nuclear weapons, but it was generally believed to be well along with their development. India, which had conducted a nuclear test in 1974, was believed by some to be in possession already of a small nuclear weapons stockpile. In the midst of the crisis, Pakistan's leading nuclear scientist, Dr. A. Q. Khan, "revealed" in an informal chat with the well-known Indian journalist, Kuldip Nayar, that Pakistan had, indeed, achieved nuclear weapons capability. His revelation, coming in the manner it did, was unlikely to have been accepted at face value by India's sophisticated atomic energy insiders. It was apparently an attempt by Pakistan to exploit the uncertainty that prevailed over the exact stage at which it stood in the fabrication of nuclear weapons. Hagerty observes that, in any event, "little evidence has yet come to light suggesting that nuclear weapon capabilities played any existential deterrent role in Indian and Pakistani crisis behavior in 1987." On the contrary, he says, "Brasstacks was essentially a prenuclear weaponization crisis," occurring at a moment when India had not yet come to view "Pakistan as a 'real' nuclear weapon state."[62] That crisis, then, at least as Hagerty understands it, can give us little insight into Kargil's specifically nuclear implications.

As for the 1990 crisis, Hagerty avers that Pakistan had acquired useable nuclear weapons by that time. The crisis developed in reaction to a massive uprising by Kashmiris against Indian rule, responsibility for which New Delhi naturally assigned to Pakistan. Once again, threatening conventional military preparations were undertaken by both sides. This time both sides sent repeated signals to one another warning of their willingness, if pushed to the wall, to resort to nuclear weapons. Some accounts of the crisis suggest that India and Pakistan came perilously close to using them. This prospect allegedly triggered international intervention, including the much-publicized dispatch to South Asia by Washington of Deputy National Security Adviser Robert Gates, in the wake of whose visit the crisis rapidly subsided.

Much debate has ensued over just how close to nuclear war India and Pakistan came in 1990. Hagerty's view is that the more alarmist accounts are of doubtful validity. Indeed, he concludes his discussion of the 1990 crisis with the observation that

> a strong case can be made that India and Pakistan were deterred from war in 1990 by the existence of nuclear weapon capabilities on both sides and the chance that, no matter what Indian and Pakistani decision-makers said or did, any direct military clash could ultimately escalate to the nuclear level.[63]

Hagerty concedes that the case for existential deterrence—the notion "that nuclear weapons deter aggression by virtue of the simple fact that they exist"[64]—can't be proven. There is a paucity of substantiated facts, for one thing, and only the 1990 episode, he concedes, can be considered a legitimate test. He maintains, nonetheless, "that existential deterrence was the most important cause of peace on the subcontinent."[65]

The heavy reliance of Hagerty's thesis on the 1990 episode focuses attention on the still unanswerable question of the actual state of nuclear readiness achieved by one or both of the two rivals by that time. Were it to turn out that the Pakistan side, at least, was actually in no condition in 1990 to launch a nuclear strike on India and, moreover, that its nuclear saber-rattling, as in 1987, was mere bluff, then Hagerty's confident assertion of linkage between subcontinental peace and the region's nuclear weaponization would have to be reappraised.

Brought in view at Kargil, of course, was yet another crisis in India-Pakistan relations, this one pitched at a higher rung on the nuclear escalation ladder—that of unambiguous demonstration by both countries in May 1998 of their possession of nuclear weapons. The question raised by Hagerty persists: Does nuclear deterrence work in South Asia? In Kargil's wake, do we find his guardedly optimistic forecast of the region's nuclear future confirmed? Or do we, taking our cue from the largely pessimistic forecasts emerging from what Hagerty calls "the logic of nonproliferation," find reason now for even greater apprehension?

No consensus is apparent in the replies observers have given to these questions. Some continue to see in the multi-angled process of nuclear weapons and ballistic missile development going on today in India and Pakistan a situation fraught with great danger. "Even before conducting its May 1998 nuclear tests and declaring itself a nuclear-weapon power," in the words of a comprehensive and authoritative report on the nuclear situation in South Asia published soon after those tests,

> India had been pressing ahead with sensitive nuclear activities in enrichment, plutonium reprocessing, and breeder reactor installation, as well as with ballistic missile development. India apparently was barely restrained by diplomatic intervention from new nuclear testing in 1995 and again, during the uncertainty of the BJP's 13–day tenure, in early 1996. India was poised to quickly resume nuclear and medium-range missile testing and to step up production and deployment of short-range missiles before the BJP came to power in April 1998. Pakistan was responding in 1996–97, trying to match each nuclear and missile development in India. Most hesitated then to label the South Asia action-reaction cycle as a full-fledged nuclear arms race, but that conclusion was unavoidable after May 1998. The immediate issue now is whether this nuclear and missile arms race can be slowed and eventually capped, short of actual war.

"Since the Kashmir issue is still unresolved," the report went on to observe, "the India-Pakistan nuclear arms competition brings the Subcontinent closer to the edge of a nuclear catastrophe."[66]

In a more recent and trenchant examination of the concept of "minimum nuclear deterrence" in South Asia, Rodney W. Jones, one of the authors of the above-quoted report, observed that

> the risk of nuclear war in South Asia is significant and not to be taken lightly. The potential for nuclear crisis instability is inherent in the conventional military imbalance between Pakistan and India. India's steadily growing conventional military superiority over Pakistan, coupled with Pakistan's geographic vulnerabilities to preemptive conventional air strikes and rapid invasion, and the fact that Pakistan's nuclear forces are smaller, means that Pakistan could be driven to use nuclear weapons during a conventional conflict [with] India. Pakistan's nuclear posture preserves a nuclear first-use option by default and therefore reflects these military and geographic asymmetries.

"Kargil," he notes in particular, "was the first unambiguous case of crisis management between India and Pakistan as nuclear-armed rivals. . . . [It] indicated to the outside world that there is a high risk of nuclear conflict in the subcontinent."[67]

The point of these remarks, in contrast with Hagerty's analysis, is that the nuclear arms competition between India and Pakistan has acquired considerable momentum. Unchecked, it promises to fuel a steadily expanding search for new and more sophisticated weaponry and delivery systems. No cap is in sight. No agreed restraints are in place. The strategic context in South Asia is thus spasmodic and unpredictable, with both sides having to struggle to match the other's advances, and with neither side, in spite of India's natural advantages, wholly confident it is keeping pace.[68] Viewed from this angle, New Delhi's release in mid-August 1999 of a controversial six-page document setting forth a draft nuclear doctrine ("Draft Report of National Security Advisory Board on Indian Nuclear Doctrine") gave compelling evidence that a perilous nuclear trend was underway. The doctrine, advocating a considerably enlarged nuclear-war fighting force structure based on a triad of nuclear strike systems, seemed to represent a hardening of Indian commitment to nuclear weapons and, as well, to mark an aggressive departure from India's past—more self-restrained—nuclear strategy. It presented Pakistani strategic planners with a very narrow set of alternative responses, from which they were most likely to choose, in Rodney Jones's phrasing, "maximally credible deterrence"—a nuclear force operational posture heavily reliant upon countervalue (cities and industry) targeting and retention of the nuclear first-strike option.[69]

In spite of these seemingly threatening nuclear developments, some professional South Asia watchers still see in the region's evolving nuclear status no reason for exceptional alarm. RAND Corporation senior policy analyst Ashley Tellis, for example, in the most meticulous and methodical published inspection thus far of India's emerging nuclear doctrine, maintains not only that a state's nuclear doctrine is a critical determinant of nuclear weapons utilization but also that, in India's case, the doctrine is reassuringly sober, enlightened, defensive, and—under existing geostrategic circumstances—proper. "In contrast to much of the extant analyses about Indian nuclear doctrine appearing in both scholarly and popular publications," he writes,

> India's emerging nuclear doctrine is fundamentally conservative in orientation and exemplifies a systematic internalization of the lessons of the "nuclear revolution." This doctrine, premised as it is on the fearsome power of nuclear weapons and the strengthening taboo against nuclear use, is judged to be appropriate, given India's specific strategic circumstances in South Asia; the conventional balance of power currently existing between India and its immediate rivals; and, the generally status quo orientation of the Indian state. All these variables are viewed as combining to create an official consensus that India's nuclear weapons are primarily pure deterrents intended to ward off political blackmail that might be mounted by local adversaries in some remote circumstances, while simultaneously providing strategic reassurance to India's political leaders if the country were to face truly dire threats to its security. *This view of the utility of nuclear weapons has resulted in a doctrine that is quite sincere about its claims to pursue a no-first-use policy and, consequently, the actual use of nuclear weapons by India is likely to occur only in retaliation against the prior use of nuclear weapons by an adversary. Further, such retaliation is likely to be slow but sure in coming, with the absence of alacrity here being entirely a function of India's desire to simultaneously: maintain its traditionally strict system of civilian control over all strategic assets; minimize the costs of maintaining a nuclear deterrent at high levels of operational readiness routinely; and maximize the survivability of its relatively modest nuclear assets by an operational posture that emphasizes extensive, but opaque, distribution of its many constituent components.*[70]

Tellis's strong faith in India's radical inversion of conventional Strangelovian logic—the offensive, nuclear-war-fighting logic that underwrites the preemptive nuclear strike—runs through his entire discussion. Nuclear weapons, he argues, are not understood by Indians as implements of war but as "antidotes to blackmail."[71] They are seen as "exclusively political instruments . . . rather than military tools . . ." [72] India's fairly modest security challenges preclude the need for "a more expansive view of the utility of nuclear weaponry."[73] India doesn't need nuclear weapons for power or prestige. India's non-war fighting doctrine of pure deterrence rests on far more, however, than its immediate security environment. On the contrary, it is firmly rooted in India's political culture, more specifically in the political morality imbedded in that culture—in what Tellis labels India's "ideational discomfort with nuclear weaponry." "Only a worldview," he says, "that treats nuclear weapons as political devices *in opposition to* their being military tools can emphasize their radical inutility and, thereby, salvage something that resembles fidelity to the country's larger commitment to non-violence as an ordering principle of political life."[74] As a consequence of all this, concludes Tellis on a notably uplifting (and disarming) note, "India's evolving nuclear doctrine is likely to be conducive to—rather than subversive of—strategic stability in South Asia."[75]

Tellis concedes that India's nuclear deterrent posture, as he defines it, "represents a unique approach to maintaining a nuclear arsenal."[76] Indeed, it is upon the strength of this claimed uniqueness—of the amount of sophistication, for instance, that Indian nuclear doctrine has actually acquired from mistakes made by earlier generations of nuclear weapon states; of the extent of moral "anguish" Indians experience as their country amasses the arsenal; or, most importantly, of the capacity acquired by India over the long haul to insulate the alleged restraint of its deterrence doctrine from the intra- and extra regional pressures upon it to change into something more aggressive—that the core of Tellis's argument ultimately rests.[77]

Even if we grant that the subcontinent's present "precarious equilibrium" is contingent to an extent upon India's unique nuclear doctrine, as Tellis asserts, or that something akin to existential nuclear deterrence helped to keep the peace on the subcontinent in the particular circumstances obtaining in 1990, as Hagerty maintains, there would still be no reason to depend on those two postulates for a working model of nuclear deterrence reliably attuned to the astonishingly turbulent strategic circumstances that present themselves in South Asia at the start of the new century. India's nuclear weapons program *may* have been primarily domestically driven, defensive, and morally restrained up until now, but its program may acquire very different characteristics and motivations in coming decades as it evolves (necessarily) interactively with the far-from-static nuclear programs of its existing or potential adversaries, China and Pakistan among them. As Stephen Cohen of the Brookings Institution has pointed out, nuclear decision making in Asia grows steadily more complex and difficult to manage. The nuclear *proliferation* chain that characterized Asia in earlier decades, he says, is giving way to "an interactive, multinational, nuclear *weapons* chain stretching from Israel to North Korea, and perhaps beyond."[78] In this kind of nuclear system, one cannot be confident that the possession of nuclear weapons will be stabilizing and relaxing. "The security of India in relation to Pakistan," he suggests, now

> depends not on the quality of the *Indian* nuclear force or the rationality of an *Indian* decision-making system, but on the integrity of *Pakistan's* chain of command. Indian lives and security ultimately rest on the calculations of the least reliable link, the least informed decision-maker, the most extremist general, and the most rabidly anti-Indian politician, who find themselves in Pakistan's decision-making system.[79]

Needless to add here, of course, is the fact that the security of Pakistan in relation to India rests on a very similar calculus.

In any event, I for one am not convinced that the "no peace, no war" code of conduct currently observed in the conflict between India and Pakistan—its "ugly stability," to use Ashley Tellis's memorable phrase[80]—will go on indefinitely. Neither do I find persuasive the argument that the agreement reached between India and Pakistan in 1999 to pull back from the brink at Kargil "suggests that each country had already learned the discipline of nuclear-induced restraint."[81] The truth of the matter, unfortunately, is that the Kargil episode, like the crises that preceded it, supplies few if any certain clues to the region's nuclear future. The nuclear deterrent may have acted in 1999 to constrain India from carrying the fight across the LOC, but it obviously did not deter Pakistan from launching a provocative military operation against India in the first place. As this is being written (in May 2002), war again menaces the subcontinent. There prevails now at least as great a threat of escalation to nuclear warfare as has existed at any time in the two adversaries' past. Both sides reportedly had moved nuclear-capable missile batteries to forward-deployed positions; and there were scarcely muted warnings that resort to the nuclear option had not been ruled out.[82] In late May and in the face of powerful international appeals for restraint, Pakistan conspicuously carried out two back-to-back nuclear missile tests.[83] Leading newspapers warned in ominous language of the imminent nuclear threat.[84] It seemed that circumstances themselves were in the nuclear saddle, not any formalized nuclear doctrine or species of deterrence logic.

As many have commented, there is a very fine line between nuclear deterrence and nuclear blackmail, and when it is crossed, the incentive to move from subnuclear to nuclear forms of warfare is increased. For any but the most sanguine analysts, the region's steady drift toward heightened nuclear weaponized status, unaccompanied by compensatory nuclear arms control agreements between India and Pakistan, cannot be viewed as a salutary development.[85]

Toward Dialogue—Cease-Fire Diplomacy and the Agra Summit

The Kargil episode endured long enough to impose fairly heavy material costs on both sides—immediately in terms of military casualties, over a longer period in terms of an inevitable increase in military expenditure. When the fighting concluded, India announced plans to create a new army corps headquarters in Kashmir (14th Corps, at Leh in Ladakh) as well as to station one of its mountain divisions permanently in the Kargil sector, steps whose financial and other requirements, given the remote and difficult mountainous terrain in that area, were bound to be substantial.[86] Few doubted that New Delhi's announcement in February 2000 of a hefty 28.2 percent increase in military spending—the largest single-year increase in India's history—owed at least some of its inspiration to Kargil.[87]

These material costs aside, had the Kargil episode, taking place against the backdrop of the region's move to overt nuclear weaponization, not dramatically highlighted the urgency of revived official dialogue between India and Pakistan? Had it not, in fact, made the most emphatic case possible for a more resolute regional commitment to Kashmir's settlement? Western observers clearly thought it should have. Even before Kargil, they were painting frightening scenarios of a South Asia

swept to the brink of nuclear holocaust via mismanaged regional conflict over Kashmir. Renewed dialogue over Kashmir, for them, was an
obvious and inescapable antidote to the nuclear threat.[88] Not even in the
wake of Kargil, however, were South Asians likely to view their circumstances in quite this light. While Kashmir unquestionably persisted as a
dominant influence on both Indian and Pakistani policymakers, tackling
the thorny problem of its resolution was unlikely to be seen by either
side as necessarily the most fruitful, much less the only, direction in
which to move in order to contain the nuclear genie. Neither side appeared unduly upset, in fact, that the genie had escaped the bottle; and
neither side, public rhetoric to the contrary notwithstanding, was likely
to believe that it could be rebottled by negotiating an end to the conflict
over Kashmir. More likely to repay diplomatic effort, they appeared to
have decided in the immediate post-Kargil period, were renewed efforts to use the Kashmir issue—by the Indians, to affix the label of
terrorist state to Pakistan and thus to isolate it internationally, by the
Pakistanis, to deepen India's reputation as a regional bully and op-
pressor of minorities—to pillory the other side and to undermine its
international standing and prestige.

Among the most immediate and conspicuous political casualties of
the sudden downslide in India-Pakistan relations brought on by Kargil,
as we have seen, was the Lahore Declaration and the momentum achieved
in the India-Pakistan dialogue associated with it. Pakistani prime minister Nawaz Sharif, even before the fighting ended, appealed for immediate revival of the Lahore process "without preconditions"; but on 12
July 1999, his Indian counterpart, facing strong criticism at home for
his alleged mishandling of the crisis and, in particular, for having lowered his guard unwisely at Lahore in a misplaced attempt to appease the
Pakistanis, abruptly jettisoned India's previous position and refused to
return to the dialogue until Pakistan had satisfied a number of rigorous
conditions. The first was that Pakistan must withdraw entirely any remnants of the Kargil armed intrusion still present on the Indian side of the
LOC. This condition Pakistan quickly satisfied. The other two were more
formidable: first, that Pakistan should reaffirm the inviolability and sanctity of the LOC, and second, that Pakistan should take clear steps to end
cross-border terrorism throughout the state of Jammu and Kashmir.
Islamabad, said an Indian Foreign Office spokesman, had to cease aiding and abetting terrorism. He was quoted as calling upon Pakistan to
"dismantle the entire network set up in Pakistani territory for this pur-

pose."[89] In this new formulation, as an Indian political analyst pointed out, "India was no longer seeking the restoration of the situation as it prevailed prior to 1999, but the one that prevailed before 1989 when insurgency broke out in Kashmir."[90] The Pakistanis, equally averse both to the notion of the LOC's "sanctity" and to the label of "terrorism" applied to their tactics in Kashmir, were bound to bristle at these demands. The Vajpayee-led interim government in New Delhi, possessing demonstrably strong grounds for doubting Pakistani sincerity[91] and facing a difficult electoral challenge in the imminent September elections, was itself in no great haste to restart the talks with Islamabad. Even when the BJP emerged victorious in the elections, however, New Delhi gave no indication that it was ready to relent from its novel demand that the preconditions be met *before* talks could resume.

In fact, it took almost exactly one year after the fighting ended at Kargil before the first major sign surfaced of any softening in the formal positions of either side on Kashmir. It came on 24 July 2000 in the form of a unilateral declaration of a three-month cease-fire by the Hizb ul-Mujahideen, one of the most powerful as well as the most indigenously rooted of the Kashmiri militant organizations. Engineered by prearrangement with Indian intelligence agencies, the cease-fire appeared to have Islamabad's at least tacit approval. It was greeted enthusiastically by New Delhi, which quickly ordered its own security forces to observe a cease-fire while at the same time initiating talks with the Hizb ul-Mujahideen commanders. The truce collapsed after only fifteen days, however, probably the result of two things: one, inadequate preparations to pave the way to negotiations; the other, severe pressure brought by hard-liners upon both the Indian and Pakistani governments. Before its collapse, however, the joyful public celebration of the moment by Kashmiris telegraphed the unmistakable message to all who were listening that the Kashmiris, at least, had had enough of fighting.[92]

A second and still more momentous sign of possible movement toward more conciliatory government (Indian *and* Pakistani) postures on Kashmir came about four months later, on 19 November, when Indian Prime Minister Vajpayee announced that Indian security forces in Jammu and Kashmir would observe a month-long unilateral cease-fire* of their own— this one set to commence on 28 November with the onset of the Islamic

---

*At its inception, the Indian cease-fire was formally described as "non-initiation of combat operations" (NICO).

holy month of Ramadan.[93] Coming on the heels of a considerable amount of public (and, one assumes, private) introspective analysis by Indian observers of the reasons for the collapse of the July cease-fire,[94] New Delhi's decision seemed carefully calibrated both to nurse along the lines of cleavage among the Kashmiri militant organizations that had been brutally exposed by the abortive July cease-fire as well as to bring Pakistan under still greater strain from international pressure.[95] Islamabad responded on 2 December with its own version of a unilateral truce offer by ordering its troops along the LOC in Jammu and Kashmir to exercise "maximum restraint in order to strengthen and stabilize the ceasefire";[96] and it followed that two days later with the conciliatory announcement that it had simultaneously decided no longer to oppose one-on-one talks between New Delhi and the Kashmiri separatists—in other words, that it was dropping its customary insistence that Pakistan had to be included from the outset of any negotiations on Kashmir.[97] The prolonged maneuvering back and forth fed deepening skepticism among observers, leading one to suggest that the activity might prove in the end to be no more than "another exercise in gimmickry."[98] An uncharacteristic silence settled upon the LOC, however, and India's repeated renewals of the cease-fire—the third, a three-month extension, came on 21 February 2001[99]—kept alive speculation that the Kashmir dispute was once again entering a hopeful stage.

Speculation ended on 23 May 2001 with yet another stunning development in the remarkably staccato relationship that India and Pakistan have maintained of late—namely the Indian government's abrupt termination of the cease-fire, by then in its sixth month, coupled with a seemingly incongruous invitation to General Pervez Musharraf, viewed in India as the architect of Kargil, to visit India. Musharraf immediately gave an affirmative response. Fifty-two days later, on 14 July, he arrived in India for talks. The talks, staged over two days at Agra, renowned as the site of the Mughal architectural gem, the Taj Mahal, were extraordinary on a number of grounds. First, in agreeing to the talks, both sides displayed uncommon political boldness—the Indian prime minister for risking not only the wrath of hard-liners in his own party but also the appearance of having succumbed to Western, especially American, pressures; the Pakistani president* for daring to tread upon diplomatic ter-

---

*Musharraf had dismissed the incumbent president and had himself declared president of Pakistan on 20 June, only weeks prior to the Agra Summit. On his arrival in India, he thus held three top posts—president, chief executive, and chief of army staff.

rain that had brought catastrophe to other rulers of Pakistan, including his immediate predecessor, Nawaz Sharif. Second, the popular media covered the talks to an extent unprecedented in the South Asian region. Body language was duly noted and subjected to minute analysis along with the leaders' spoken remarks. For the first time ever, however, the populations of India and Pakistan were treated to a simultaneous exchange by both print and electronic media of exhaustive and often frank commentary on their countries' troubled relationship—a development likely to widen (albeit not necessarily to render more constructive) the role of public opinion in the shaping of both countries' foreign policies. Third, for between eight and nine hours over the two days the two top leaders met in what were billed as one-on-one meetings.* This signaled a level of confidence in one another far out of keeping with hostile official propaganda circulated by both sides in the post-Kargil period. Less positively, it signaled at the same time a level of confidence in each one's senior foreign affairs and/or military colleagues far below what would likely be required to achieve a significant breakthrough. Fourth, and in some ways most astonishing, was the summit's overwhelming focus on Kashmir. The Indian prime minister had taken pains in his opening remarks at Agra to emphasize the need to address "all outstanding issues" and to take "a comprehensive view" of the relationship between the two countries. He welcomed a full exchange of views on Kashmir, but in the few minutes it took to make his remarks he significantly qualified that concession with three explicit references to terrorism and terrorists.[100] When all was said and done, however, even the Indian side had to acknowledge that Kashmir had won the lion's share of attention—not only in the popular media but also in the official talks themselves.

Not extraordinary, by South Asian standards, was the outcome of the summit. It ended abruptly late in the evening of 16 July without agreement having been reached on the wording of a declaration or joint statement, without a joint press conference, and, indeed, without even a photographed final handshake. Pakistani officials, in particular, sought to depict the summit as a "hopeful" first step, thwarted by hardliners in the ranks of the Indian government, but still promising, since

---

*Since note-takers were present, the meetings were only nominally one-on-one. Absolute candor, such as some observers anticipated from the arrangement, was unlikely under the circumstances.

in the course of it the two sides had narrowed their differences down to a mere handful of words.[101] Indian officials generally struck a more discordant note, contending that the two sides remained leagues apart on the Kashmir issue.[102] When it came to characterizing this issue in the text of a draft joint statement, the two leaders and their negotiating teams did appear to have reached a dead end. Neither side was willing to stray too far from long-standing maximalist official formulations—India's that Kashmir had to be linked with cross-border terrorism, Pakistan's that Kashmir was primarily a problem of human rights and self-determination.[103] "Pakistan's effort to incorporate words into the joint statement suggesting that India would ascertain the will of the people," according to a senior Indian analyst, "was really designed to smuggle in the plebiscite modality that Pakistan has been plugging for over the last half century. India's desire to introduce words suggesting that Pakistan had conceded the need for moderating cross-border terrorism was unacceptable to Pakistan as it would have amounted to a confession of guilt before the international community."[104] Before departing for home, Musharraf extended an invitation to Vajpayee to make a return visit to Pakistan. Vajpayee promptly accepted, without specifying a date. If nothing else, there was the promise of continued dialogue.

Just two months later, even that promise was dealt a severe setback when Vajpayee, reacting to a speech by Musharraf broadcast nationwide in Pakistan on 19 September, canceled his planned visit to Pakistan.[105] Musharraf, seeking to explain to his citizens the reasons for his decision to support Washington's counterterrorist campaign against Afghanistan, peppered his speech liberally with remarks that in India were understood—correctly—to be highly unfriendly, even belligerent, toward Pakistan's eastern neighbor.[106]

War on Terrorism—Common Cause Against Osama and the Taliban?

Having been the principal ally and strategic beneficiary of Afghanistan's maverick Taliban regime from its founding in 1994 up until September 2001, when the Bush administration's stark "join us or suffer the consequences" ultimatum forced it to break the relationship, Pakistan's government was severely jolted by the suddenness of the Taliban's total military collapse over the next few months. The Taliban's vanquishing had all the trappings, in fact, of a debacle for Pakistan—the worst since its defeat by India in the Bangladesh war of 1971. True, in a technical sense Pakistan had found itself thrust virtually overnight into the novel position of "alliance" with its Indian adversary in the global war on terrorism. The alliance was entirely nominal, however, for both the swiftness of the Taliban's fall and the—for Pakistan—highly adverse geopolitical developments its fall immediately gave rise to practically ensured a steep rise in India-Pakistan tensions. To be sure, the war on terrorism brought considerable material and political gains to Pakistan, but strengthened grounds for reconciliation with India were clearly not among them.

Among the immediately visible adverse consequences for India-Pakistan relations of the war on terrorism, two stood out. First, America's rout of the Taliban opened a vast new front in Afghanistan for India-Pakistan rivalry. So long as Afghanistan was ruled by the Taliban, the opportunity for India to influence events there was sharply limited—not only by Pakistan's privileged geographic, ethno-religious, and military standing in Afghanistan but also by the immense ideological gap between the religiously extremist Taliban rulers and India's democratic and secular-inclined leadership. Postwar Afghanistan presented India with a vastly changed and clearly more inviting set of circumstances. Gone were Pakistan's Taliban allies. In their place was a patchwork interim government—the product of an accord stitched together at a UN-sponsored conference in Bonn, Germany—that was clearly dominated by non-Pashtun (and strongly anti-Pakistan) elements of the triumphant Northern Alliance, a motley assortment of Tajik, Uzbek, and Hazara militias, among whose backers India in recent years had been prominent. The situation thus clearly favored India's engagement on the side of Afghanistan's post-Taliban rulers, and New Delhi, together with its Russian ally, was quick to respond to Kabul's appeal for international assistance with reconstruction.[107] For Islamabad, in contrast, the new circumstances presented huge headaches. The severance of its ties with the Taliban, notwithstanding the notably problematic eccentricities of the Taliban leaders, was unquestionably a painful step for Islamabad to take.[108] For one thing, the Taliban's replacement by non-Pashtuns politically oriented to co-ethnic Central Asian states to the north of Afghanistan threw a wrench into whatever slender prospect there might have been for Pakistan's economic development to be "decisively accelerated" by the creation of road, rail, and energy linkages between itself and Central Asia.[109] For another, it meant that territorially narrow Pakistan had just lost what some of its military analysts considered the principal benefit of its alliance with Afghanistan—strategic depth against India. An almost certain outcome of the Taliban's demise, in any event, was the birth of a new and very likely fierce contest between New Delhi and Islamabad—the Indian side seeking to make the most of the unexpected opportunity offered to it by the war on terrorism, the Pakistan side, in its turn, striving desperately to stem the hemorrhaging of its failed Afghan policy.

Second, the war on terrorism threatened to make enormously more volatile an already existing front for intense India-Pakistan rivalry—that of Kashmir. How? To begin with, the war on terrorism had created the grounds for an extraordinarily awkward contradiction in Pakistan's strategic posture: To the west, it stood in the frontline against terrorism; to the east, it supported a movement some of whose activities inevitably lent themselves to characterization, by Americans among others, as terrorism.[110] Widespread acceptance of this characterization had the potential, of course, to shift the international antiterrorist spotlight not only onto Pakistan itself, which would then face powerful international pressure to "resolve" the contradiction in its strategic posture, but also onto its militant allies in Kashmir, whose claim to represent the internationally sanctioned cause of self-determination would thus be discredited. Thanks to a dramatic terrorist attack in New Delhi, the shift wasn't long in coming.

The 13 December 2001 terrorist attack on the Indian parliament building, in which fourteen people lost their lives (including five terrorists), resulted in the instantaneous and pitiless exposure of Pakistan's awkward position. The Indian government asserted that the terrorists were Pakistanis and that they were in some way linked to Pakistan's Inter-Services Intelligence Directorate (ISI), an organization that New Delhi had for long portrayed as the mastermind of terrorist activities in Kashmir. The Indians claimed to have evidence that the terrorists were tied to the Pakistan-headquartered Lashkar-e-Taiba (LeT) and Jaish-e-Mohammad (JeM) organizations, groups New Delhi had singled out as the principal instigators of terrorist violence in Kashmir. The Indians demanded that Islamabad take forceful steps to curb them by arresting their leaders and, once and for all, shutting down entirely their operations in Kashmir. Under enormous American pressure and anxious to forestall war with India, the Pakistanis, while denying any official complicity in the attack, arrested the leaders of both organizations and agreed to bring charges of terrorism against them upon production of actionable evidence.[111]

Meanwhile, skirmishing intensified along the Line of Control and in the Siachen Glacier area. The Indian government, surprising even its Indian sympathizers with its willingness to resort to coercive diplomacy and even nuclear brinkmanship, gave every appearance that this time it meant business.[112] For the first time in thirty years, it recalled its ambassador to Pakistan. It also ended rail and bus service between the two countries, banned Pakistani commercial aircraft use of Indian airspace, and, by the end of December 2001, had mobilized hundreds of thousands of troops along the 1,800-mile border between the two countries—the largest hostile military concentration ever faced by Pakistan.[113] With many observers still unconvinced that New Delhi's maneuvering was any more than bluff, the chance of open warfare, nevertheless, seemed to be mounting swiftly.

The Bush administration grew increasingly anxious that the crisis in India-Pakistan relations might hinder its efforts to capture fleeing Taliban and Al Qaeda remnants.[114] In the face of potential calamity, Washington sought to defuse tensions by implementing a series of measures that culminated on 26 December with the addition of both the LeT and JeM to a State Department list of "designated terrorist organizations"—a momentous step that Washington had long sought to avoid taking.[115] Washington orchestrated its action in a manner Indians believed, rightly, was intended to pacify India without excessive embarrassment to Pakistan.[116] An inevitable result of its action, however, was to reinforce India's contention that Pakistan's support for the Kashmiri separatist movement was illegitimate. As a correspondent for the New York Times speculated, President Bush appeared to be siding with India, telling the Pakistanis "that any further backing for armed Islamic militant groups operating in Kashmir will be tantamount to supporting terrorism. . . . Pakistan, after more than 50 years of battling India over Kashmir, must now abandon the armed struggle there, and rely henceforth on political means of confronting India."[117]

Pulling the rug out from under the Jihadist forces operating in Afghanistan was one thing, however, abandoning the armed struggle in Kashmir was quite another. That step, even if the Musharraf regime were minded to take it, seemed extremely unlikely. All that could be said with any certainty at the end of 2001, in fact, was that India and Pakistan were far closer to war than to an agreement over the future of Kashmir.

Nuclear Stalemate Over Kashmir

India and Pakistan thus moved into the year 2002 with few grounds for thinking that peaceful settlement of the Kashmir dispute lay just ahead. Nevertheless, many observers clung to the belief that most parties to the Kashmir dispute had reached a point of exhaustion and were thus extremely reluctant to abandon the negotiating process. Whether any such commitment to a negotiated solution really existed or, even if it did, whether it would survive for long on the prevailing seesaw agenda of postnuclear tests talks between India and Pakistan was anyone's guess. If the past record was any guide, however, then a truly formidable set of obstacles lay ahead.

The first and most obvious of these fell into the category of domestic politics, specifically under the heading of unstable or even chaotic politics. In autumn 1999, India and Pakistan had put on virtually back-to-back exhibitions of this species of politics—generically labeled their "crisis of governance." The less convulsive of the two was on the Indian side. Scarcely thirteen months after the BJP came to power in New Delhi at the head of an ideologically disparate, regionally based, and extraordinarily fractious nineteen-party grouping, it was driven from office in the middle of April 1999 after losing a parliamentary confidence ballot by just one vote. The BJP coalition, a victim as much of the treachery of some of its partners as of the conniving of its opponents, was the third government to try its hand at running India in as many years. Unfortunately, the record of longevity compiled by India's governments—in particular its *coalition* governments—over the past decade or so was not one to inspire much hope for the regular emergence of full-term government anytime in the future. In the list of prime ministers below, one may observe that of the seven governments that headed India in the decade preceding the 1999 balloting, only one—the Congress-led government of Narasimha Rao—survived a full term:

- V. P. Singh, December 1989 to November 1990 (11 months)
- Chandra Shekhar, November 1990 to March 1991 (4 months)
- P. V. Narasimha Rao, June 1991 to May 1996 (5 years)

- Atal Behari Vajpayee, May 1996 (13 days)
- H. D. Deve Gowda, June 1996 to April 1997 (10 months)
- I. K. Gujral, April 1997 to November 1997 (7 months)
- Atal Behari Vajpayee, March 1998 to April 1999 (13 months)

Predictions by BJP leaders that India's thirteenth general elections in September-October 1999 would see the emergence of the desired majority government were fulfilled: the 24-party National Democratic Alliance cobbled together by the BJP succeeded in winning 298 seats—nearly 55 percent of the total—in the lower house of parliament. Nevertheless, the elections confirmed that the fragmented circumstances of the 12th Lok Sabha, in which 45 political parties were represented, would persist in large part in the 13th. India's regional parties outstripped both the Congress (I) and BJP in these elections, in fact, having raised their total in the parliament from 150 seats to about 200.[118] Barring the unforeseen, in other words, the Indian government would likely continue indefinitely to be held hostage to the whims and ambitions of regional groupings and parties.

Indians can take comfort, of course, from the fact that the country's political instability is measured, at least to an important extent, in the frequency of democratic elections. Pakistanis can boast of nothing comparable. The "systemic flaws" in Pakistan's domestic political situation, mentioned earlier, include not only the inherently precarious position of elected governments, a condition shared with their Indian counterparts, but the unique vulnerability of these governments to military coup. This particular flaw leaves Islamabad with quite modest leeway when it comes to matters affecting its relationship with India. True, the Pakistan Muslim League (PML) government of Prime Minister Nawaz Sharif had an obvious political advantage over its BJP counterpart when the two sides entered upon negotiations in 1998 in that it commanded nearly two-thirds of the seats in the National Assembly. Its Kashmir policy, in theory at least, was thus insulated by its super-majority and technically free of the formidable encumbrance of a hung parliament. Widely acknowledged in Pakistan, however, is that on certain key public matters—Kashmir policy definitely being one of them—the civilian government is compelled to defer to the army generals, whose views on Kashmir are bound to reflect not only the army's corporate (and, not infrequently, self-aggrandizing) interests but also its acute awareness of India's across-the-board military superiority. The Kargil debacle, as we've already noted, appears to have stretched this civil-military "understanding" of spheres of policy responsibility to the breaking point. The Nawaz Sharif government's post-Kargil efforts to rectify the situation by bringing the army to heel eventually brought the army's wrath down upon it. The army's stunning ouster of Nawaz Sharif on 12 October 1999 was the result. Of the impact of this ouster on the long-term stability of the Pakistan government, few would claim that another round of military rule was likely to herald a new dawn in Pakistan's governance. Conspicuous among the burdens Musharraf brought along with him to Agra, in fact, was the curse of illegitimacy and the heightened requirement that imposed for nursing his natural army constituency. While it was certainly an exaggeration, the belief of many Indian writers that Musharraf had come to Agra primarily not to make peace but to buttress his limited domestic constituencies, especially the army, is not without merit.[119]

Beyond this fundamental institutional impairment of the Pakistan state are the legion of unresolved constitutional, economic, ethno-sectarian, and political crises that for years have undermined every sector of Pakistan's civil life and, more recently, have threatened to weld to Pakistan the unenviable reputation for being a "failed" or "failing" state. Crippling the government's will and ability to mount and sustain consistent and forceful policies targeted at any of the country's problems, these chronic and multiplying crises, since they inevitably sap the confidence of Pakistan's foreign interlocutors, have the added and most unfortunate effect of subverting whatever willingness might exist on the Indian side for tackling seriously the bilateral matters outstanding between the two countries. The Pakistan government's clumsily handled crackdown in spring 1999 on the country's print media, in particular the arrest of the *Friday Times* editor, Najam Sethi, ostensibly for making near "treasonous" remarks in a speech given in New Delhi at the India International Centre, is symptomatic both of Pakistan's political frailty and of the potential of this frailty for damaging bilateral diplomacy aimed at normalization.[120]

Of crucial importance in assessing the domestic political constraints on either India or Pakistan is, of course, the state of public opinion. Abundant signs that it was changing, in particular that it was warming to the idea of India-Pakistan reconciliation and to greater regional cooperation in general, were apparent in both India and Pakistan in the post-tests—but pre-Kargil—period. In the months before Kargil broke into the news, a parade of *privately* arranged India-Pakistan events—

including wildly popular cricket and hockey matches, an unprecedented three-day conference mixing nearly 100 Indian and Pakistani parliamentarians, and even the founding of a joint India-Pakistan Chamber of Commerce and Industry![121]—threatened to overtake the *public* diplomacy the events were designed to promote. More than a little skepticism is warranted, however, in regard to the depth and durability of those trends in public attitudes. One must allow, in the political circumstances prevailing in that region of the earth, for a considerable volatility in them. Once Kargil appeared on the scene, they vanished—alike in India and Pakistan, I hasten to add—as quickly as they had appeared.

Even had there been no Kargil crisis, one should note, the assumption would not have been warranted that public support of increased cross-border contacts—by artistic performers, lawyers, athletes, politicians, or business interests, for instance—necessarily translated into firm public support of governmental initiatives embodying *major* concessions in either side's Kashmir policy. This is not to say that there are not pockets of thought, perhaps fairly large pockets of thought, in both Pakistan and India where the wisdom and practicality of existing policy is seriously questioned. But it doesn't take too many Kargils to drive such questioning underground. It is worth contemplating, for instance, whether the editorial comment on Kashmir made on 30 May 1999 in a venerable English-language daily published in Calcutta—before Kargil's eventual cost in Indian casualties could have been predicted—would have been printed even one month later. I quote it here at some length:

> India, the bigger and arguably the more mature of the two [countries], must take the lead [in heading off an arms race]. And no lead is better than a grand policy on Kashmir. . . . India should respond to Pakistan's tests and the possibility of escalating tensions by making a unilateral posture on Kashmir. It can announce that the government will exhume the nearly five decades old United Nations proposal to hold a referendum on the question of the valley's (Jammu and Kashmir) territorial loyalty.
>
> This will seem preposterous to the BJP, indeed to many Indians. But an astute political party—the BJP has shown it can be one—does not remain a prisoner of conventional wisdom. More, a referendum on and in Kashmir, internationally supervised, will again put India in a different league from one defined by sub-continental squabbles—a status the BJP thinks the country deserves. The "worst" possibility is that Kashmir may not choose to remain with India. Is that too bad a prospect compared to the price India pays in blood, money, and a general marring of reputation

when the troops "occasionally" misbehave? A Kashmir referendum will also blunt global condemnation of the sub-continent as a mad hatter area full of nuke-wielding hot-heads. As well as force Pakistan to drop its belligerence, both verbal and clandestine. These are benefits that can be grabbed only by a government with vision and courage. . . . [122]

At the present time a significant public constituency supportive of the unconventional approach outlined in this editorial simply doesn't exist in India. It did not exist before Kargil. On the contrary, as a very senior Indian foreign affairs bureaucrat bluntly put it at a meeting in New Delhi attended by the author in spring 1998, there simply wasn't much public interest in Kashmir at all in India. "Indians," he observed, "were not sufficiently interested in its solution." India's agenda was extremely crowded, he explained; Kashmir held fairly low priority on it. There was, he said, a "lack of a peace constituency in India, especially on the Pakistan front." Youthful Indians would demonstrate about a lot of things, he said, but they won't go into the streets on the Kashmir issue. There was simply no political reward in India for those who would attempt to mobilize a peace constituency. Appreciation for former prime minister Inder Kumar Gujral's much-publicized peace initiative, he noted by way of example, "did not extend beyond the [narrow intellectual confines of] the India International Centre." Gujral, together with his initiative, vanished from the headlines once he stepped down from the prime ministership.[123] No doubt, interest in Kashmir has grown substantially in India since Kargil; the centrality of that issue in the national elections would have seen to that. But if the "peace constituency" was fairly miniscule *before* Kargil, do we have any good grounds for confidence that it has grown *since?*

A second obstacle to sustained commitment by New Delhi and Islamabad to bilateral dialogue over the Kashmir dispute in the wake of the dispute's nuclearization relates directly to the nuclear tests themselves: it is, namely, that the territorial dispute over Kashmir was not likely to have been the dominant consideration, and it may not have been even a major consideration, among either side's motivations for testing. Formal statements of India's motives, to take a look at them first, do, indeed, allow some space to Kashmir. In his letter to President Bill Clinton on 12 May 1998, for instance, in which he explained the rationale underlying India's initial series of tests, Prime Minister Vajpayee complained of India's "deteriorating security environment" and, without naming Pakistan, of India's having been "for the last ten years . . . the victim of unremitting terrorism and militancy sponsored by it in several parts of [the] country, specially Punjab and Jammu and Kashmir."[124] Nevertheless, he apportioned the responsibility for this situation about evenly between Pakistan and China. The latter he described in multiple terms as an overt nuclear weapon power on India's border, a party to an unresolved boundary conflict, the perpetrator of armed aggression against India in 1962, and Pakistan's covert nuclear weapons benefactor.

The political opposition to the then-ruling BJP, alleging that India's relations with China had, in fact, been on the mend for some years, laid blame for the tests almost wholly at the feet of the BJP's domestic political ambitions.[125] BJP leaders themselves, presumably perturbed at seeing the suddenly nuclearized Kashmir danger flashing ominously in so many international forums, soon came around to alternative explanations. When party spokesman Jaswant Singh visited the United States on a damage-control mission in the second week of June 1998, he reportedly claimed that the deterioration in India's security environment had come about "as much from global realignment as from complicity of the guardians of non-proliferation," implying that India's decision to test was mainly an effort by a nuclear have-not to neutralize the coercive diplomacy of the existing nuclear powers.[126] India's conflict with Pakistan over Kashmir had pretty much dropped through the floorboards.[127] Singh's unusually blunt *Foreign Affairs* article, written a few months later, in which he spelled out India's case for nuclear weapons, considerably embellished the "global *apartheid*" theme that had come to characterize the Indian position. In what was the most carefully crafted inventory yet of Indian motivations, India-Pakistan rivalry, in that still pre-Kargil period, fell to a distinctly subordinate position among them. "Faced as India was," observed Singh,

> with a legitimization of nuclear weapons by the haves, a global nuclear security paradigm from which it was excluded, trends toward disequilibrium in the Asian balance of power, and a neighborhood in which two nuclear weapons countries [China and Pakistan] act in concert, India had to protect its future by exercising its nuclear option.[128]

Interestingly, in an article that filled twelve pages of the journal, the sole mention of "Kashmir" occurred in an editor-inserted map inset.

In their public rhetoric, Pakistani leaders, in their turn, naturally sought to exploit to the hilt the opportunity handed them to publicize Pakistan's troubles with India over Kashmir by ringing the nuclear alarm and calling for international mediation of the Kashmir dispute at every opportunity.[129] These deliberate efforts to nuclearize—and, thus, to internationalize—the dispute were patently self-serving, however, and, when it came to Pakistan's motivation for testing, they were beside the point: Faced with the overwhelming military-strategic imperative to maintain a semblance of nuclear parity with India, the primary motivations of Pakistani leaders for countering India's nuclear testing by conducting a series of their own were never really in doubt.

A third obstacle to sustained commitment to bilateral diplomacy over Kashmir is that Pakistan's bargaining position relative to India has steadily declined in recent years, a product of India's success in enlisting considerably increased international political support for its stand on Kashmir (a subject pursued in detail in Chapter 2) while at the same time chipping away at the bonds of allegiance between Pakistan and its militant confederates within Kashmir itself. Especially since Kargil, incentives to make political concessions to Kashmiri Muslims in order to win Pakistan's agreement to a settlement have been largely replaced by incentives to force Pakistan's withdrawal of military support to the insurgents as well as to drive a political wedge, on the one hand, between the insurgents and Pakistan and, on the other, between hard- and soft-line elements among the insurgents themselves. An increase in the number of foreigners (mainly Pakistanis) fighting alongside the Kashmiri insurgents in the last few years has reinforced New Delhi's claim that the separatist movement had been hijacked. The threat to Kashmir lends itself now—following the terrorist catastrophe of 11 September 2001—more easily than ever to description as essentially of *external* origin, a condition that strengthens India's moral position to about the same degree that it weakens Pakistan's. In these circumstances, the odds for Pakistan's achievement of a reasonably favorable outcome from renewed bilateral dialogue are likely diminished.

As formidable as they may appear, all of the above reasons for the failure of the region's altered nuclear circumstances to guarantee a break in the existing diplomatic stalemate over Kashmir between India and Pakistan fade, I believe, in the face of a fourth and final feature of the South Asian region. This feature is the glaring power imbalance between the two sides and the resulting divergence in their basic national interests that this imbalance produces. Inevitably, this imbalance generates insecurity in the outlook of Pakistani strategic planners. It generates in the outlook of Indian strategic planners, at the same time and just as inevitably, aspirations for unalloyed regional dominance and Great Power status. No doubt, Pakistani fears and Indian ambitions could be eased or facilitated, as the case may be, with implementation of agreements such as those chalked out at Lahore in February 1999. It would be a huge mistake, however, to think that technical measures for avoidance of incidents at sea involving the two sides' navies or for the enhancement of a "hot line" between the military operations directorates of the two sides' armies, to mention two such proposed agreements, can somehow eliminate Pakistan as an impediment to Indian aspirations, on the one hand, or compensate Pakistan for India's vastly greater physical size, population, wealth, military strength, and future potential, on the other. Like it or not, these "structural" realities—in the absence of either India's or Pakistan's unlikely disintegration and collapse—are permanent features of the region's security architecture and they inevitably exert powerful influence on those—Pakistanis and Indians alike—who chart the region's security policies.

This circumstance is a familiar one to Indian and Pakistani writers on regional security. The Indian point of view on it has been expressed succinctly by Rajesh Rajagopalan, Research Fellow at the Institute for Defence Studies and Analyses, best known simply as "IDSA"—a government-subsidized think tank in New Delhi that has often been at the center of policy controversies. Rajagopalan, in an essay written *after* the Lahore Summit but *before* Kargil, commented on the improbability of a sudden diplomatic breakthrough resulting from the diplomatic initiatives undertaken by India and Pakistan. I quote him here at some length:

> The failure to understand the real sources of Pakistan's insecurity is a leading cause for the inflated expectations [of regional diplomacy] and the consequent cynicism. The tendency is to identify the salient dispute of the day as the root cause of the problem. The current favourite is the Kashmir dispute. Despite Islamabad's claims to the contrary, Kashmir is not the root cause of the India-Pakistan problem. Indeed, between the 1965 war and the outbreak of the Kashmir insurgency in the late 1980s, Kashmir was just another item in the laundry list of Pakistani complaints. Its centrality in bilateral relations in the 1990s was the result of Pakistan's diplomatic exploitation of the insurgency problem, not the result of any intrinsic merit in or importance of the dispute itself. Other disputes have at other times been as important as Kashmir is today. If Kashmir is iden-

tified as a threat because of its potential for escalation today, that potential was present in equal measure, for example, in the arms race in the subcontinent in the 1980s, an issue that is now all but forgotten.

Pakistan's insecurity lies in the natural imbalance of power in South Asia. India is several times the size of Pakistan and, in material terms, vastly better endowed. Pakistan's unremitting concern over the last half-a-century has been to correct this gross imbalance and its India policy has reflected this concern. It has tried to offset the imbalance through military alliances and disproportionately large defence budgets. But burdened as it is by fickle allies and a weak economy, such efforts have bred more frustration than promoting security. *The India-Pakistan conflict is the consequence of Islamabad's frantic quest for a balance with India, not the consequence of India's actions.*[130]

The writer's concluding remark, acquitting India of responsibility for the chronic hostility between India and Pakistan, recalls a similar comment made years ago by IDSA's erstwhile and famously combative director, K. Subrahmanyam. According to him, "most of Pakistan's security problems, and the haunting sense of insecurity of the country's rulers are inherent in the nature of the Pakistani state and the relationship between rulers and ruled." India, he claimed, "can do nothing about it."[131]

Barring this standard and transparently self-serving IDSA sentiment on culpability, Rajagopalan's broad observation does, nevertheless, contain a crucial element of the South Asian security dynamic—namely, its asymmetric power configuration. This configuration breeds suspicion and watchfulness—not uncommonly, also an inclination to dabble in worst-case scenarios—on the Pakistani side, where reticence to gamble on diplomacy's capacity for ensuring Pakistan's future security is an essential, even if at times paralyzing, strategic virtue. On the Indian side, it tends, just as ineluctably, to breed national assertiveness—behavior that might strike its neighbors as "aggressive," "bullying," or "hegemonistic."[132] Brought face to face with this core truth—the centrality of unequal power in India-Pakistan relations and the divergence in fundamental national interests that this inequality breeds—the confidence-building measures proposed by the two countries at Lahore in 1999 and then by India prior to the Agra Summit in 2001 seem feeble remedy indeed.[133] Time will tell whether any of the peace initiatives hesitatingly put in place by India and Pakistan at the turn of the millennium will survive long enough for less feeble remedies to be discovered.

* * *

When it comes to relations between India and Pakistan, there is no dearth of arguments to the effect that they simply cannot afford any longer the costly enterprise of regional rivalry. India, for example, a correspondent of the *New York Times* some time ago reminded us, was set to pass the one billion mark in population in August 1999 with still about a third of that figure "abjectly poor people unable to muster an income equivalent to the $1 a day needed to buy basic foods."[134] Promising diplomatic initiatives, a Pakistani writer commented at the same time, seemed always to end with the two states unsheathing their weapons and exchanging bitter invective—"adrift in a sea of animosity," in his words.[135] "While the decision makers of South Asia remain obsessed with mountain tops, body-counts, demarcation of glaciers and rocks, nuances of press statements from the other side, and similar other trifles," he observed despairingly,

> the gathering socioeconomic storm would become more and more menacing, regardless of the path that the LoC may or may not follow. The population will not stop growing, the infrastructure will not stop decaying, unemployment will not be contained, the tensions between various segments of society will not ease, governance will not reform itself on its own, poverty will not be alleviated, and hunger and ignorance will not have been banished.[136]

Accompanying and sometimes threatening to drown out these often painful exercises in self-examination, however, was a substantial amount of nationalist bluster and bravado—on the Indian side conveying the chest-thumping triumphalist message of India's finally having come of age as a unified and proud nation,[137] on the Pakistan side conveying the remarkably disingenuous and self-deluding message that what looked on the surface like defeat at Kargil was, beneath it all, a major victory.[138]

No more than the nuclear tests crisis of 1998, the Kargil crisis of 1999 thus far has yielded no certain signs that a determined push for peace lies just ahead in South Asia. The Agra Summit of 2001 unquestionably bore witness to the existence in that region of fairly widespread fatigue with the Kashmir dispute, but it testified eloquently at the same time not only to that dispute's continued intractability but also to the glaring infirmities of the bilateral approach to its resolution. One might, perhaps, derive some comfort in this circumstance from Kargil's presumed "validation" of the deterrent value of nuclear weapons, but, as we have seen, this validation rests on the thinnest of evidence and a paucity of comparable cases. That nuclear deterrence "works" in South Asia is clearly a matter of faith, not fact. Another round of subcontinental warfare—this time governed by fewer restraints than existed at Kargil—simply cannot be ruled out.

The tortured history of bilateral diplomacy in this part of the globe allows for no more than modest optimism, in fact, that it will somehow be reinvented in a new and more effective form in time to forestall yet another catastrophe in India-Pakistan relations. In this circumstance, the focus inevitably turns to the international community—in particular, to the United States and the other Great Powers and the question of the role they may play in forestalling or, conversely, actuating such a catastrophe. Can they, in this post–Cold War moment of extraordinary turbulence in global political alignments, find a way to pursue their own interests in the South Asian region without compounding the dilemmas imbedded in the bilateral rivalry between India and Pakistan? To that question and to the issue of the "internationalization" of the Kashmir dispute, we now turn.

2

The Problem of Global Intervention

The "Internationalization" of the Kashmir Dispute

We observed in the preceding chapter that the Pakistani desire to internationalize the Kashmir dispute—that is (as Pakistanis understand the term) to offset India's natural advantages in any bilateral diplomatic setting by securing an increase in international involvement—has been tagged by many observers as perhaps the key motive behind Pakistan's Kargil project. After all, the argument goes, Pakistan's repeated appeals for international support of its position on Kashmir had failed to make any headway in the decade of the 1990s in spite of a popular uprising of Kashmiri Muslims against Indian rule. The Pakistan government had finally decided to gamble that a major flare-up in fighting in Kashmir would trigger prompt intervention by an international community growing increasingly uneasy over the South Asian region's steady slide toward nuclear weaponization. According to this view, the Pakistanis expected not only that internationalization would occur but that, yoked to world nuclear anxieties, it would work in Pakistan's favor by pushing recalcitrant Indians to accept serious negotiation of the Kashmir territorial dispute. This formulation of the Kargil operation describes Pakistan's objective as political rather than military. It implies that the abrupt vacating of Indian-occupied territory by Pakistani forces was no reason for shame. I noted in the earlier discussion my view that this argument reeked of alibi or rationalization—that its assertion, at least when made by Pakistani officials, was an effort to camouflage an outcome that bore the hallmarks of a military and diplomatic fiasco. In the face of virtually inevitable bewilderment, disappointment, humiliation, and anger among Pakistan's cognoscenti and within its armed forces about the government's sudden about-face on the Kargil operation in early July, the "object-was-internationaliza-tion" spin on events had obvious practical utility.[1]

Whether or not deliberate internationalization figured among initial Pakistani objectives in undertaking the Kargil venture, there can be no doubt that Kargil's occurrence kindled unusually strong international re-actions. The most sensational of these was the hastily arranged meeting between President Bill Clinton and Prime Minister Nawaz Sharif in Wash-ington on 4 July 1999. This meeting led directly to withdrawal from Kargil of Pakistani forces. The shockwave from that produced a number of after-effects, among them the intensification of debate, already in progress in the wake of the nuclear tests crisis, over the kind of role, if any, the inter-national community might play in the search for a resolution to the Kash-mir dispute. This debate, whose participants included not only the two rival South Asian governments but their domestic critics and foreign on-lookers, prompted animated discussion at the time about whether Clinton's personal effort to bring an end to fighting at Kargil amounted to media-tion. A far more favorable reception for this concept was likely in Islamabad, of course, than in either Washington or New Delhi. A more pressing topic in this debate, however, focused on which of the two South Asian adversaries, if either, had emerged the "winner" in this most recent round of the region's high-stakes contest for international approval and backing. Highlighted in this connection was the enormous disparity in the economic, political, and military power of India and Pakistan, as well as the impact this lopsidedness was likely to have on their relationship as the new century dawned. Also highlighted was the supreme importance attached to the definition of the Kashmir dispute that would ultimately be accepted as standard by the international community. What would this definition emphasize—that Kashmir signified the sinister spread of terrorism? The oppression of a religious minority and denial of human rights? Or the menace of nuclear weapons? Inevitably, differing points of view emerged in the debate on the expected or preferred role of the United States in South Asia. Was the United States, as the world's sole super-power, finally ready to "engage" South Asia in a manner befitting the region's importance? Were its recent actions in regard to South Asia proof that it was moving decisively away from the preoccupations that domi-nated America's South Asia policy during the Cold War? Was there, in particular, a decipherable change underway in American—and, indeed, in Western—understanding (or "appreciation") of India that was likely to impinge fundamentally not only upon the regional balance of power but upon the future fate of Kashmir?

This is obviously a multifaceted and important debate. It has been rendered all the more complicated by the changes in global power alignment that have come in the wake of the September 11, 2001 terrorist attack on the United States. The review of it that follows will advance three propositions—one, that internationalization of the Kashmir dispute, while perhaps less in scale and more limited and ephemeral in form than what some were claiming, nevertheless made some progress in the last few years; two, that whatever progress was made in its internationalization— if it went no further than it had to date—was unlikely to move the Kashmir dispute any closer to settlement; and three, that only a radical change in the way the Kashmir dispute is understood by the international community would enable internationalization of it in a way that would improve prospects for its negotiated resolution. We begin our examination of the debate by returning for a moment to the Kargil episode, in particular to the chain of events that brought it to a close.

Global Diplomacy—The "Virtual" Mediation of Kargil

Within less than a month of the outbreak of fighting between Indian and Pakistani forces in the Kargil sector in May 1999, two things became plain. One was that the human and material costs of protracted fighting were going to be very high. This applied to both sides. True, the Indian military had assembled massive firepower, and that it would eventually erode the intruders' ability to cling to the seized terrain was never really in doubt. Nevertheless, rapid dislodgement of the intruders from Indian territory, assuming the Indians weren't willing to absorb horrendous casualties, simply wasn't possible without cutting off their resupply from Pakistan. That meant crossing the LOC and inviting a still wider conflict, a step New Delhi was loath to take. The other was that India and Pakistan were coming under increasingly strong global diplomatic pressures, including personal letters (the first on 3 June) and repeated telephone calls to both prime ministers from President Bill Clinton imploring them to stop the fighting. In Pakistan's case, the pressures included scarcely veiled threats to withhold urgently needed IMF and World Bank loans. These circumstances combined to prompt the two sides to resume bilateral contacts with one another.

A number of telephone calls between the two prime ministers led, first, to Pakistani Foreign Minister Sartaj Aziz's apparently fruitless visit to New Delhi on 11 June to meet with Indian leaders, and then to the two final and fruitless "back-channel" exchanges at the end of June that we took note of in the preceding chapter. Focused on the arrangement of a cease-fire and timetable for the intruders' safe withdrawal, these hectic exchanges ended in complete failure. Hopes for a bilateral resolution to the crisis ended with them.

The Washington Joint Statement

Even while both the formal and informal bilateral attempts to defuse the Kargil crisis were in progress, New Delhi had set in motion an alternative —international—strategy having the same objective. An initial step in this strategy was the hand-delivery on 18 June by Brajesh Mishra, Vajpayee's principal secretary and advisor on national security, to Sandy Berger, Mishra's counterpart in the Clinton administration, of a personal letter from Vajpayee to Clinton on the subject of Kargil. Reportedly warning Clinton of the gravity of the situation on the LOC and of the mounting pressure on India to retaliate directly against Pakistan, the letter was a transparent attempt to induce Clinton "to turn up the pressure on Pakistan" in order to avoid collapse of his administration's year-long efforts to fashion a more constructive relationship with the two South Asian rivals.[2] Clinton complied. According to an account in the *Washington Post*, Clinton first obtained a formal condemnation of the armed intrusion from the G-8 countries, then meeting at Cologne. Their statement, forming part of the meeting's final communiqué, pointedly demanded "full respect" for the LOC. Clinton followed that with the dispatch to Islamabad on 22 June of General Anthony Zinni, commander of the U.S. Central Command, who reportedly communicated directly to Pakistani leaders the urgency of pulling the intruders back to the Pakistani side of the LOC.[3] With Zinni was Gibson Lanpher, deputy assistant secretary of state, who went on to New Delhi on 26 June (curiously, the same day on which Niaz Naik arrived there on his separate mission) to brief Indian leaders on the results of Zinni's talks in Pakistan.

The startling result of these maneuvers was Clinton's three-hour-long meeting with the Pakistani prime minister at Blair House on 4 July. The meeting was extraordinary both for its timing—held on the American side's national holiday—and for the alacrity with which it was arranged, within one day of Nawaz Sharif's urgent telephoned appeal to Clinton. No less extraordinary, however, was the way in which it was conducted— the Pakistani and American delegations breaking down into multiple small discussion groups in separate rooms for about forty minutes, a one-on-one discussion midway in the proceedings involving the president and Prime Minister, an extended break during which Clinton telephoned New Delhi and held a "brief ten-minute conversation with prime minister Vajpayee of India to keep him fully apprised of the discussion," then another round of delegation discussions and exchanges, and, finally, wrapping up with a telephone call by Sandy Berger to Brajesh Mishra "to bring him up to date on the results of [the day's] activity."[4] The meeting was followed with release of a brief "Joint Statement by President Clinton and Prime Minister Sharif of Pakistan," whose contents, since they have figured prominently in subsequent discussion of the ramifications of the Kargil episode, I reproduce here in full:

> President Clinton and Prime Minister Sharif share the view that the current fighting in the Kargil region of Kashmir is dangerous and contains the seeds of a wider conflict. They also agreed that it was vital for the peace of South Asia that the Line of Control in Kashmir be respected by both parties, in accordance with their 1972 Simla Accord. It was agreed between the President and the Prime Minister that concrete steps will be taken for the restoration of the line of control in accordance with the Simla Agreement. The President urged an immediate cessation of the hostilities once these steps are taken. The Prime Minister and President agreed that the bilateral dialogue begun in Lahore in February provides the best forum for resolving all issues dividing India and Pakistan, including Kashmir. The President said he would take a personal interest in encouraging an expeditious resumption and intensification of those bilateral efforts, once the sanctity of the Line of Control has been fully restored. The President reaffirmed his intent to pay an early visit to South Asia.[5]

This joint statement was frequently cited by spokesmen for the Nawaz Sharif government to support the prime minister's contention that Kargil produced the desired internationalization of the Kashmir dispute. On the surface, at least, their claim had merit. After all, it is apparent that the Clinton administration did go to unusual lengths to broker a deal that paved the way for the 11 July agreement between the Indian and Pakistani armies providing for temporary cease-fire and safe conduct guarantees during the withdrawal of the intruding forces from Indian territory. Spokespersons for the Clinton administration took pains at the time to describe its role in brokering the agreement as being focused on "the immediate crisis"—in other words, on Kargil and not on the Kashmir dispute proper. However, the details of its role leave little room for doubt that a species of mediation took place. It matters little in this age of electronic communication marvels that India's leaders were not physically present in Washington, since it was explicitly conceded at the time that Prime Minister Vajpayee was kept "fully informed"—before, during, and immediately following the meeting—about what was being discussed.[6] Indeed, if the allegation of a former chief of Pakistan's Inter-Services Intelligence Directorate can be believed, the draft Clinton-Sharif accord was actually faxed for approval to Vajpayee, who sent it back before public release of the joint statement with the word "sanctity" added to the document's comment on restoring the LOC.[7] In any event, that the Indians had at least some "voice" in the proceedings can hardly be denied. It is also undeniable, of course, that they too, along with the Pakistanis, played a major role at the outset in precipitating American involvement. They very likely did not anticipate that it would take quite the form it did. However, by adding their appeal for Washington's intercession to that of the Pakistanis, and then by playing an active (albeit telephonic and third-party mediated) role in the discussions, the Indians inadvertently satisfied Washington's longstanding condition for its assumption of an intermediary role in regard to Kashmir—that both sides request it.

Washington's mediation of the crisis, if mediation it was, was hardly an unalloyed triumph for Pakistan. In the first place, the obvious haste in which Nawaz Sharif's meeting with Clinton was arranged inevitably lent to his request for the meeting a panicked and undignified appearance—even, since he was faced with the threat of being diplomatically outmaneuvered by New Delhi, that he had had to beg for it. In the second place, by acquiescing to the joint statement's assertion of the need to restore the "sanctity" of the LOC, Nawaz Sharif lent legitimacy to the LOC, thus pulling the rug from under Pakistan's official position that it was a strictly temporary arrangement without the status of a hardened permanent boundary. "The Washington statement's emphasis on the LoC sanctity," complained Dr. Maleeha Lodhi in the July 1999 issue of *Newsline*, which resonated in the G-8 communiqué and virtually every statement of key countries, suggests that turning the LoC into a de jure international border could be the basis along which a solution may be sought. In committing Pakistan to take concrete steps to restore the LoC, the statement obligated Islamabad to unilaterally defuse the crisis in compliance with U.S.-endorsed Indian terms. In agreeing to this declaration, Sharif failed to ensure the inclusion of key formulations safeguarding Pakistan's long-standing position on Kashmir. Implicit acceptance of the sanctity of the LoC without the qualifying "without prejudice to its position" (the language of the Simla Agreement) represented an avoidable dilution of Pakistan's declaratory position.[8]

In the third place, while the joint statement itself mercifully did not make explicit mention of the Pakistani-backed intruders and spoke only in general terms of "concrete steps" that needed to be taken to assure "restoration of the line of control," Clinton administration spokesmen themselves didn't mince words when it came to clarifying the administration's own understanding of those words. The administration position, one official put it, "has been that the forces that are across the line of control need to be returned to the Pakistani side."[9] India was clearly being let off the hook. Seen in this light, President Clinton's thin commitment in the joint statement to "take a personal interest" in the resumption of the bilateral dialogue begun in Lahore could give only cold comfort to Pakistanis. No wonder, then, that at least for some of them what Islamabad was proudly hailing as internationalization resembled more than anything an abject diplomatic surrender.[10]

Misgivings about the role played by Washington in the Kargil episode were also expressed on the Indian side. We've already noted A.G. Noorani's reservations at the time about the broad strategic implications of New Delhi's seemingly deliberate straying from the bilateral track. Others, too, expressed awareness that the manner in which the Kargil crisis developed carried with it an unavoidable and, in some respects, worrisome element of internationalization. The well-known journalist Amit Baruah, for example, suggested that the United States, not India or Pakistan, was "the net gainer from Kargil. . . . The July 4 statement and what followed reflect the growing U.S. clout in South Asia. . . . Today, the door for mediation, notwithstanding repeated official rejections by India, has been opened."[11] For the most part, however, Indian reactions to Washington's intercession over Kargil were positive, in some instances nearly gleeful. Indeed, not a few commentators claimed that what happened in the context of Kargil helped to solidify a major—and, for India, largely advantageous—strategic realignment with the West. A leading journalist-spokesman for this point of view, the strategic analyst (and international affairs editor for *The Hindu*) C. Raja Mohan, maintained, for example, that India's Kargil stance symbolized what he called "a new pragmatism" in Indian foreign policy circles—a willingness, in other words, to show some flexibility, to shed "the past anti-Western prejudices," and to work for "a comprehensive engagement with the U.S."[12]

From Mohan's ideologically mainstream point of view, the Indian government's handling of Kargil was proof of sorts that India was finally coming of age. It was no longer strapped, in other words, to non-alignment's requirement for knee-jerk rejection of Western involvement in the region. Now, if this was true, that New Delhi was prepared to experiment with a tentative "tilt" to the West, was the West, in its turn, prepared to assume a new and more influential role in South Asian affairs? Was Clinton's intercession at Kargil a harbinger, in particular, of a new American activism in the region? Was India likely to be, as many Indians appeared to believe, the principal beneficiary of this activism? And did all of this mean that the Kashmir dispute was finally being pushed irreversibly in the direction of a settlement—one that India might very well be able to live with?

Kashmir on the International Agenda—Reticence to the Rescue

The Kashmir dispute has undoubtedly taken an upward turn in the last few years on Great Power and international organization policy agendas. It comes up for public discussion more frequently, and is a stimulus for more official statements and declarations, than at almost anytime in the past. All the attention has resulted so far, however, in no major international initiative—no *visible* initiative, at least—aimed at settling the Kashmir dispute proper. In this light, it is tempting, of course, to view America's innovative role during the Kargil episode as prelude to a new and more interventionist American engagement with South Asia, one that might perhaps hasten Kashmir's ripening for resolution. America's intervention in regard to Kargil is too recent, however, and too narrow in scope by itself to supply a reliable guide to the future of U.S. involvement in South Asia. For that, a broader perspective on America's evolving interest in the region, including that generated by the deadly terrorist attack on America in September 2001, is needed. We will focus on that enormously important matter later in this chapter. For the moment, we defer consideration of it, taking up first the matter of the international community's transparent reticence, to date, to act decisively in regard to Kashmir.

Expectations of a major or sudden turn toward genuinely enlarged international engagement in the search for a settlement of Kashmir shot upward with the much-publicized highlighting of the Kashmir dispute, discussed in Chapter 1, that went along with the world's alarmed reaction to the nuclear tests of May 1998. The alarm held no assurances, however, either that international interest in Kashmir would be sustained or that it would eventuate in substantive international undertakings in regard to Kashmir. Pakistan's repeated appeals at the time for international mediation of the Kashmir dispute fell largely on deaf ears.[13] The Clinton administration pressed for the resumption of bilateral talks on Kashmir, but it carefully coupled its appeals in this regard with repeated and emphatic disavowals of any desire to mediate the dispute itself.[14] Indian editorial writers and columnists, responding to the P-5 statement in Geneva at that time, observed with understandable delight that the final version was much watered-down on the subject of Kashmir and that it didn't deliver what Pakistan sought. The following *The Times of India* editorial comment was typical:

> Much to the surprise of the doomsayers in India and abroad, the joint statement issued in Geneva by the five permanent members of the Security Council on the nuclear tests conducted by India and Pakistan did not invoke the threat of intervention in the Kashmir dispute. The omission, however, was only to be expected. With Tibet and Chechenya [sic] on their hands, China and Russia respectively cannot afford to open the door to Security Council intervention in such disputes. The UN Secretary General had proposed the removal of Kashmir from the forum's agenda as the issue had not come up for discussion in the past three decades. It is only to placate Pakistan that the UN dhobi [laundry] list still formally retains Kashmir; the rest of the world is thoroughly bored with it. Further, to reopen Kashmir would inevitably unleash mischievous chimeras like the "two nation theory," which is an earlier version of the "clash of civilisations" thesis; that would also promote ethno-nationalism, the bane of the current world. So the P-5 have wisely called for the resumption of direct dialogue between India and Pakistan.[15]

The Indians could take additional comfort from the fact that, as was noted earlier, only a relatively small number of nations joined in the imposition of economic sanctions against India and Pakistan—and even more from the fact that, only weeks after the nuclear tests, these same nations displayed unmistakable signs of retreat. When the Clinton administration put its sanctions into effect on 18 June 1998, it was clear that they had been crafted to soften their impact;[16] and when the World Bank approved major loans for India scarcely six weeks after the tests, it did so with the blessings of the Clinton administration.[17] There were— *very early in the game*—clear grounds for skepticism, in other words, about the likelihood that the sanctions would ever be applied forcefully enough or remain in place long enough to prove sufficient to push India and Pakistan into serious discussions over anything, including Kashmir. Nothing in the history of these sanctions since then, most conspicuously Washington's terrorism-inspired decision in September 2001 to waive all nuclear-related sanctions against India and Pakistan under the Glenn, Symington, and Pressler amendments,[18] has given any reason to question the skepticism.

The reasons for pronounced global reticence to go beyond rhetorical involvement when it comes to the Kashmir dispute are not wholly obvious. After all, at the dispute's onset in the 1940s, when it posed very little threat to anyone outside of the South Asian environment, it found itself suddenly a star attraction on the agenda of the newly formed UN Security Council, and it remained just that, an active and prominent issue on that agenda, for nearly a decade. The UN peacekeeping group brought into being by the Security Council in those early days—the UN Military Observer Group in India and Pakistan (UNMOGIP)—remains at its task today, the next to oldest of all UN peacekeeping missions. The Kashmir dispute's neglect is thus not likely the product of the world's ignorance of it. Neither could its neglect, in the face of the heightened nuclear threat and widespread acknowledgment of Kashmir as a potential nuclear flashpoint, be written off very easily as a product of the world community's lack of appreciation for the dangers inherent in its continued festering.

From what, then, does the reticence stem? The most obvious reason, perhaps, is that global powers have little if any urgent and direct *material* stake in Kashmir itself to lure them in. It is a geographically remote region, landlocked, with a population scarcely 1 percent of the South Asian regional total. Moreover, in sharp contrast with fellow Muslim-majority and separatist-bedeviled territories in the Caucasus, like Dagestan and Chechnya, Kashmir lies well outside the geostrategically vital and increasingly contested Eurasian energy corridor.

Two additional reasons spring to mind. One relates to the disunity and disarray of *global* powers, the other to the inescapably dominant position of India within the South Asian *region*. These merit closer examination.

Great Power Disarray

The turbulent last years of the twentieth century witnessed their full share of threats to the unity and ability to function even of such pillars of cooperative global security as the Security Council of the United Nations and the North Atlantic Treaty Organization. The threats to these bodies were severe enough, in fact, to draw warnings from respected observers of their potential for irreparable decay, even final demise.[19] Thus, it hardly seems necessary to point out that global capacity for international cooperation on a host of so-called "world order" issues—among which the resolution of regional conflicts like Kashmir would certainly be included—has been running for some years at fairly low tide. Washington's success with present efforts to build an enduring global coalition against "terrorism with a global reach" would, of course, represent a welcome reversal of the trend. About the probability of such an outcome, it is far too early to speak with any certainty. One can be fairly certain, however, that mobilizing at this point any significant portion of the international community in support of a direct international assault on the Kashmir problem would likely draw down reserves of patience (and political capital) in amounts that few governments would find attractive. One would risk considerable embarrassment, in fact, in the present circumstances to give serious endorsement to formation of an "International Kashmir Committee," as has been urged by a branch of the Jammu and Kashmir Liberation Front, that would consist of a strikingly heterogeneous collection of official representatives (one each, the proposal recommends) drawn from the United Nations Secretary General, the P-5, Germany, Japan, the Organization of the Islamic Conference (OIC), and (two representatives in this instance) the Non-Aligned Movement (NAM).[20] Even a Kashmir-focused "contact group" of external powers, as recommmended by a Washington, D.C.-based task force in 1997,[21] or, indeed, any other joint multilateral initiative in regard to Kashmir that would require bridging the enormous political and strategic cleavages that now stand revealed before us, risks seeming impractical.

With the passing of the Cold War and the rigid ideological polarities that went with it, it had seemed to many that an opportunity was present for vastly greater cooperation among nations on common global, including security, problems. That may yet prove possible. America's unprecedented efforts in autumn 2001 to build a lasting global coalition against terrorism were clearly a major test of this possibility. At the moment, however, there is in progress a fundamental reshuffling, or at least rethinking, of practically all of the world's existing power balances and alliance strategies. The rethinking has been accelerated, of course, by political pressures stemming from recent terrorism-related developments, but it did not originate with them. It has been readily visible in Asia, in fact, for a number of years. Some of the offshoots of this process, like the erstwhile Russian prime minister Yevgeny Primakov's suggested "strategic triangle" of Russia, China, and India, appear improvised, even outrageous, and are quite unlikely to get off the ground.[22] Others, including the revival of close arms ties between Russia and India, as well as the conspicuous recommitment by China and Pakistan to their long-standing military cooperation, are more carefully premeditated and long-term developments and deserve close scrutiny. While one cannot speak confidently at this time of an emerging Asian power axis, with clear lines of accord and discord, one can be certain that *all* major Asian powers—so long as the rethinking continues and alliance structures remain blurry—will step gingerly around the volatile issue of Kashmir.

This circumstance does not preclude the world's major foreign offices from conceding the menacing nature of the Kashmir dispute, but their recognition of this fact doesn't translate in any important world capitals into enthusiasm for an earnest extra-regional project of conflict resolution. In spite of the official, nuclear-alarmist rhetoric over Kashmir, in other words, the truth is that Kashmir continues to be viewed practically everywhere fundamentally as a bilateral matter, to be settled (or not) by India and Pakistan in direct bilateral talks. *Accordingly, the international community's main contribution to the process, by virtue of its own structurally induced paralysis, has consisted up to the present, at least, to no small extent of cheering the region's diplomats on from the sidelines.* One must conclude, then, that any concerted effort by global powers to bring pressure on India and Pakistan to bring their dispute over Kashmir finally to an end would have to overcome this initial and formidable inertial barrier.

Indian Regional Dominance

A yet more powerful explanation for the still prevalent pattern of global reticence to risk entanglement in Kashmir, *especially in an uninvited capacity*, is the inescapable fact of Indian regional dominance. This dominance invites from India's courtiers a certain amount of strategic deference. The deference seems natural for a number of reasons, including India's growing economic clout and the relatively stable performance of India's political system, but towering over them all are the natural advantages built into India's vastly greater size and resources relative to Pakistan. Up until the present decade, these advantages were held in check by political hindrances arising from Cold War rivalries. With the Cold War's end, as Sandy Gordon suggested a few years ago, they've been unbuckled. The strategic deference or "tilt" is now more prominent than ever: India, freed of its Soviet baggage, has emerged the winner in the post–Cold War strategic realignment, and Pakistan, stripped of the historic grounds for its alliance with the West, the loser. "Far from having lost out as a result of the end of the Cold War," Gordon wrote,

> India is poised to emerge in the early 21st century as a far more important and influential power in the Indian Ocean region, and even globally, than it was in the latter part of the 20th. Some of the constraining factors in India's rise to power, particularly domestic and regional South Asian instability, are still present and will continue to snap at India's heels for some years to come. But the end of the Cold War has also enabled India to jettison some of the more burdensome foreign and economic policies that had constrained it in the past.

In sharp contrast, he pointed out, "Pakistan, which has long been India's only serious competitor in South Asia, has lost out seriously as a result of the end of the Cold War. While India suffers from internal instability, Pakistan's problems are potentially far more serious."[23]

The result is that courting India has evolved into a cottage industry in some countries, most notably, perhaps, in the United States. Dubbed in the middle of the 1990s a "big emerging market" by the Commerce Department, India is held up to Americans as a potentially vast economic opportunity for trade and investment. It is also held up, albeit

more circumspectly, as an opportunity for political and military collaboration on a wide range of subjects, from the environment to anti-
terrorism. This trend we examine in a moment.

While India has thus been quite successful in recent years in recruiting international supporters, Pakistan—prior to September 2001, at
least—could boast of only a very brief list. Its diplomatic isolation, on
practically all points of the compass, has been more complete in recent
years, in fact, than at any previous time in its history. Notably, its list of
supporters does include China, which has maintained an unusually close
military partnership with Pakistan without a break since 1963. Unfortunately, this seemingly durable alliance with Beijing brings Pakistan under suspicion for consorting with a state that is under powerful attack
nowadays from anti-China forces, especially in the United States. Targeted, in particular, is alleged Sino-Pakistani violation of global norms
covering nuclear weapons and ballistic missiles development.[24] Ironically, the "Chinese threat" to Western interests is sometimes invoked to
justify American acquiescence to India's emergence as a nuclear weapons power—a development running directly counter to Pakistan's interests.[25] Pakistan's satisfaction with China's friendship, we must add, does
not extend to Beijing's position on the Kashmir dispute, which has in
recent years displayed a reticence barely distinguishable from that of
the rest of the world community.

India's dominant regional position unquestionably helps to explain
the world's customary reticence to get involved in Kashmir. Faced with
India's now billion-plus population, the world isn't likely to reverse that
position heedlessly. The question addressed in this chapter goes well
beyond reticence, however, to consider the possibility that reticence to
act is yielding ground to something quite different—a new resolve to
intervene in regard to Kashmir *but in support of one side in the dispute.*
This question pertains to quite recent clues, largely stemming from the
Kargil episode, that the international community, led by the United States,
has been moving slowly but surely to take the *Indian* side in the dispute.
Obviously, the implications of any such move, particularly insofar as
Pakistan is concerned, are vast. The clues need to be carefully sifted.

Kashmir in American Foreign Policy—Taking Sides?

In its first term (1993–1997), the Clinton administration, a 1996 report
prepared for Congress observed, "followed the general policy of recent

preceding administrations of treating the Kashmir issue as a bilateral problem between India and Pakistan." While affirming its availability for mediation of the Kashmir dispute, it consistently insisted, said the report, that the invitation to serve in that role had to come from both India and Pakistan.[26] Pakistani spokespersons labored to clarify that this stipulation, given New Delhi's well-known preference for bilateralism, worked inevitably in India's favor. They generally were able to discount it, however, since the Clinton White House seemed equally inclined, especially during its first term in office, to draw attention routinely to Indian human rights abuses in Kashmir, and, from time to time, to issue blunt reminders to New Delhi that Kashmir was still understood, from Washington's point of view, as a disputed territory. The most barefaced instance of this—the observation in October 1993 by the Clinton-appointed Assistant Secretary of State for South Asia Robin Lynn Raphel that "we [the U.S. government] view Kashmir as a disputed territory and that means that we do not recognise that Instrument of Accession as meaning that Kashmir is forever more an integral part of India"—detonated a nearly unprecedented explosion of irate commentary in the Indian press.[27] Gleefully welcomed in Pakistan, Raphel's seemingly artless shot across India's bow did not, in any event, signal a change in Washington's Kashmir policy. As before, it continued to seek a middle ground between the two sides, tilting conspicuously to neither.

The Clinton administration's second term (1997–2001) was buffeted by a trio of unusually convulsive developments in South Asia, all of them impinging upon and acting directly to reshape the way in which Washington viewed its relationships with India and Pakistan, in general, and its position on the Kashmir dispute, in particular. First, of course, came the severe jolt to the White House of the nuclear tests of May 1998. U.S. intelligence had failed to detect Indian plans for the tests, and Clinton's unusually aggressive efforts to dissuade Islamabad from going ahead with its own matching series, once the Indians had gone ahead with theirs, proved fruitless. When the tests were finished, in the judgment of a great many observers, a fair portion of Washington's pains-takingly erected nonproliferation policy toward that region lay in ruins. In its place had occurred an alarming advance up the escalation ladder toward full nuclear weaponization in a region where two neighboring states were still locked in a major and unresolved territorial dispute.

Hardly more than a year later came the Kargil crisis, with calamitous consequences for the budding India-Pakistan entente that had seemingly just been born a few months earlier at Lahore. A grave betrayal of trust, as interpreted by New Delhi, Kargil turned the emotional excitement and media extravagance surrounding the Lahore Summit into a major and potentially disastrous political embarrassment for Interim Prime Minister Atal Bihari Vajpayee, whose government had just fallen in a parliamentary vote of no confidence. Kargil acted at the same time, and no less forcefully, to give substance to American fears of a deepening and dangerous connection between the Kashmir dispute and the region's drive for nuclear weapons.

Within months of the Kargil crisis, and closely related to it, came the third in the trio of upheavals—the Pakistan army's seizure on 12 October 1999 of the reins of government in Islamabad. The fourth military coup in the country's history, it resulted in the jailing of Prime Minister Nawaz Sharif, winner in the massive 1997 election landslide and cosignatory of the Lahore Declaration, and the assumption of supreme power for an indefinite period by General Pervez Musharraf, the Chief of Army Staff and—in the judgment of most Pakistan-watchers—one of the masterminds of the Kargil invasion. The Clinton administration revealed no sign of deep regret over the discarding of the elected government, but its tacit acquiescence in the military takeover did not occur oblivious of the bald contrast the army's action made with India's recently concluded thirteenth national elections. When General Musharraf bluntly confessed in his first major address to the nation following the seizure of power that Pakistan had "hit rock bottom,"[28] he unavoidably added strength to the Indian complaint that New Delhi should not be criticized for its reluctance to negotiate over Kashmir with a government that, virtually by its own admission, deserved the title of "failed state."

These three developments impacted rather differently on the Clinton administration's thinking about Kashmir. The first of them, the nuclear tests, naturally acted to heighten the administration's concern for the South Asian region's dogged defiance of the global nonproliferation regime; it also, just as naturally, intensified the administration's concern that a solution be found to the region's most chronic conflict and potential flashpoint—Kashmir. The two concerns were formally yoked together in an extraordinary White House diplomatic initiative begun almost immediately following the tests. Headed by Deputy Secretary of State Strobe Talbott, the initiative consisted of a prolonged and intensive series of diplomatic dialogues stretching from June 1998 to January 2000, a grand total by the end of the Clinton administration of twelve rounds—

ten of them parallel talks engaging (separately) both the Indians and the Pakistanis, the remainder, the Indians alone. The approach of the Americans was to offer to relax sanctions in return for Indian and Pakistani agreement to take five practical steps—demands, really, or what the Americans preferred to call "benchmarks." These were:

- Observe a nuclear test ban, and both sign and ratify the Comprehensive Test Ban Treaty (CTBT) without conditions;
- Refrain from production of fissile material for nuclear weapons, and join talks in Geneva on a fissile material cutoff treaty to permanently ban such production;
- Accept a strategic restraint regime covering the development and deployment of missiles and aircraft capable of carrying weapons of mass destruction;
- Tighten export controls on sensitive materials and technologies used in developing weapons of mass destruction; and
- Enter into direct, high-level, frequent, and serious negotiations with one another over long-standing tensions and disputes, including Kashmir.[29]

The fifth and Kashmir-related provision, which tacked a staple Pakistani policy priority to the four nonproliferation measures, mildly signaled the administration's impatience with New Delhi's Kashmir policy. The reproach was understandable: It was the Indians, after all, who had led the way with the nuclear tests. In return for the lifting of U.S. sanctions inflicted on both India and Pakistan as punishment for violating nonproliferation norms, India, in effect, was being directed to enter into negotiations with its archenemy on an issue New Delhi held was both irrelevant to the nuclear issue and entirely its own business.

Kargil, the second of the three South Asian upheavals to jar the Clinton administration's second term, had a sharply different impact upon American perceptions of the Kashmir problem. On the one hand, the outbreak of unusually severe fighting on the LOC seemed to Americans to give unequivocal vindication to the administration's inclusion of "serious negotiations" over Kashmir among its five benchmarks. On the other hand, since in this instance it was Pakistan that appeared to have led the way with an egregious transgressing of the territorial status quo on the LOC, the pendulum of administration displeasure swung predictably and pitilessly against Pakistan. Pakistani pleadings that the intruders were, in fact, indigenous "freedom-fighters" met not only with Washington's justifiable skepticism over their national origins but with a feeling of alarm, shared fairly widely in some Washington circles, that the intrusion drew at least some of its inspiration from a rising regional tide of Islamic extremist-driven international terrorism. Assiduously shepherded along by New Delhi, this latter notion threatened to brand Pakistan with the reputation of a "rogue state" while at the same time it stained Kashmiri self-determination with illegitimacy. Yet more ominous, from the Pakistani point of view, were indications that Kargil had reinforced already existing reservations in the United States over the advisability of striving for evenhandedness in Washington's dealings with India and Pakistan.

One such indication came on 20 July 1999, while Pakistan's withdrawal of its forces from Indian-held territory was still in progress, in the course of a policy address made in Washington by Mathew Daley, the State Department's Senior Advisor for South Asia, to a meeting of the Indian-American Friendship Council. In his assessment of the Clinton administration's post-Kargil objectives in South Asia, Daley disclosed to the largely Indian audience what appeared to some observers to be an important shift in U.S. policy toward India and Pakistan—a shift that ruled out a return to the pre-Kargil pattern of relations and that placed them on a distinctly new footing. "In the past," he was reported to have said,

> there have been attempts to impose intellectual constructs such as balance or even-handedness on American foreign policy towards India and Pakistan. . . . Those days are over, if indeed they ever existed. America's relations with India and Pakistan are going to have their own separate vectors, trajectories and velocities. At any given moment, on any given topic, we might appear to be even-handed, but that will be an incidental outcome of a policy, not the objective of a policy.[30]

Daley's prominent position in the U.S. policymaking establishment, together with the fact that he had participated as a member of Talbott's team in multiple rounds of diplomatic dialogue with the Indian and Pakistani governments, inevitably drew added attention to his remarks. Administration spokespersons denied that these remarks represented a change in U.S. policy.[31] To South Asian observers, reared in a government-manipulated informational environment in which even the most casual or nebulous remarks of leaders are earnestly sifted for clues to pending policy decisions, the disclaimers were unlikely to be persuasive. Daley, after all, was a seasoned diplomat, and his remarks were made within two weeks of Clinton's 4 July meeting with the Pakistani prime minister. Moreover, his remarks seemed in line with earlier reappraisals of the U.S. approach to South Asia that had been surfacing with some regularity in the public observations of Clinton administration officials long before Kargil. It was the apparent hardening of these earlier assessments in Daley's address that caught South Asian attention.[32]

Pakistan's military coup, the third development helping to shape Clinton administration thinking about Kashmir, obviously lent itself to the discrediting of Pakistan in Western eyes—a phenomenon already far advanced, as we have seen, in the wake of Kargil. However, the coup's impact went well beyond reinforcement of Pakistan's reputation for misgovernment. A no less important consequence, in fact, was the shattering of any lingering illusions in Washington that an end to the conflict over Kashmir could be bought fairly quickly or cheaply—in other words, by winning Pakistan's consent to a settlement formula granting at least tacit approval to the LOC's conversion into a permanent international border. Such a formula had long been favored by New Delhi, of course, and there had been occasional, albeit usually discreet, hints given by ranking officials of the Nawaz Sharif government since its return to power in February 1997 that the conversion option was not entirely outside the realm of possibility from Islamabad's point of view also. In fact, the author's own interviews with senior (both retired and active) members of Pakistan's bureaucratic and political Establishment in the late spring of that year turned up a surprising number of individuals, including at least one member of the prime minister's inner circle of advisers, willing to contemplate Pakistan's eventual acceptance of the LOC option.[33] Two years later, with his government severely shaken both by Pakistan's military setback at Kargil as well as by its virtual economic bankruptcy, Nawaz Sharif was unquestionably more vulnerable than ever to Washington's pressure along these lines. It has been rumored but not confirmed that Washington applied such pressure at the time.[34] In any event, any suggestion that a weakened Islamabad might be ready to cave in on Kashmir was squashed almost immediately by the army's October 1999 takeover.

General Pervez Musharraf, self-appointed chief executive of the new military-run government of Pakistan, moved swiftly, in fact, to dispel any notion that Islamabad was ready to scrap its traditional stand on Kashmir. In a televised address to the nation on 17 October, he offered India what he termed a "meaningful confidence-building measure"—the announcement of "a unilateral military de-escalation on [Pakistan's] international borders with India and [the initiation of] the return of all [Pakistan's] forces moved to the borders in the recent past." He affirmed as well his interest in "unconditional, equitable and result-oriented dialogue with India." For the most part, however, his characterization of his country's Kashmir policy showed no sign of appeasement. Kashmir, he said, remained "the core issue" between India and Pakistan. Pakistan, he asserted, resorting to stock phrases long viewed in New Delhi as thin camouflage for the Pakistan army's massive material support to the Kashmiri militants, would "continue [its] unflinching moral, political and diplomatic support to [its] Kashmiri brethren in their struggle to achieve their right of self-determination." The UN resolutions pertaining to Kashmir had to be honored, he observed, and Indian repression of the Kashmiri people ended.[35] In a statement made in the capital of Azad Kashmir in late December, Musharraf appeared to adopt an even more assertive and unyielding position on Kashmir. "I want to reiterate that there is a change in the policy with India," he was reported to have said by the official Pakistani news agency. "Earlier we used to say that we will negotiate all issues including Kashmir. But now we will discuss the Kashmir issue first [while] including all other issues."[36]

Neither was there anything in Musharraf's initial official appointments to signal an interest in accommodating India on Kashmir. To the important post of foreign minister, for example, he named former Foreign secretary and high commissioner to India Abdus Sattar, an articulate and polished diplomat closely identified for many years with hard-line factions in the Pakistani foreign affairs bureaucracy. Even more revealing of the new regime's intentions, at least from New Delhi's perspective, was continued infiltration by militants across the LOC, the increasingly bold attacks by militants on Indian security forces deployed in Kashmir, and Islamabad's turning a blind eye to the recruiting activities and loud anti-India propaganda attacks staged on Pakistani soil by hard-line militant Kashmiri separatist outfits like the Lashkar-e-Taiba, the Harkat-ul-Mujahideen, and the Hizbul Mujahideen.[37]

Deprived of any likelihood that a beleaguered, and thus tractable, Pakistan might be brought around in a timely fashion to a bilaterally negotiated Kashmir settlement, the Clinton administration, in its final year at the helm of affairs, found itself in the coils of the South Asian region's notorious complexity.

Two stubborn problems confronted the administration. One was that prospects for either one or both of the nuclear-weaponized South Asian rivals to comply voluntarily with all, or even most, of the five benchmarks that had been designated vital prerequisites to the relaxation of sanctions seemed virtually zero. Widely circulated Central Intelligence Agency reports in autumn 1999 of uninterrupted ballistic missile advances in the South Asian region left no room for doubt, in fact, that India and Pakistan, more than a year after the May 1998 nuclear tests, remained relentlessly determined to carry on with their nuclear weapons programs.[38] The White House itself made no secret of the lack of progress in regard to its proliferation benchmarks. In his annual report to Congress on the proliferation of weapons of mass destuction (WMD) and their means of delivery, released on 10 November 1999, President Clinton conceded that Washington's high-level dialogues with the Indian and Pakistani governments had "yielded little progress." There were "no indications," he said, "that India or Pakistan played helpful 'behind the scenes' roles" in the Geneva discussions on fissile material cut off. Moreover, he commented, New Delhi's August 1999 release of its draft nuclear doctrine "suggests that India intends to make nuclear weapons an integral part of the national defense."[39]

In regard to the accuracy of this last comment by Clinton, seasoned Indian security analysts, whether pro- or anti-bomb, left little room for doubt. Among the former, for instance, was K. Subrahmanyam, the notoriously hawkish co-author of the draft nuclear doctrine. Admittedly, Subrahmanyam added his influential voice to those in late 1999 urging the Indian government's signing of the Comprehensive Test Ban Treaty (CTBT). He made it clear in the course of his discussion, however, that he favored signing provided that it "be done after ensuring that India gets the maximum benefit" out of it and without generating "an impression that India is doing it under pressure." By signing, in other words, India needn't necessarily give anything away. On the contrary, explained Subrahmanyam, signing meant that the United States would have to agree

> to lifting all the sanctions imposed on India since 1974 and to work towards admitting India into various multilateral nuclear and missile arms control arrangements. The U.S. should recognise formally India's role as a democratic balancer and stabiliser in Asia.

In any event, India would only be agreeing to *sign* the CTBT, he pointed out, not to *ratify* it. Ratification itself "will follow those by the U.S., Russia and China"—and only after full debate in both houses of parliament.[40] Noteworthy in Subrahmanyam's discussion was the complete absence of any indication that Indian nuclear concessions might go beyond the CTBT to include the other benchmarks. Adroit playing of India's "nuclear card," he seemed to be saying, would leave India's nuclear weaponization program virtually untouched. Understood in Subrahmanyam's terms, of course, signing the CTBT was a ticket of admission *into* not *out of* the prized company of internationally acknowledged nuclear weapon states—a status, we should recall, that was explicitly and emphatically ruled out in the appeals to India and Pakistan for unconditional signature of the CTBT made by the Group of Eight and the Security Council in June 1998.

Nuclear moderates in India, in their turn, were not any more encouraging in this regard. Arguing that only one of Washington's five proliferation benchmarks—calling for restraint in exporting sensitive technologies—was likely to face relatively clear sailing in the ongoing Indo–U.S. dialogue, P. R. Chari, Director of the Institute of Peace and Conflict Studies in New Delhi and one of India's most senior and respected security analysts, observed that when it came to India's adherence to the White House–advocated strategic restraint regime governing the development and deployment of missiles and aircraft capable of carrying weapons of mass destruction, agreement was "most problematical." The strategic restraint benchmark, he said,

> questions the logic of the nuclear tests, the BJP's ideology of military power premised on nuclear weapons, and the influence within the government of the defence-nuclear-scientific lobby. The enunciation of the nuclear doctrine, currently in draft form, commits the government to pursuing the deployment of nuclear weapons and missile systems for equipping itself with a "credible minimum deterrent"; its structure is no different from that of the other nuclear weapon powers. The present government cannot halt that process; to cap that process, however, is an article of faith for the United States. There is nothing to suggest, at present, that either government is prepared to compromise on this basic issue.

"In this milieu," he concluded, "it is difficult to see how Indo–U.S. relations can improve in the final months of the Clinton administration."[41]

The second problem that confronted the administration was that its ability to compel compliance with its nonproliferation objectives had already been substantially undermined by the lack of consensus within foreign policy circles in the United States itself on either the utility or wisdom of sanctions. Stiffening the sanctions, in the face of substantial skepticism in regard to their material effectiveness, especially in India's case, didn't appear to be an option at all.[42] Easing them, an option the administration resorted to sporadically, in fact, virtually from the moment they were first put in place, threatened to cancel whatever limited leverage the administration still retained while at the same time risking the appearance of succumbing to nuclear blackmail. Beset with increasingly insistent domestic pressures not only to ease the sanctions but to do away with them entirely, those against India in particular, the White House seemed to be inching slowly but inexorably in that direction. One signpost of many was its strategically timed removal in mid-December 1999, on the eve of renewed Indo-U.S. nuclear dialogue, of 51 Indian entities from the list of 200 entities originally sanctioned following the Pokhran nuclear tests.[43]

Among the domestic forces chipping away at the Clinton administration's resolve to cling to its nonproliferation goals in South Asia was a formidable pro-India lobby. From fairly modest beginnings, this lobby had expanded in the United States in little more than a decade into one whose size, savvy, and apparent clout earned depiction of it in the *Washington Post* "as a powerful and effective domestic lobby—one that aspires to the level of influence that American Jews have exerted on behalf of Israel. . . ."[44] Its influence had spread noticeably into Congress, the federal bureaucracy, and the media, as well as into major academic institutions and think tanks. The formally organized legislative arm of this lobby, the Congressional Caucus on India and Indian Americans, was formed in 1993. It claimed about 115 members. The Brooklyn Democrat who helped found it, Representative Gary L. Ackerman, has been celebrated in the Indian media as "Mr. India" of Capitol Hill, as the "Man for All Reasons," and "as India's staunchest backer."[45] Support for congressional lobbying efforts came from the well-heeled and increasingly politicized 1.6-million-strong Indian diaspora in the United States,* organized into such groups as the Indian American Political Advocacy Council (IAPAC), the Indian American Forum for Political

---

*According to the official 2000 Census, the Indian diaspora population in the United States had approximately doubled since the 1990 Census.

Education (IAFPE), the India Abroad Center for Political Awareness (IACPA), the American Association of Physicians of Indian Origin (AAPIO), the Network of South Asian Professionals (NSAP), and the Indo-American Democratic Committee (IADC). One visible sign of the flourishing of this lobby was the surfacing in Congress less than a year after the May 1998 nuclear tests of a strongly backed legislative initiative, called the Brownback-Harkin amendment in the Senate version, that sought—against the explicit objections of the Clinton White House—to de-link the suspension of economic sanctions from the requirement for Indian and Pakistani signatures on the CTBT and, at the same time, limit the discretionary authority of the executive branch to lift the sanctions selectively.[46] Predictably, an argument made on the initiative's behalf stressed "India's huge middle class" and the market opportunities this represented for American companies.[47] Another straw in the wind was the mention by prominent congressional visitors to India in the same period of the U.S. government's need to "deepen its appreciation of Indian security concerns"—among them, as reportedly included in the comments of a leading member of Congress and perennial presidential aspirant, Richard Gephardt, during a visit to New Delhi late in March 1999, that India "'is fully capable of advancing the cause of peace without intervention of outside powers.'"[48] The allusion here to India's preference for bilateralism in regard to Kashmir was unmistakable.

The smaller pro-Pakistan lobby in the United States, drawing, like its pro-India counterpart, on a well-heeled, increasingly active and well-organized diaspora community, has proven itself too, at least on occasion, no less adept at the lobbying game. Indeed, it registered a surprising success in a strenuous effort in 1999 to win sizeable congressional support for aggressive White House mediation of the Kashmir dispute. That initiative, which sought to take advantage of heightened American anxieties over Kashmir's emergence, in Kargil's wake, as a potentially dangerous nuclear flashpoint, was spearheaded by paid lobbying firms in alliance with a Washington-based group calling itself the Americans for Peace and Justice in South Asia, a consortium of nine Pakistani and Kashmiri-American organizations. Months of effort culminated in the signing by over sixty congressmen of two similarly worded letters to President Clinton—a Senate version (dated 21 July) that finally contained fifteen signatures and a House version (dated 29 July) with forty-six—urging the President "to: 1) consider appointment of a Special Envoy who could recommend to you ways of ascertaining the wishes of the

Kashmiri people and reaching a just and lasting settlement of the Kashmir issue; and 2) propose strengthening the UN Military Observers Group to monitor the situation along the Line of Control."[49] Signed by members of both the Democratic and Republican parties, and including the names of a number of prominent legislators generally considered on the Indian side, the letters unleashed a cascade of agitated commentary in the Indian press. Finally delivered to the president near the end of September, they drew a scathing rebuke from *The Times of India*, which labeled their proposals "ill-conceived," "ill-informed," and "harebrained."[50] The Pakistani press, exulting over the pro-Pakistan lobby's achievement, hailed the letter campaign a "major diplomatic success."[51] The White House, urged on by Congressman Ackerman and others, promptly and unsurprisingly rejected the proposals.[52] For the pro-India lobby, the campaign, even after its White House snubbing, was naturally judged a setback. The setback was unlikely to be enduring, however, given the considerable political assets remaining with the pro-India lobby. It immediately launched its own congressional letter-writing campaign, provoking one Indian newspaper to muse about the onset of "Kargil II"—a war of letters in Washington.[53] As well, it brought pressure to bear, apparently not without bearing some fruit, even on some of those who had already signed a letter calling for a special envoy. The abrupt, last-minute withdrawal of his signature from the Senate letter by Daniel Patrick Moynihan, a leading Democrat and former ambassador to India, was just one sign that the pro-India lobby, while perhaps momentarily down, was definitely not out.[54]

Reassuring to India, no doubt, was that support for White House mediation of the Kashmir dispute, notwithstanding the impressively orchestrated appeal for a special envoy, was far from substantial in either official or unofficial foreign policy circles in the United States. A pronounced India-friendly preference for bilateral over either multilateral or third-party approaches to Kashmir had been showing up with noticeable regularity for years, in fact, in most public discussions of the issue among America's South Asia–focused policy advocates. With but rare exception, such advocates, typically coming from bureaucratic, diplomatic, journalistic, or academic backgrounds and lodged in prestigious and influential think tanks, have urged the United States to play a helpful "background" role in regard to Kashmir, by encouraging the two sides to seek peaceful resolution, for instance, but they have generally coupled this advice with the persistent appeal that the United States itself, unless expressly invited to take an active role by *both* New Delhi and Islamabad, maintain a strictly "hands-off" policy on Kashmir. This was the gist of former ambassador Teresita C. Schaffer's testimony, for instance, in October 1999 before the House International Relations Sub-committee on Asia and the Pacific. Schaffer, who joined Georgetown University's Center for Strategic and International Studies as Director for South Asia in August 1998, commented that "the work of settling [Kashmir] has to be done by [India and Pakistan]. I oppose naming a special envoy on Kashmir. The administration is right, I believe, to conclude that a U.S. third-party role can be effective only if both countries accept it." In suggesting that the Pakistanis needed to recognize "that they will not be able to wrest Kashmir from India and may need to build a political consensus around a solution that doesn't significantly change today's territorial allocation," Schaffer gave virtual endorsement to New Delhi's preference for conversion of the Line of Control into a permanent international boundary.[55]

The fact of the matter is that practically every privately sponsored task force on the South Asian region assembled under the auspices of major think tanks in the United States in the decade of the 1990s took an unequivocal stand against direct U.S. involvement in the Kashmir dispute. This rule holds for groups sponsored singly or jointly by the Asia Society, the Carnegie Endowment for International Peace, the Council on Foreign Relations, and the Brookings Institution. In a 1998 report sponsored jointly by the latter two organizations, for instance, the authors held themselves to urging the United States to help in "calming Kashmir" by encouraging India and Pakistan to take a number of fairly modest bilateral steps, including, for example, to refrain from provocative public rhetoric and to accept an increase in the number of international peacekeepers on the LOC. They conceded without equivocation that "Kashmir remains the most dangerous point of contention between India and Pakistan. It is the issue with the greatest potential to trigger a conventional or even nuclear war." Adopting a puzzling mixture of certitude and resignation, however, they immediately added the following caveat:

> That said, the dispute is not ripe for final resolution. It is not even ripe for mediation by the United States or anyone else. Consistent with these realities, diplomacy aimed at now resolving the permanent political status of Kashmir is bound to fail.[56]

Contributing to Washington's seeming tilt toward New Delhi was the conviction of many professional South Asia watchers that the world's largest and oldest democracies had acquired in the post–Cold War circumstances plausible grounds for constructing a multifaceted "strategic partnership." A concept more liberal in its invocation than rigorous in its definition, strategic partnership implied—in the South Asian context—that the international agendas of the United States and India had come to overlap one another sufficiently to warrant India's classification as an ally, not in the classical military sense necessarily, but in regard to a fairly extensive list of shared world order and South Asian regional concerns. Also implied, at least in the way Indian analysts chose to interpret the term, was the absence of a similar partnership with (meaning the tacit strategic downgrading of) America's erstwhile ally, Pakistan.

Conspicuous on the list of concerns presumed shared by India and the United States at the turn of the century was religion-motivated terrorism. Washington's concerns in this regard, geographic and otherwise, naturally extended well beyond New Delhi's. However, the coming to power in Afghanistan in 1996 of the religiously radical Taliban regime supplied practical grounds for the convergence of interests and possible policy coordination focused on counterterrorism. Washington's initially equivocal view of the Taliban yielded fairly quickly to one of utter disdain. Angered, in particular, by Kabul's sheltering of Osama bin Laden, the alleged Saudi Arabia–born mastermind of the deadly 1998 bombings of two American embassies in Africa, Washington took to dubbing Afghanistan a rogue state and a breeding ground for global terrorists. India, no less angered by Kabul's alleged covert aid to the insurgency in Kashmir, in its turn broadcast to the world Pakistan's role as a backer of the Taliban. To the dismay of Pakistanis, Taliban-aided separatist militancy in Kashmir lent itself handily to designation as Islamic terrorism, a label that converted with equal ease into designation of Pakistan itself as one of Islamic terrorism's prime exporters. In this way, talk of strategic partnership between India and the United States led ineluctably to consideration of Kashmir's terrorist element. It also led, just as ineluctably, to consideration of this element's relevance to Washington's Kashmir policy. Menacing to Pakistan's policymakers in this connection was the Clinton administration's increasingly explicit naming of Osama bin Laden, as was reportedly done in a statement to South Asian correspondents by Assistant Secretary of

State Karl F. Inderfurth in late December 1999, as an abettor of terrorism specifically in Kashmir.[57]

The Taliban-Kashmir connection surfaced again at the time of the December 1999 hijacking of an Indian Airlines Airbus A300 bound for New Delhi from Katmandu, Nepal, with 189 mainly Indian passengers and crew on board. Five masked and well-armed hijackers, declaring themselves supporters of Kashmir's independence of India, seized control of the aircraft soon after take off on 24 December. Apparently low on fuel, the ill-fated plane made brief stops at Amritsar, Lahore, and then Dubai—at which point the hijackers released twenty-six passengers and off-loaded the body of a slain male Indian passenger, the only hostage to lose his life in the course of the hijacking—before continuing on to Kandahar. There, at the spiritual center of Taliban-ruled Afghanistan, the ill-fated plane ended its five-nation forced odyssey parked on the airport runway. With Taliban officials acting as intermediaries, a team of Indian diplomats dispatched to Afghanistan by New Delhi engaged the hijackers in five days of arduous negotiations that ended on 31 December with India's capitulation to the hijackers' key demand—the release from Indian captivity of three notorious Kashmiri militants.[58] The hijackers, placing themselves in the custody of Taliban officials along with the trio of freed militants flown from India, disappeared without having revealed either their identities or nationalities. The remaining passengers and crew, their eight-day ordeal finally over, walked to freedom.[59]

The Indian government came under unusually severe domestic attack for its handling of the crisis. Numerous respected analysts, including even some normally allied with the government on security issues, declared the hijacking's outcome a major defeat for India.[60] The noted journalist Prem Shankar Jha, indulging in hyperbole, no doubt, but mirroring, nevertheless, the frustrations felt in many quarters, asserted that "India has just been handed its most serious psychological defeat of the entire Kashmir war."[61] The Vajpayee government fought back with charges of its own, directed for the most part against its old adversary Pakistan. Senior Indian officials, including the Prime Minister's National Security Advisor Brajesh Mishra and External Affairs Minister Jaswant Singh, unleashed a barrage of public charges identifying Pakistan as the mastermind of—or at least perfidious accomplice to—the Christmas eve hijacking. Their allegations included: that the hijackers had flown to Katmandu earlier on the day of the hijacking onboard a Pakistan International Airways flight from Karachi; that they were assisted at the airport in Katmandu by Pakistani diplomats or intelligence agents; that the hijackers were all Pakistani nationals; that the militants in Indian jails whose release the hijackers sought were largely Pakistanis; that the hijackers had been in constant touch by cell phone or wireless radio with "a third force"—presumably their Pakistani handlers—throughout the negotiations at Kandahar; and, when the crisis ended, that they naturally fled across the border into waiting arms in Pakistan.[62] India's prime minister publicly called upon the United States to name Pakistan a terrorist state.[63] Pakistani leaders, in their turn, denied all the charges, describing them as New Delhi's panicked reaction to its self-induced political weakness. General Musharraf seized the occasion to remind the world in a CNN broadcast that Pakistan was prepared to use its nuclear weapons in the event of a dire threat to the country's security. Disquieted Pakistani analysts, reflecting on the huge scale and intensity of the propaganda war between India and Pakistan that had been triggered by the hijacking, warned darkly of its potential consequences. The end-of-century hijacking incident, observed Hasan-Askari Rizvi, was "the most unfortunate and serious crisis in [India-Pakistan] relations in the decade of the nineties."[64]

Any collaborative measures that India and the United States ultimately decided to take in regard to what they jointly considered was a terrorist threat in Kashmir would technically qualify, of course, as a step toward the "internationalization" of the Kashmir dispute. In principle, of course, precisely such a step is what the government of Pakistan has been seeking for decades. The Pakistani perception, however, is that Indo-U.S. counterterrorist collaboration would be internationalization of the most perverse, counterproductive, and unwelcome kind. Instead of contributing to a negotiated and equitable settlement, it would, from the Pakistani perspective, only make matters worse: It would betray a decade of Kashmiri Muslim sufferings at the hands of Indian security forces, stiffen Indian resistance to accommodation of any sort (whether with the Kashmiris or the Pakistanis), and, in the end, simply deepen the paralysis that has inhibited the search for resolution for decades.

When it came to the South Asian region, whether considered as a whole or specifically in regard to Kashmir, the Clinton administration, through two terms of office, seemed torn by conflicting policy priorities. It did appear keen to chart a new course for U.S. policy in the region. It was attracted, in particular, by the potential benefits of closer bilateral cooperation with India—a choice that inevitably lent itself to interpretation by South Asians, Indians and Pakistanis alike, as "taking sides." The Clinton administration was naturally hesitant, however, to

place at risk the nonproliferation objectives to which Washington has
been committed for most of the last half century. Any vacillation on that
score met up with resistance from a powerful domestic arms control
lobby that opposed both expansion in the number of nuclear weapon
powers and casual dilution of existing arms control agreements. Stalwarts of this lobby—disparaged in India as "arms control ayatollahs"
and "non-proliferation fundamentalists"[65]—viewed the administration's
nuclear benchmarks essentially as nonnegotiable. The predictable end
product of this tug of war between rival policy groups was a fairly lengthy
period of drift and indecision. In the events surrounding the exchange of
official, high-level visits that took place in the last year of the Clinton
White House (President Clinton's visit to Bangladesh, India, and Pakistan in March 2000, Prime Minister Vajpayee's return visit to the United
States in September the same year), the tug of war seemed to be nearing
an end—with pro-India elements of the American foreign policymaking
community appearing within sight of victory. By the time Clinton left
office, however, the scale of this victory was already in doubt. The new
George W. Bush administration took the reins of government, in fact,
with the issue of "taking sides" still not fully resolved. This point requires some additional clarification.

India vs. Pakistan: From Clinton to Bush

Clinton's visit to South Asia in March 2000—not only the visit itself
and the agreements that accompanied it, but the months of agonized
discussion in the United States that preceded it over the visit's anticipated costs and benefits—was remarkable in a number of ways. One
was the fact that it took place at all. In spite of strong urging by various
public interest groups that the president visit the region and make up for
decades of unwarranted neglect, the proposed visit had been repeatedly
postponed.[66] When it finally did occur, it was the first visit to the region
by an incumbent American chief executive in twenty-two years, the first
to Pakistan in thirty-one years, and the first ever to Bangladesh. Another
remarkable aspect of the visit was the fact that details of the president's
itinerary in South Asia—in particular, whether or not Pakistan was to be
included on it, and, if it was, for how long—became the focus of a lengthy,
public, heated, and, at times, even international discussion. In the United
States, lobbyists for India and Pakistan worked frantically to build support either for an "India-Bangladesh only" or "Pakistan also" resolution

of the itinerary crisis. America's First Lady, Hillary Rodham Clinton, found herself the target of bitter criticism when she was reported to have "interfered" with White House decision making by making a public appeal to the president—at a $1,000-a-plate fund-raising dinner in New York staged for her Senate campaign in late February by a group of Pakistani-Americans—to include Pakistan on his tour.[67] The Indian government itself officially ventured into the "battle of the itinerary" controversy with the reported warning of its foreign secretary during a mid-February visit to Washington that "as friends, we thought we should bring to [U.S. officials'] notice that [inclusion of Pakistan on the president's itinerary will bring] a public reaction (in India) and this has been conveyed to them."[68] In what by any standard was an extraordinary display of presidential procrastination (and a display, as well, of the growing clout of the South Asian ethnic lobbies discussed earlier), the White House did not reveal its final decision in regard to Pakistan's inclusion on Clinton's South Asia itinerary until 7 March—just twelve days short of the date of departure for New Delhi.

A third way in which President Clinton's March visit to South Asia was remarkable lies in the actual unfolding of the event itself—in particular, in the stark contrast that developed in both symbolic and substantive content between the Indian and Pakistani legs of the visit.* By all accounts, the visit to India was a public relations extravaganza, light in major agreements, to be sure, but heavy with public ceremony and opportunities for the American president to flatter the host country and to herald a new era in India–United States relations. The official hyperbole went significantly beyond the stock exaggerations one expects in banquet speeches and communiqués issued at the conclusion of meetings of heads of state; it had to have had a dampening impact on the leaders of India's western neighbor, already busy by then with their own preparations for the American president's imminent arrival. On 21 March, the first full day of the presidential visit to India, Clinton and Vajpayee released a so-called "vision" statement, painstakingly crafted well in advance of the trip, entitled "India-U.S. Relations: A Vision for the 21st Century." The statement frankly admitted that differences persisted be-

---

*Clinton's visit to South Asia, which began with his arrival in New Delhi the evening of 19 March, was distributed in the following manner: over four full days of official visit in India (21–25 March), one day in Bangladesh (20 March, daytime visit only), and roughly five hours in Pakistan (25 March) on the way home.

tween the two countries, especially when it came to nuclear arms control. However, mention of differences was significantly softened by the stress given to the potential for what the statement called a "qualitatively new relationship." The statement pledged the two governments to "be partners in peace, with a common interest in and complementary responsibility for ensuring regional and international security." It committed them to "regular consultations on, and work together and with others for, strategic stability in Asia and beyond." It said the two countries would "bolster joint efforts to counter terrorism and meet other challenges to regional peace." Nowhere in the statement did the word Kashmir appear, and, in a sentence obviously crafted to placate the strong Indian aversion to foreign meddling in the Kashmir dispute, it registered the acknowledgment "that tensions in South Asia can only be resolved by the nations of South Asia."[69]

Clinton's short stopover in Pakistan on 25 March could not have presented a more contrasting spectacle. Far from demonstrating the president's keen admiration for the country's political and economic prowess and progress, the visit sent the clearest signals possible of Clinton's reluctance to be there, of his disdain for Pakistan's tradition of military rule, of his government's belief in Pakistan's extreme vulnerability to terrorism, and, by no means least, of his strong disapproval of Islamabad's Kashmir policy. Almost unprecedented security arrangements were made in conjunction with the visit, conveying the unmistakable message to watching world audiences that the Pakistan government couldn't be counted upon to protect its distinguished visitor. Restrictions were in place to prevent unwanted media photos of the president meeting with the Pakistani chief executive, General Pervez Musharraf. An American journalist observed that Clinton, having just come from courting India for five days with "unconditional affection" and "with the ardor of a smitten suitor," spent a half a day treating its old Cold War ally Pakistan "like an old girlfriend who is part of the past."[70] In his televised address to the people of Pakistan, actually videotaped before his departure from Bombay, the president delivered a remarkably blunt lecture on the revolutionary realities of "a new and changing world" and on the urgent need for Pakistan to face up to the "hard choices" ahead. "For this era," he advised,

> does not reward [those] who struggle in vain to redraw borders with blood. It belongs to those with the vision to look beyond borders for partners in

commerce and trade. It does not favor nations where governments claim all the power to solve every problem. Instead, it favors nations where the people have the freedom and responsibility to shape their own destinies.

Employing language in the talk stunningly indifferent to Pakistan's political culture and markedly harsher than anything he had said in his address to the Indian parliament, Clinton admonished his listeners to recognize "that no grievance, no cause, no system of belief can ever justify deliberate killing of innocents. Those who bomb bus stations, target embassies and kill those who uphold the law are not heroes." He noted Pakistan's "tragic squandering of effort, energy and wealth on policies that make [it] poorer but not safer." On Kashmir, he urged restraint and respect for the Line of Control. He called attention to what he designated "a stark truth," specifically that "there is no military solution to Kashmir," then added the biting moral admonition that "it is wrong to support attacks against civilians across the Line of Control." If there were any left among Clinton's Pakistani listeners that day who still hoped for a comforting signal of some sort on the all-important matter of Kashmir, Clinton removed all doubt with the steely disclaimer: "We cannot and will not mediate or resolve the dispute in Kashmir. Only you and India can do that through dialogue."[71]

There were ample indications in the immediate wake of Clinton's visit that a great many Indian and practically all Pakistani analysts considered India to have emerged as by far the greater beneficiary of the visit, at least in the public relations battle it stirred up. A characteristic theme in much of the Indian press was that the visit marked a "boom time" in India-U.S. relations and that "it could not have gone off better."[72] In the Pakistani press, no less characteristic was the correspondingly gloomy assessment of Salahuddin K. Leghari, writing in *Dawn*, that the South Asian region, described by Clinton before the trip as "the most dangerous place in the world," had become even more dangerous in the trip's wake. "President Clinton's heavy 'tilt' towards India on the Kashmir issue," he said, "will further embolden [India] to continue with its repressive policy of forced occupation of Kashmir."[73]

More sober analyses suggested that the existence of persistent discontinuities in the strategic outlooks of New Delhi and Washington would certainly slow down, if not entirely prevent, the emergence of a true meeting of the minds between the two governments. Such was the theme of an acerbic editorial in the prestigious *The Times of India*, appearing on the first day of Clinton's visit to India, which suggested that Clinton and his hosts would be better off sticking "to the digital realm by seeing the whole show as a virtual visit of a virtual VVIP to an equally virtual destination. In other words, a highly enjoyable tamasha [spectacle] but a write-off, really if not virtually. Truly, a case of a mouse that roared."[74]

Vajpayee's return visit to the United States the following September was in most respects a replay of Clinton's visit to India—a dazzling spectacle of pomp and ceremony, including a rare address to a joint session of Congress by the Indian prime minister, accompanied by a number of quite modest agreements aimed at promoting increased trade and investment as well as increased cooperation in fields such as health, technology, narcotics, law enforcement, and counterterrorism. Largely echoing the "vision statement" signed in New Delhi, the joint statement released by the two leaders during Vajpayee's visit to Washington made no direct mention of either Pakistan or Kashmir. The two leaders once again "reaffirmed their belief that tensions in South Asia can only be resolved by the nations of South Asia. . . ."[75] Once again, opinion was divided on the significance of the visit, the more sober commentaries pointing out that the red carpet had been rolled out for Vajpayee by an administration truly on its last legs, and, moreover, that the palpable results of the visit fell conspicuously short of a breakthrough.[76]

Breakthrough or not, the Clinton administration ended its second term with India-United States relations clearly at an unprecedented high point and with foundations seemingly in place for continued improvement. Continued improvement faced at least three formidable obstacles, however, and even as George W. Bush was taking the helm in Washington, there were ample signs that improvement was far from assured. Noted by many observers of the region, for one, was that the exchange of high-level visitors had resulted in virtually no progress on the nuclear weapons issue. The two sides simply agreed to disagree. Had the disagreement been over an issue other than that of nuclear weapons, it might not have mattered so much. President Bush entered the White House, however, in the midst of a chorus of warnings about the mounting nuclear danger in South Asia that seemed at the time bound to forestall any sudden or serious departure from long-standing American nonproliferation policies in the region. One such warning came in the publication in December 2000 of a Central Intelligence Agency–compiled analysis entitled *Global Trends 2015: A Dialogue About the Future with Nongovernment*

Experts, a report based on a distillation of private specialists' views and issued under the authority of the National Intelligence Council. When it came to South Asia's nuclear circumstances, the language used in this major assessment was chilling. "The threat of major conflict between India and Pakistan," it said,

> will overshadow all other regional issues during the next 15 years. Continued turmoil in Afghanistan and Pakistan will spill over into Kashmir and other areas of the subcontinent, prompting Indian leaders to take more aggressive preemptive and retaliatory actions. India's conventional military advantage over Pakistan will widen as a result of New Delhi's superior economic position. India will also continue to build up its ocean-going navy to dominate the Indian Ocean transit routes used for delivery of Persian Gulf oil to Asia. *The decisive shift in conventional military power in India's favor over the coming years potentially will make the region more volatile and unstable. Both India and Pakistan will see weapons of mass destruction as a strategic imperative and will continue to amass nuclear warheads and build a variety of missile delivery systems.*[77]

Two similarly bleak proliferation warnings followed in quick succession. The first was a Department of Defense report, *Proliferation: Threat and Response*, released in January 2001 just weeks before the Bush administration took over. It concluded its section on South Asia with the forecast that

> in South Asia, India and Pakistan are in a period of accelerated nuclear weapons and missile development. Political tensions and domestic politics have driven the two countries to test nuclear weapons in 1998, and to develop and test longer-range missiles in 1998 and 1999. Tensions in the region likely will remain high. . . . Given the long-standing hostility between the two countries, even a minor conflict runs the risk of escalating into an exchange of missiles with nuclear warheads, which would have disastrous consequences for the region and beyond. . . . Additional nuclear tests are possible. . . . [M]ore missile tests are likely. . . . [T]he potential for the proliferation of technologies and expertise will increase in the future, as both countries become more self-sufficient in the production of nuclear weapons and missiles and subsequently become potential suppliers.[78]

The second warning came on 7 February, soon after the Bush administration was launched, in testimony before the Senate Select Committee on Intelligence by the director of the Defense Intelligence Agency,

Navy Vice Admiral Thomas Wilson. In his testimony, he said that "the United States must guard against an expanded military conflict between India and Pakistan over Kashmir. This is more serious now since both India and Pakistan have nuclear weapons and the means to deliver them. Both sides," he added, "operate from 'zero-sum perspectives,' retain large forces, in close proximity, across a tense line of control. . . . The potential for mistake and miscalculation remains relatively high."[79]

A second major obstacle to continued improvement in India-United States relations stemmed from the possibility that Washington's always overcrowded foreign interest agenda might turn out to have little more space for India in the present decade than it had in the 1990s. There was a hint of this possibility, in fact, even before the Bush administration had formally taken over the White House on 20 January 2001. In his confirmation hearing before the Senate Foreign Relations Committee on 17 January, the then secretary of state–designate Colin Powell, in formal testimony that filled nine single-spaced, typed pages, cited (by rough count) at least 33 separate geographical locations, 23 separate countries, including 16 references to China (24 if Taiwan is included). There were no references whatsoever to South Asia, a dubious distinction awarded to no other global region apart from the Antarctic. This was in testimony that concluded, by the way, with Powell's revealing observation that "I wanted to touch on some of the areas and particular relationships that I know are of greatest importance to you."[80] Notwithstanding India's success with political democracy, its geographical distance from the United States and the relatively modest level of economic activity between the two countries both remained fairly substantial material barriers to their much-touted "strategic partnership." The fact is that while India is often held up as a potential counterweight to China in the reckonings of American strategic analysts, U.S. economic ties with China—both in trade and investment—were far and away greater than they were with India.[81]

A third major obstacle to improved India–United States relations is Pakistan—specifically, Pakistan's continuing strategic appeal and apparent importance to Washington. This is, to say the least, a profoundly ironic circumstance. Without a doubt, the Bush presidency began with India having taken a commanding lead over Pakistan in the business of courting American favor and with signs mounting that the movement of the Clinton administration during its second term to take India's side in regard to Kashmir might be continued under Bush. This was certainly likely to be the outcome, in any event, if one were judging the matter entirely in terms of the expressed preferences of Washington's leading think tanks. In the comprehensive report (*Transition 2001*) of a blue ribbon panel presented to the Bush administration in its first weeks in office by the Rand Corporation, for example, the recommendation to continue the tilt to India was unequivocally expressed. The report warned that

> Pakistan is in serious crisis and is pursuing policies counter to important U.S. interests. The United States should increase pressure on Islamabad to stop support for the Taliban, to cooperate in the fight against terrorism, to show restraint in Kashmir, and to focus on solving its own internal problems. . . . Pakistan continues to be beset by unhealthy political, economic, and strategic trends. . . . The most disturbing of these trends has been the growth of Islamic extremism. Extremist groups thrive because of Pakistan's continuing state failures and because they are intentionally supported by the Pakistan military and secret services in the pursuit of the latter's goals in Kashmir and Afghanistan.
> . . . Pakistan refuses to roll back its nuclear program. . . . [I]t appears committed to using its emerging nuclear capabilities for strategic cover as it challenges India through its support for insurgents in Kashmir. . . .

Especially ominous from the Pakistani perspective, I think, was the report's concluding advice to the Bush administration on the South Asian region. It said:

> We recommend that your South Asian policy proceed from a decoupling of India and Pakistan in U.S. calculations. That is, U.S. relations with each state must be governed by an objective assessment of the intrinsic value of each country to American interests in this new era. This means recognizing that India is on its way to becoming a major Asian power and therefore warrants both a level of engagement far greater than the previous norm and an appreciation of its potential for both collaboration and resistance across a much larger canvas than simply South Asia. In the case of Pakistan, it means recognizing that this is a country in serious crisis and that it is pursuing policies that run counter to important U.S. interests.[82]

Just how much inclined was the Bush administration to follow this advice? On this count, the evidence suggests that there was considerable ambivalence present. On the one hand, the administration moved with surprising alacrity to solidify Washington's ties with India, promising a presidential visit, dispatching an unprecedented number of high-level military and civilian officials to New Delhi, and, in general, moving to give substance to the promised new relationship. Helping to motivate the administration's favorable slant on India, no doubt, was New Delhi's relatively strong and exceptional endorsement of Washington's proposed Ballistic Missile Defense initiative—viewed widely as anti-Chinese in concept. On the other hand, among those helping to shape the Bush administration's South Asia policy were some who cautioned against pursuing a lopsidedly pro-Indian policy. One of these was Robert D. Blackwill, a Harvard professor who had played a major role on Bush's foreign policy advisory team during the election campaign and who was subsequently appointed ambassador to India. In a book published during the campaign, Blackwill had evinced some disdain for careless talk about the potential contours of an Indo-U.S. strategic partnership. He acknowledged that there was "new interest" in India and suggested that "this is all to the good. . . . It was a mistake in the 1990s for the United States to have viewed India primarily through the prism of its confrontation with Pakistan." In language that was arrestingly prophetic, he went on to suggest, however, that

> this preoccupation with India should not obscure the fact that, for the next five years, developments in Pakistan are likely to have a greater impact on allied national interests than those in India. Pakistan today is on the edge of fulfilling the classic definition of a failed state. Its very survival as a nation is in question. If its state structures were to give way, WMD proliferation and Islamic terrorism could become Pakistan's most important exports, and the risk of war between Pakistan and India would rise. *So the giddy talk in the United States and elsewhere regarding India as a potential strategic partner should not weaken the allies' determination to do all they can to avoid a violent collapse of Pakistan. Allied policies that seek to isolate Pakistan and treat it as a pariah because of its problems in democratic governance could help to produce a catastrophe in South Asia and in the region.*[83]

Much the same sentiment was voiced in late August 2001, by the way, only a few weeks before the terrorist onslaught (again, somewhat prophetically), by a senior Pentagon official—Peter Rodman, assistant secretary of defense for international affairs. In a meeting with media representatives, Rodman was quoted in a Pakistani newspaper account as saying that "our relationship with Pakistan is valuable to us. And I don't think this administration is going to lose sight of that." He went on to say that "our relationship with India is different, but Pakistan has been an ally over many decades. I don't think we, as a great power, should be dispensing with allies when . . . we think conditions have changed. . . . It's an Islamic country in a very complicated region of the world. I think it is useful to the United States to have a friend in that part of the world." Speaking on U.S.-India relations, he suggested that their scope was limited. "India," he said, "is not going to become an ally of the United States. I think India values its independence. It values its nonalignment. So I don't think anybody should expect that India is going to collude with us."[84]

The events of 11 September swept much of the Bush administration's ambivalence over Pakistan—at least temporarily—out the door. Within days of the terrorists' attacks on New York and Washington, D.C., Pakistan's stock had risen dramatically in American eyes. Called on to "prove itself" as an ally against terrorism, Islamabad responded with an amazingly unqualified endorsement of President Bush's war on terrorism and a nearly unconditional offer to open its airspace as well as to give logistical assistance, air-base facilities, and intelligence information to U.S. forces in their efforts to pry arch-terrorist Osama bin Laden loose from his Afghanistan sanctuary. The decision unquestionably placed Pakistan's leader, Pervez Musharraf, in a politically exposed position.[85] It did, however, bring immediate material relief to Pakistan in the form of rescheduled debt and the lifting of sanctions. For Pakistan's Indian neighbors, the unexpected and stunning train of events forced an agonizing reappraisal of its still infant strategic partnership with Washington.[86] As for Kashmir, it was readily apparent that the global war on terrorism was bound to give an additional major boost to the process of its internationalization. Not clear at all, however, was the direction in which this phase of internationalization was going to move.

In Afghanistan's Shadow—The Deepening Contradictions of Kashmir

We have observed so far in this chapter that the process of internationalizing the Kashmir dispute in the decade or so prior to 11 September 2001 had gone through a number of phases, the first triggered at the end of the 1980s by the onset of the Kashmiri Uprising and its attendant mobilizing of world opinion focused on human rights abuses, and the last triggered near the end of the 1990s by the region's move to overt nuclear weaponization, a development that brought to Kashmir world-wide recognition as a "nuclear flashpoint." In the wake of 11 September, the process of internationalizing the Kashmir dispute has turned yet another corner, this one almost certain to intensify international interest in Kashmir even more. The loose-knit American-led global coalition formed to fight the war on terrorism included, after all, not only countries physically adjacent to Kashmir and with an immediate and palpable strategic stake in it (India and Pakistan, of course, but China as well), but also others (like Russia, Iran, and Saudi Arabia) with less direct but not necessarily unimportant stakes. To this had to be added recognition that Kashmir's own interconnectedness with Afghanistan, the primary initial target of American wrath, went far beyond mere geographic contiguity and religious affinity to include, among other things, significant cross-border organizational and ideological linkages. As a result, virtually from the outset of Washington's war on terrorism the issue of Kashmir's resemblance to Afghanistan—whether it, too, was a site of *globe-menacing* terrorist activity and, thus, was also in need of corrective intervention—claimed steadily greater attention on the international agenda. Pakistan's military-ruled government, in explaining to Pakistani citizens its abrupt decision to join the antiterrorist coalition, justified its stance, in part, with the argument that ending support of the Taliban militia in Afghanistan would act to shield from international criticism Pakistan's domestically popular backing for guerrilla war in Kashmir.[87] At the same time, New Delhi was pressuring Washington to acknowledge that India was also a major victim of terrorist activity. The combined arguments of the two sides put Washington in an unusually awkward position.[88] Thus, the rising visibility of the Kashmir dispute had, for Kashmiri separatists, a distinctly dark side: it carried with it the prospect of a fundamentally reversed global appreciation of Kashmir, one in which sympathy for an oppressed separatist minority struggling to cast off an oppressive government would have to compete with an understanding dominated by fear of and a determination to eradicate Islamic extremism and terrorism. To put it simply, the Kashmiri freedom struggle was being increasingly conflated with, and was in grave danger of being understood largely in terms of, terrorism.

Kashmiri separatists have always faced major handicaps in attracting and sustaining world sympathy and legitimate involvement in their cause. In the wake of the Taliban's crushing defeat, these handicaps threatened to multiply. The most obvious among the threatened new handicaps was attrition in the ranks of Kashmiri separatism's most important foreign backers. Without question, the defeat and replacement of Afghanistan's Taliban rulers had reduced the ranks of these backers at least by one. It was a safe bet that whatever government managed to establish itself in Kabul when the fighting was finished would, for the foreseeable future, discontinue Afghanistan's crucial role during most of the past decade as a recruiting and training ground for would-be Kashmiri guerrilla fighters. The array of regional states that demanded the Taliban's total exclusion from a successor government—among which India was, of course, a particularly vocal member—could be counted upon to make every effort to ensure that that government would not include forces eager to resume jihadist activities in Kashmir. To a lesser degree, perhaps, but with nearly equal certainty, Saudi Arabia's ability to carry on either as banker or spiritual guide to the Kashmiri separatists also seemed bound to experience curtailment. Alleged covert patronage by the Saudi kingdom of groups linked to Osama bin Laden's Al Qaeda organization has recently drawn intensified international scrutiny and criticism.[89] Some of these groups have been openly headquartered in Pakistan and active in Kashmir. Considerably less welcome since September 11, one suspects, would be Saudi sponsorship in Kashmir of *madrasahs* (religious schools or seminaries), under suspicion more widely than ever now as primary incubators of extremism.

More vital by far to the Kashmiri cause than either Afghanistan or Saudi Arabia, of course, has been Pakistan. As we've noted, its army-dominated government in September 2001 simultaneously renounced its support for the Taliban while, at the same time, enlisting itself as a frontline state in the global war on terrorism. This implied the government's belated recognition of what innumerable Pakistani political commentators had been warning of for years, namely that Pakistan's post-Soviet-era Afghan policy threatened Islamabad with nearly total international isolation. In any event, Islamabad's actions created an unusually awkward and embarrassing situation for Pakistan: On its western border, it stood in the frontline against terrorism; on its eastern border, it continued to voice support of a movement whose activities inevitably lent themselves to charges, by Indians and others, of terrorism. Pakistan's Indian critics naturally delighted in Islamabad's discomfort.[90] Stunned by the government's policy volte-face, the Musharraf regime's domestic critics, right-wing stalwarts of the jettisoned Afghan policy foremost among them, were hardly more merciful.

Even to neutral observers, Pakistan's position appeared deeply contradictory. Islamabad had made use of Afghanistan as a recruitment, training, and transit point for guerrilla fighters in Kashmir for some time in advance of the Taliban's arrival on the scene in 1994. Once the Taliban had taken power in Kabul in 1996, however, this role was substantially expanded with Islamabad's active assistance. Pakistan, after all, had been the Taliban's principal foreign backer and de facto military ally virtually from the start. The mutually supportive arrangement thus constructed between Afghanistan and Pakistan encouraged the proliferation of jihadist organizations on Pakistan's own soil. Their mounting strength posed a threat to Pakistan's political stability. Into that volatile environment burst the war on terrorism, practically overnight bringing Islamabad under extraordinary global scrutiny along with strong pressures to curtail, if not to pull the rug out entirely from under, the organizational infrastructure of extremist forces it had long tolerated.[91]

New Delhi was quick to exploit Islamabad's predicament. In the weeks immediately following the 11 September attacks, it sought without success to get Washington to add a number of militant groups headquartered in Pakistan and active in Kashmir—in particular, the Jaish-e-Muhammad (JeM) and Lashkar-e-Taiba (LeT)—to its list of proscribed foreign terrorist organizations. The effort failed.[92] The Bush administration at that moment was far more concerned with ensuring Pakistan's collaboration with America's high-priority counterterrorist campaign against Osama bin Laden and the Taliban than with raking up the messy issue of Pakistan's own covert connections with groups New Delhi insisted were also terrorist. Nevertheless, media reports persisted on the contradictions implicit in Pakistan's simultaneous roles as a frontline player in an unprecedented global struggle against terrorism *and* as a safe haven for groups judged by many to be terrorist.[93] The Taliban were flushed from their last bastions of power by early December. When five terrorists made a brazen suicide attack on India's parliament building on 13 December, New Delhi's complaint about Pakistani ties to groups engaged in terrorist actions against its eastern neighbor finally got a serious hearing.

The attack, in which fourteen people lost their lives (including five terrorists), resulted in the instantaneous and pitiless exposure of Pakistan's awkward position. The Indian government asserted that the terrorists were Pakistanis and that they were in some way linked to Pakistan's Inter-Services Intelligence Directorate (ISI), an organization that New

Delhi had for long portrayed as the mastermind of terrorist activities in Kashmir. The Indians claimed to have evidence that the terrorists were tied to the Pakistan-based LeT and JeM organizations, groups New Delhi had already claimed were responsible for most of the terrorist violence in Kashmir. They demanded that Islamabad turn over the groups' leaders to India for trial and that their operations in Kashmir be entirely shut down. Not surprisingly, the Pakistanis resisted the demands, arguing that New Delhi had turned over no concrete evidence of the groups' involvement. Meanwhile, skirmishing intensified along the Line of Control and in the Siachen Glacier area; New Delhi, for the first time in thirty years, recalled its ambassador to Pakistan; bus and rail transport links were severed; and both countries mobilized elements of their armed forces. Pakistan faced the largest concentration of hostile armed forces in its history. The chance of open warfare seemed to be mounting swiftly.[94]

In this circumstance, the Bush administration sought to cool Indian tempers by adding both the JeM and LeT to a State Department list of "designated terrorist organizations"—a gesture that technically froze the groups' assets in the United States but that also, more importantly, called upon Islamabad to shut them down.[95] Washington orchestrated its action in a manner Indians believed, rightly, was intended to pacify India without excessive embarrassment to Pakistan.[96] An inevitable result of its action, however, was to lend weight to India's contention that Pakistan's support for the Kashmiri separatist movement was illegitimate. As a correspondent for the *New York Times* speculated, President Bush appeared to be siding with India, telling the Pakistanis "that any further backing for armed Islamic militant groups operating in Kashmir will be tantamount to supporting terrorism. . . . Pakistan, after more than 50 years of battling India over Kashmir, must now abandon the armed struggle there, and rely henceforth on political means of confronting India."[97]

Pakistan reacted by taking a number of unprecedented steps of its own. It arrested the leaders of the two groups named by Washington and claimed, at the same time, to have ordered the ISI to terminate support for nonindigenous militant groups fighting in Kashmir. It promised that in the future Pakistan would confine its support of the Kashmir cause to groups with roots in Kashmir.[98]

Worrisome, of course, to those in charge of government in Islamabad was not only the immediate threat of Indian military action against Pakistan but also the possibility that the collapse of the Taliban, together with the unresolved contradictions implicit in Pakistan's Kashmir policy, would serve to remove the incentives that had motivated Washington to forge a renewed strategic partnership with Pakistan in the first place. They clearly had grounds for worry. Apart from the inevitable suspicions in Washington stemming from Pakistan's previous close ties to the Taliban, there remained between Pakistan and the United States a number of additional unsettled issues relating to the restoration of democracy in Pakistan as well as to Pakistan's nuclear weapons program. Pakistan was highly vulnerable to pressure in regard to either of these other issues, and either of them, on its own, could conceivably trigger a major upheaval in Islamabad's equation with Washington. Seymour Hersch's sensationalist article "Watching the Warheads," published in a prominent periodical at the height of the bombing campaign in Afghanistan, was symptomatic of the danger. In it, he alleged that joint training of American and Israeli commando teams was under way in the United States in preparation for possible surprise raids on Pakistan's nuclear weapons facilities. The raids were being contemplated, Hersch said, as a prophylactic measure for implementation if required to keep Pakistan's nuclear weapons from falling into extremist hands in the event of an Islamist takeover of the government.[99] In regard to that particular eventuality, Washington was already rife with speculation. Reports at the time that retired Pakistani nuclear scientists were actively supplying their expertise to the Taliban contributed to fears of an in-house attempt by Taliban sympathizers within Pakistan's vast nuclear establishment to confiscate Pakistani bombs or radioactive materials.[100] Nothing, in fact, posed a more severe threat to continued strategic cooperation between the United States and Pakistan than the prospect that what was still only speculation would eventually be converted to firm conviction. If this happened, the equation of the Kashmiri separatist movement with terrorism would, of course, be virtually complete. How the Kashmir dispute was ultimately internationalized in the wake of 11 September, in other words, depended far less on the merits of the separatist cause than on how observers perceived Pakistan's relationship to global terrorism. In this regard, no issue was more controversial than the *motivation* for Pakistan's involvement on the Indian side of the Line of Control.

Pakistan: Frontline Ally or Axis of the Islamic Jehad?

As a matter of policy, the Pakistan government had all along routinely claimed that it gave no more than diplomatic, political, and moral support—all internationally legitimate activities—to the Kashmiri separatist movement. Ironclad proof to the contrary was difficult, if not impossible, for the ordinary observer to come by. Circumstantial evidence of Pakistan's *material* aid to the separatists was fairly abundant, however, and appeared to confirm Indian allegations of mounting foreign involvement in the fighting. The Pakistan army, in particular its shadowy Inter-Services Intelligence Directorate (ISI), seemed to many observers, in fact, to be the separatists' indispensable ally, providing them with weaponry, training, sanctuary, and—of growing importance since the mid-1990s in the face of the Indian army's vastly improved counterinsurgent capabilities—foreign mercenaries, some of them battle-hardened, imported mainly from neighboring Islamic countries. Figures released in October 1998 by Indian Home (Interior) Minister Lal Krishna Advani alleged, for example, that 216 (32 percent) of 677 militants killed by Indian security forces in Kashmir in the first nine months of 1998 were foreign mercenaries, and that of the grand total of 866 foreign mercenaries killed in the state up to that point in the decade, Pakistan and what Indians call Pakistan Occupied Kashmir (POK) accounted for the majority of them, Afghanistan for 123, and places like Sudan, Egypt, Lebanon, and Chechnya for the remaining.[101] A year or so later, estimates circulating in India in regard to the foreign component of militant forces had gone up considerably: 70 percent of all militants operating in Kashmir Valley "could be foreign militants" said one report;[102] and "nearly half" of the 700-odd militants killed in the Valley in 1999 were of foreign origin, said another.[103] Still another estimate placed the number of what it called "hard-core terrorists" active in Jammu and Kashmir in 1999 at about 2,300, of which 900 (39 percent) were claimed to be foreign mercenaries.[104]

Figures of this kind lent support, of course, to the "sponsored terrorism" thesis that Indian officialdom has long propagated as the leading source of Kashmiri disaffection.* In the view of some observers, however, these figures point to something far more menacing than Pakistan's geographically narrow fixation on Kashmir—merely one staging ground among many, as they see it, in a massive pan-Islamic geostrategic enterprise. Kashmiri separatism's overt links with such Pakistan-based, politically Islamist organizations as the Jama'at-i-Islami, coming on top

---

*We examine this thesis in some detail in Chapter 3.

of alleged covert links with the likes of Osama bin-Laden's Al Qaeda network in Afghanistan, confirm for these observers the existence of something far more alarming than a mere terrorist threat—a "fundamentalist specter" hovering not only over the subcontinent but over the West as well. As they see it, the movement for territorial secession in Kashmir is mainly a local disguise, in other words, for a deep-rooted and massive Islam-wide conspiracy, mobilized under the banner of the "brotherhood of Islam" and aimed at undermining the West's control of the modern world order. Yielding to the separatists' demands in Kashmir amounts to a betrayal of this order. The self-styled separatist "freedom-fighters" are dubbed religious zealots and terrorists—the harbingers of Kashmir's impending talibanization; and Pakistan, where an officially supported campaign to Islamicize society has been under way for years, is tagged as their chief sponsor. Obviously, were this image of Pakistan to prevail over the "frontline ally" image put forth after 11 September 2001, the process of internationalizing the Kashmir dispute would likely take on a wholly different character.

One of the most prolific and certainly among the most colorful of Western writers propounding such a sinister image of Pakistan is Yossef Bodansky, a contributing editor of the Washington-based journal *Defense and Foreign Affairs Strategic Policy* and director of the U.S. Congress–sponsored Task Force on Terrorism and Unconventional Warfare, who in a string of essays in recent years has relentlessly warned of a China-orchestrated and conspiracy-infested trans-Asiatic "arc of crisis" in which are happening a "myriad of clashes between Islamist forces and the various Armed Forces [of the states in the neighborhood] stretched between the Caucasus and Kashmir [constituting] a coherent dynamic of grand strategic, if not historical, significance."[105] In the events of this arc of crisis, Pakistan—in particular its ISI organization—plays a pivotal role.

In an essay first published in 1995, Bodansky described Pakistan's Kashmir policy in terms archly reminiscent of classic geopolitical writings common in the first half of the twentieth century. Islamabad, he said,

> has consciously linked its own strategic vision to that of Beijing, whose present and near-future grand strategy considers the revival of the Silk Road as a primary regional strategic entity. The on-land transportation system—stretching along the traditional Silk Road—is of crucial significance to the consolidation of the Trans-Asian Axis—Beijing's key to glo-

bal power posture and strategic safety. The PRC's self-acknowledged naval inferiority reduces the strategic use of the Indian Ocean, thus only increasing the importance of the on-land lines of communications—the Silk Road—for the consolidation and enhancement of the Trans-Asian Axis.[106]

For its part, Islamabad, reckoning that it can piggyback on Beijing's strategy to its own advantage and having at its command a war-seasoned ISI apparatus,

> has launched a major campaign to consolidate control over the Silk Road's traditional gateways to China. Fully aware of the major strategic importance of the regional transportation system, Islamabad sees in its control over these key segments of the regional road system the key to its future and fortunes. . . . The Pakistani strategic calculation is that if Pakistan is the dominant or hegemonic power over the western gateways to China—a crucial component of both the Silk Road (actually) and the Trans-Asian Axis (strategically, metaphysically)—Islamabad will be in a position to exert influence over the entire Trans-Asian Axis. Such a position, reinforcing Pakistan's already unique position as the linch-pin between the PRC and the Tehran-led Islamic Bloc, will enable Pakistan [to] enjoy economic and political benefits in the process way beyond what it could have hoped to gain on the basis of the country's objective economic, scientific-technological, and population posture, and even the realistic future potential. Essentially, the Pakistani strategic logic behind the drive to control the western gateways to China is to transform Islamabad's strategic position as the linch-pin between the Islamic Bloc and China into a tangible reality on the ground.

In pursuit of these goals, Bodansky pointed out, Islamabad had to bring under its sway the access routes to China's western gateways. This meant taking control of, or at least extending its hegemony in territories currently held by Tajikistan, Afghanistan, and India. Undeterred by the boldness of this vision, the ISI, Bodansky claimed,

> has recently launched a relentless drive to ensure that local Islamist irregular forces—most of them already Pakistan's protégés for they are sponsored by the ISI—will control all key roads and axes in order to create a regional dependence on Islamabad to ensure safety of traffic—in other words, recognize Islamabad's hegemony over the western gateways of China.

Recognition that "the path to the future and strategic salvation of Pakistan" passed through Indian Kashmir only dawned on Pakistan's strategic thinkers, says Bodansky, in 1993. The dawning, he claims, led to a marked change in the focus and substance of the armed struggle in Indian-controlled Kashmir. Specifically, it soon manifested itself "in the evolution of the Islamist terrorist and subversion struggle in the region." The dramatic escalation in ISI support for the Kashmiri insurgents was thus, according to Bodansky, "a direct by-product of Pakistan's national security policy and grand strategy," including, he claims, "the centrality of the annexation of the entire Kashmir for the long-term development of Pakistan." As Bodansky put it in a companion essay, "Islamabad uses the escalation in Kashmir as a cover for the overall expansion of the terrorist training and support system for operations in Central Asia and elsewhere in the world."[107]

Lending weight to Bodansky's argument, as we noted above, have been the reported tallies of foreign or "guest" militants in Kashmir. While the motives of such persons may or may not coincide with Islamabad's strategic ambitions, as Bodansky conceives them, their presence in Kashmir has for long been virtually impossible to deny. Washington's naming in 1998 of one Pakistan-based group active in Kashmir—the Harkat-ul-Ansar—as a terrorist organization inevitably fueled suspicion of Pakistan. Washington's cruise missile strike against alleged terrorist training camps (at least some of them with acknowledged ties to Pakistan and Kashmir) along the eastern border of Afghanistan in August 1998 even more clangorously drew the world's attention to the lethal cross-border activities of the Kashmiri militants' co-religionists.[108] Islam-oriented Pakistani political groups, for their part, made little effort to conceal their sponsorship of these activities. For example, the escape from an Indian jail in Jammu and the return to Pakistan in late October 1998 of three Pakistan-born mercenary fighters was openly hailed in Pakistan, where a leading right-wing opposition political figure told a massive rally that it was Pakistan's "duty and right to send help to the Kashmiris who are fighting against illegal occupation."[109] Scarcely a month later, the leading Pakistani daily, *Dawn*, reported an alleged interview with a Taliban (Afghan) mercenary commander somewhere in Indian-administered Kashmir, in which he claimed that his group was running twenty-eight secret guerrilla camps in "held" Kashmir, where some 1,350 recruits were being trained in guerrilla warfare. The Taliban troops were in Kashmir, he said, "to give a steel frame to Kashmir militancy."[110]

Dramatically highlighting Pakistan's role as a potential recruiting ground for Islamist warriors was the hijacking incident of late December 1999. In the days following the release of the hostages, the Indian government took pains to publicize worldwide the claim that the five hijackers themselves were all Pakistanis and that as many as thirty-three of the thirty-six prisoners whose release the hijackers sought at one point in the negotiations were also Pakistanis.[111] One of the three militants actually released—and the main prize, apparently, of the hijacking operation—was Pakistani-born Maulana Masood Azhar, a religious cleric and erstwhile leader of a radical Kashmiri separatist group called Harkat-ul-Mujahideen (the rechristened Harkat-ul-Ansar). Within days of his release, Azhar turned up in public in Pakistan. He gave a fiery public speech in a Karachi suburb, in which he was quoted as saying that he would "not rest in peace until Kashmir [was] liberated" and "that Muslims should not rest in peace until [they] have destroyed America and India." In reply, the crowd, estimated at about 10,000, reportedly roared "God is great!" and "Death to India, death to the United States!"[112] In a public speech soon thereafter at Bahawalpur, his hometown in the Punjab, Azhar was reported to have announced an audacious plan to recruit a force of a half million men from all over Pakistan to fight Indian rule in Kashmir.[113] That plan, though naturally on a much lesser scale, evolved with surprising swiftness into formation of a new group, the Jaish-e-Muhammad, whose mainly non-Kashmiri membership apparently came largely from the disintegrating ranks of its parent—the Harkat-ul-Mujahideen.*

Azhar's inflammatory remarks were grist, of course, for the Indian propaganda mills, which concentrated their efforts increasingly on pinning the Pakistan government with responsibility for official sponsorship of the cross-border terrorist activity. Naturally, these efforts, which had begun in earnest during the Kargil episode and reached a peak at the time of the hijacking of the Indian Airlines flight, sparked Pakistani countercharges no less blistering in content. The result at the turn of century was a full-blown propaganda war between India and Pakistan, with alleged international Islamic terrorism the focal point of contention. This "war on airwaves," as a Pakistani writer described it, took advantage of the South Asian region's revolutionary expansion in electronic media.[114] Inevitably, the propaganda attacks obscured as much as they revealed in regard to the real importance of either terrorist or for-

---

*Azhar was placed under arrest again in December 2001.

eign mercenary activity—whether or not part of a region-wide strategic plan hatched in Islamabad—in the overall balance sheet of the Kashmir dispute. The fact remained, nevertheless, that the propaganda battle posed a palpable threat to Kashmiri separatism's appeal to the world as a righteous movement of ethnic self-determination.

What is one to make of Bodansky-like arguments? Admittedly, they have an appealing simplicity and nearly absolute clarity missing from most other explanations. This they achieve, however, through blithe disregard of the huge improbability that many of Pakistan's leaders ever came to strategic conclusions at once so outrageous and so contemptuous of Pakistan's real-world capabilities and limitations. That they merit skepticism, I think, goes without saying. There is one sense, however, in which they deserve attention: They highlight in the most dramatic way possible the urgent requirement for the routine suspension of belief in the face of widespread procrustean tendencies when it comes to the dimensions and dynamics of the so-called Islamic fundamentalist threat. The truth is that we are presently confronted with cascades of allegedly "factual" information about this threat that, upon inspection, turns out not to be so incontrovertible after all.

In the case of reported tallies of the number of foreign militants operating in Kashmir, for instance, whether the number given represents either a majority or minority of the total militant forces (or whether the foreign militants, whatever their number, are presently setting the agenda for the insurgent forces) will certainly make a considerable difference to one's eagerness to buy into the Bodansky thesis. If the number (and corresponding clout) of foreigners is very large and growing, then the argument gains strength that the Kashmiri uprising has been *hijacked* by Pakistan for its own strategic objectives; if the number is not so large, however, and does not seem to be growing, then the possibility exists that the uprising is basically *indigenous* in its origins and persists because of the determination of the Kashmiri Muslims to secure their own objectives—which may, of course, not coincide exactly with those of Islamabad. A finding of this latter sort would, of course, help shield the Kashmir dispute from an *international* finding that it was no longer rooted in a legitimate quest for self-determination but was, instead, an outgrowth of the global terrorist cancer. All of this merely serves to remind us that the statistics of Islamic radicalism, not surprisingly, are an integral part of the global debate over the measures needed to cope with it. Sumantra Bose, of the London School of Economics and Political Science, deftly makes this point in a recent essay under the heading of "The Convoluted Realities of Kashmir." Noting that Kashmir brings together a "fluid mix" of ethnic, confessional, and local group identities, Bose points out that "recognition of these multiple layers of ambiguity, fluidity and complexity is essential to any informed understanding of the Kashmir problem and to any policy designed to address [it]." Amplifying the point, he argues that "the importance of non-local Islamist radical groups in this crisis is being exaggerated by at least three different sources: the *jehadi* spokesmen, Indian spokesmen and officials, and, most recently, official and some non-official quarters in the United States." Official Indian government statistics, he offers in evidence, "clearly reveal that the Kashmir insurgency is mostly composed of local militants." To illustrate, he notes that

> in the first eight months of 1999, . . . 617 guerrillas are said to have died at the hands of Indian security forces; of these, 167 (27%) were identified as "foreigners." During the corresponding period in 2000, 941 militants were killed, of whom 261 (28%) were foreigners. In both 1999 and 2000, then, local cadres comprised more than 70% of slain insurgents in Jammu and Kashmir.

Even in foreigner-infested areas (like Rajouri and Poonch districts), Bose adds, "almost half of insurgent casualties consisted of local people."[115] As is the case with most observers, Bose's judgment here is necessarily based on official Indian statistics, and these statistics obviously can be read—and *are* routinely read—in more than one way.

We face exactly the same "multiple layers of ambiguity, fluidity and complexity," by the way, when it comes to estimating the extent to which Pakistan itself has been undergoing a process of "talibanization" —a drift, in other words, toward increasing influence of Islamic extremism upon state and society (akin to the Afghanistan model). Obviously, the estimate one reaches in this matter is far from being merely academic. If the process is well along the way, Pakistan's ability to market itself as a politically stable ally of the West is correspondingly reduced. The consequences of any such reduction would likely be far-reaching.

One potentially fruitful indicator of religious extremism's progress in Pakistan that many observers have focused upon has been the spread of *madrasahs*—traditional Islamic centers of education. Also called *madaris*, the *madrasahs* have typically been defined as religious semi-naries or academies. A number of excellent scholarly accounts of their origins and contemporary evolution in the countries of South Asia exist.[116] When it comes to Pakistan, these accounts agree that the rise in the number of *madrasahs* in recent decades has been phenomenal. Nasr, for instance, reports that from a total of 137 *madrasahs* in all of Pakistan at the time of partition in 1947, their number in the Punjab alone had grown by 1996 to 2,463—an eighteenfold increase. Begun in the mid-1970s, he says, their proliferation "has continued at a phenomenal pace since."[117] There is nearly universal agreement among observers, too, that the *madrasahs* are generally organized into networks along sectarian lines, that the more aggressively oriented of them feed the country's mounting incidence of sectarian violence, that their curricula are largely medieval in content and woefully neglectful of modern subjects, that they have an enormous impact upon Muslim mass opinion, that they have been routinely and cynically exploited for political purposes by the country's military rulers, that they have been generously financed by the Gulf Arab states, especially Saudi Arabia, and, finally, that they are presently a destabilizing influence on Pakistani society. The government of President Pervez Musharraf has given every indication that he also subscribes to most of these findings.

Unfortunately, these findings fall well short of clinching the case either for or against the alleged talibanization of Pakistan. *Madrasahs*, it turns out upon inspection, come in several varieties and do not have a commonly accepted definition. In fact, in common usage they have often been confused with the lowly part-time "parochial" schools affiliated with local mosques. Such schools may have very little to do, if anything, with sponsorship of the Islamic jihad. Thus, it is not an easy matter, especially for outsiders, to acquire reliable and current figures on the number, type, enrollments, regional distribution, sectarian affiliation, and source of financial support of these *madrasahs*. More difficult yet, one suspects, would be determining exactly how many of them have acted as political platforms for imparting extremist ideology and arms training to youthful Pakistanis (as "jihadi prep schools," as one writer phased it),[118] how effective and operationally useful has been the training, how many "products" have been graduated so far from these institutions and presumably now stand ready to serve as zealous soldiers on the front lines of the Islamic jihad, how many of them have been armed (and how well), and, finally, how many of these youthful cadres have been dispatched in recent years to Kashmir or to Afghanistan. Most difficult of all, I suspect, would be determining the extent to which religious extremism in Pakistan was actually institutionally dependent on the *madrasahs*, how much sense of unity and common purpose existed to activate a common "extremist" agenda among them, and what actually motivated the people who enrolled their children in them. In the face of the universally acknowledged inadequacy of Pakistan's government-run schools, the *madrasahs* obviously service a huge public need. But is the need one strictly or even mainly of religious extremism?

These almost insuperable difficulties encountered in coming to grips intellectually with the *madrasah* phenomenon help to account for the tremendous discrepancies and/or rampant generalizations one finds in recent commentaries on them. A correspondent for *Jane's Intelligence Review* in New Delhi, for instance, stated that "reports reveal that around 1.75 million Pakistani youngsters are undergoing religious and basic military training in around 7,000 madrassahs (Islamic seminaries) across the country. These trainees are dispatched to Kashmir and other parts of the world to wage jihad against infidels."[119] Upon her return from a visit to Pakistan in late 2000, Jessica Stern, a lecturer in public policy at Harvard University's Kennedy School of Government, reported in the pages of *Foreign Affairs* that there were "tens of thousands of madrasahs" in Pakistan and that "only about 4,350 of the estimated 40,000 to 50,000 madrasahs in Pakistan have registered with the government." Official estimates of the proportion of these institutions espousing "extremist ideologies," she said, ranged between 10 and 15 percent.[120] Kuldip Nayar, a noted Indian journalist, reported:

> Nearly 20,000 madressas, according to Islamabad's interior ministry, operate in Pakistan. They belch out every year 30 lakh [3 million] students, aged four and above. At the current rate of growth, the number of madressas in the next decade will be equal to the government-run primary and secondary schools in the country. The instruction is a dose of extremism dinned into each student to evoke blind obedience and the arrogance of faith.[121]

All three of these writers observed, correctly, that the consequences for Pakistan of an out-of-control "jihad culture" could well be catastrophic. How closely Pakistan currently approximated such a culture none could say with any precision.

A question related to the *madrasah* issue and of no less importance is: How far has talibanization crept into the Pakistan armed forces—into its officer corps, in particular, and how far up the chain of command? Sumit Ganguly, a South Asia specialist at the University of Texas, says: Quite far indeed. According to him, "many midlevel officers raised under Zia [ul-Haq] share the religious zeal of the fundamentalists."[122] Samina Ahmed, a Pakistan-born analyst with the International Crisis Group, disagrees. According to an account in the *Los Angeles Times*, she considers the notion of a powerful Islamic element within the army to be misplaced, arguing instead that the army's long-standing support for jihad groups had generally been tactical rather than philosophical.[123] Settling the issue empirically is likely to be daunting. After all, the Pakistan army, with over 500,000 troops, has an officer corps numbering in the tens of thousands. One may safely assume, in view of recent history, that many of them harbor some resentment toward the West, the United States in particular. But how would one go about securing credible evidence of the quantum of "religious zeal" among them that approximated that of the "fundamentalists"?

Responsible observers have reported that Pakistan "is drifting toward religious extremism."[124] Since the events of 11 September 2001, reports of this kind have multiplied astronomically. The government of Pakistan itself, by taking the steps it has to bring Islamic militant groups under greater control, has given credence to these reports.[125] At issue, of course, was Pakistan's suitability for its newly assigned role in the West's front line against global terrorism. Was Pakistan, as its Indian adversaries were inclined to believe, a part of the problem, not of its solution?[126] If the former, what was an appropriate remedy? There were increasingly blunt warnings toward the end of 2001 that Pakistan's alleged tolerance of religious extremism was meeting up with rapidly growing annoyance in the United States. Editorial writers at the *New York Times* and the *Washington Post* demanded that Pakistan crack down on homegrown terrorist groups.[127] A university-based specialist on South Asian security issues called for the dispatch of American troops to Pakistan to compel Islamabad to take action against terrorist forces within its borders. "We should hold the Pakistanis' feet to the fire," he was quoted as saying.[128] India, all the while, issued call after call for international support of its efforts to force a Pakistani crackdown on militant forces.[129] Undoubtedly, stepped-up pressure on Islamabad to bring extremist forces to heel would have major region-wide consequences. Not the least of these consequences, we have taken pains to underscore in these pages, would likely be yet further entrenchment of a terrorism-inclined global understanding of the Kashmir dispute.

* * *

What conclusions can one safely draw from the discussion this far? One, the focus of Chapter 1, is that the prospects for significant progress on the Kashmir front to emerge from strictly *bilateral* dialogue between India and Pakistan are bleak to nonexistent. The more than three years that have passed since the nuclear tests of May 1998 have been witness to the relentless development and testing by both sides of advanced ballistic missiles, the eventual nuclear arming and deployment of which seem bound both to increase the fragility of their relationship as well as deepen the distrust between them. The Lahore Declaration of February 1999, though it raised hopes of resolution even in sober observers, was followed almost immediately by events—the fierce fighting in summer 1999 between Indian and Pakistani forces in the Kargil sector only the most conspicuous among them—that threatened to make a mockery of its contents. Far from acting as a catalyst of deliberate steps toward its resolution, the nuclearization of the Kashmir dispute appeared instead mainly to have added to the dispute's existing profound complexity.

A second, the focus of Chapter 2, is that, while there exists today no sign of a major reversal of the international community's customary reticence to act at all in regard to Kashmir, whatever movement there was in that direction, at least up until the terrorist attack on the United States in September 2001, seemed to be at Pakistan's expense. The reticence prevails in spite of the fact that practically every major successful bilateral agreement between India and Pakistan during the past fifty years—the 1949 Karachi Agreement ending the first Indo-Pakistan war, the 1960 Indus Waters Treaty, the 1966 Tashkent Agreement, the 1968 Sind-Kutch Boundary Settlement, to mention four such instances—entailed, in one form or another, major international intervention. Thus far, the palpable spin-off on Kashmir of the September 11 terrorist attack has been relatively minor: It is too early to tell which side, if either, will gain permanent advantage from the region's changed geopolitical context. The governments of India and Pakistan were both aggressively searching for signs of Washington's favor.[130] At the end of November 2001, at least one Indian observer was insisting that Washington, notwithstanding appearances, for all practical purposes was "at war with Pakistan."[131] Very likely the dominant view in Washington at that time was the belief that "once the 'Afghan dust' settles, in all likelihood the U.S. overall agenda in South Asia will return to something closer to what it was early in this [Bush] administration"—namely, one focused on the growing convergence between United States and Indian security perspectives on Asia and the Indian Ocean.[132] In any event, one thing was clear: A heavy tilt to either side in the wake of the attack would almost certainly sound the death knell for a peacefully negotiated *bilateral* settlement of Kashmir.

Obviously, decisions made by Washington in this regard will have a major impact. Taking sides with India, as we have seen, has powerful advocates in the United States. India accounts for about 80 percent of the South Asian region's Gross Domestic Product. India's liberalized economy—and, in particular, its remarkably successful information technology industry—has formidable potential in an integrated global market. Its military might is unsurpassed among Indian Ocean states and could be a stabilizing influence in an especially volatile area of the globe. It is a potential counterweight to China, as we have noted, should the need for the latter's containment by Western powers grow. As some see it, the logical corollary to enlisting India on the side of the West in regard to concerns such as these would be to take India's side in regard to Kashmir. The terrorist issue, expanded from Afghanistan to include Kashmir, is an obvious point at which to make the trade-off. Equally obvious, however, is that making common cause with India by siding with New Delhi's position on terrorism in Kashmir can't be done without serious costs—to India-Pakistan and U.S.-Pakistan relations, certainly, but perhaps also to the global human rights and nuclear nonproliferation regimes.

We have the option at this point, of course, of throwing up our hands in despair and declaring Kashmir still mired in the quicksand of unending regional conflicts, one whose settlement must await a future and fundamental change in circumstances. This is not an attractive or even realistic option, however, unless one is prepared to accept at face value— as I am not—the routine assurances of Indian and Pakistani leaders that they have no aggressive intentions against one another and that there thus need be no anxiety over their growing conventional and nuclear arsenals. Even without the added feature of nuclear weapons, the economic, political, cultural, and environmental costs of the Kashmir dispute are demonstrably heavy. The dispute's nuclearization seems bound to make them heavier still.

I would suggest, therefore, that a third conclusion needs to be drawn from the above discussion, namely that there is an urgent need for the region's well-wishers to take a fresh look at the Kashmir dispute and, if warranted, to jettison whatever formulae or principles presently governing understanding of it that turn out, upon examination, to get in the way of its swift and methodical removal from the category of "nuclear flashpoint." Needed, in particular, is an earnest attempt to identify precisely what it is that we think fuels this dispute and blocks a settlement of it. Assuming a reasonable answer to that is forthcoming, what do we believe can most practically and swiftly accomplish the dismantling of that block? This is no small task. It will require our examination of the dispute from at least two additional angles. The first relates to demography. It pertains to the ethno-religious composition of Kashmir itself. It is concerned primarily with the role of religious identity in the dispute—with its role, on the one hand, in motivating the Kashmiri Muslim separatist movement and, on the other, in driving the state strategies of India and Pakistan toward Kashmir. Is Kashmir to be understood, we ask, fundamentally as a *religious* problem? Is it fair or useful to describe it, in particular, as a problem of religious extremism, fanaticism, or *fundamentalism?* What characterizes the manner in which India and Pakistan integrate religious identity into their state strategies toward Kashmir? To what extent do these strategies differ? To what extent do they incorporate or rely upon terrorism? And what are the consequences of these strategies for India-Pakistan relations?

The second angle is prescriptive and pertains to the potential applicability to Kashmir of existing plans and models of conflict resolution. What are the major alternatives, we ask, and which of them puts up the most practical antidote to the dispute's continued festering? How much of the solution is to be found in unilateral state action? How much in bilateral agreement? When and how, if at all, should the international community intervene?

These two angles—that of religious identity and that of policy prescription—we take up, respectively, in Chapters 3 and 4.

3

The Problem of Religious Identity
Faultline Politics in a Disputed Territory

The Kashmir dispute, we have already taken note of in preceding chapters, involves considerably more than religious identity. Other factors, extending all the way from the imperatives of strategic alliance construction to the banalities of human greed, are clearly involved. Religion has always played a visible role in the dispute, however, and no discussion of it that omitted the religious aspect entirely could be taken seriously. This is so, no matter what the focus of discussion happens to be—whether the dispute's origins, for instance, its impact on the electoral maneuvers and fortunes of regional politicians, or, as has lately become overwhelmingly apparent, its linkages to global terrorism. The dispute was still in its infancy, in fact, when religion took the stage. Religious communal majority was the demographic device explicitly singled out by the British on the eve of partition in 1947 for the fashioning of fresh boundaries between the designated successor states of India and Pakistan and it was the religion-related expectations of the new and already deeply hostile governments of these two states in regard to possession of the Hindu-ruled but Muslim-majority princely state of Jammu and Kashmir that soon boiled over into the first Indo-Pakistan war. From that point on, religion's inclusion among the dispute's staple ingredients was more or less assured. One is not bound to go beyond historical origins, in other words, to justify inclusion of religion's role in the Kashmir dispute in this book's reexamination of it.

Inquiry into the manner and extent of religion's intersection with the persistent rivalry of India and Pakistan over Kashmir requires even less argument, of course, in the wake of the terrorist assault on the United States in September 2001 and Washington's retaliatory attacks on Afghanistan—aimed both at Osama bin Laden's Al Qaeda terrorist leadership and infrastructure in Afghanistan as well as at Afghanistan's religiously radical and politically oppressive Taliban rulers—launched a month later. As we observed in Chapter 2, the Kashmir dispute remained for the most part on the sidelines of these events, at least initially; but that it was unlikely to avoid being implicated in them—and heavily so—became patently clear by the end of 2001 when India, prompted by a suicide attack on the Indian Parliament House in New Delhi, threatened military retaliation of its own against Pakistan.

Still further justification for a focus on religious identity in the Kashmir dispute may be found, of course, in its nuclearization. While it may once have seemed reasonable to set intractable identity issues aside, leaving them for later generations to settle, now that a potential finger on the nuclear trigger might belong to someone for whom matters of religious identity are neither minor nor fit for postponement compels us to acknowledge that neglect of such matters could be disastrous.

The prolonged episode of Kashmiri Muslim separatist militancy that began in the Indian state of Jammu and Kashmir nearly a decade before the nuclear turning point of 1998 had, of course, already rekindled interest in the role of religious identity in the Kashmir dispute. There is not much disagreement among contemporary analysts of the situation in Kashmir, in fact, that mobilization of the Kashmiri separatist movement in the 1990s took place along ethno-religious lines and that, as Sumantra Bose put it, "the central importance of a deeply-felt collective Muslim identity in the Kashmiri struggle for 'self-determination' cannot, and need not, be denied."[1] Neither has there been much disagreement over the multilayered character of the movement's connectedness to religious identity issues—that it was entangled, in other words, not only in the religious cleavages spawned locally within Kashmir itself but in those both of its immediate neighbors, India and Pakistan, and of the wider regional and global arenas.[2]

No consensus has ever developed, however, over just how *much* attention religious identity should be paid when the Kashmir dispute is under discussion and nothing even remotely like a consensus has ever emerged either over *how* religious identity has exerted whatever influence it wielded. Disagreement arises sharply, for instance, over the extent to which the political imaginations of Kashmiris have actually been fired by religious identity. Does Kashmiri separatism have its roots, in other words, primarily in the Islamic religion or in Kashmiri ethno-nationalism? Disagreement is no less sharp, we should note, when it comes to the exact manner in which religious identity has been mobilized in support of separatism. How much weight should be attached, for instance, to the impact on the Kashmiri Muslim minority of pan-Islamic radicalism? Or to the Machiavellian maneuvers of Pakistani intelligence organizations? Or to Kashmiri Muslim resentment of the rising tide of militant Hinduism in India?

Perhaps the most profound source of disagreement, however, stems from rival late-modern understandings of religious identity itself—of the depth of its entrenchment in human nature and society; of its compatibility with the secular, rational, and individualist values of the Enlightenment; and of the extent of its susceptibility to modification and change. Disagreement of this sort features rival ideological camps— secular-minded mainstream liberals on the one side, typically, and a diverse assortment of more-or-less dissenting conservatives, communitarians, "primordialists," postmodernists, neo-Marxists, and post-colonialists, among others, on the other—as contestants in a fiercely fought philosophical battle, raging now practically everywhere in the world, over the sources, potency, political consequences, and, of course, presumed virtues of cultural identity. In this battle, the Kashmir dispute sometimes has seemed important less in its own right than as a site for a surrogate trial of strength among these competing world views.

This contemporary interpretative struggle over the importance to the global order of religious identity has generated a growing corpus of literature. One of the most provocative products of this literature is the "clash of civilizations" thesis put forward by Samuel Huntington.[3] Challenging the prevailing wisdom that global politics is increasingly to be written in the language of market economics, Huntington's thesis elevates religion to a commanding position among the most probable determinants of the emerging world order. According to his thesis, civilizational identity— designated by Huntington the highest level of cultural identity—is mounting rapidly in importance. Patterns of international conflict and cooperation in the next—the twenty-first—century, in his judgment, would be increasingly dominated by it. Most of the nine extant civilizations he identified are primarily religion-based. Three of these religion-based civilizations— Hindu, Islamic, and Buddhist—comprise the cultural core of Jammu and Kashmir. Two of them—the Hindu and Islamic—have been in a state of full- or quasi-belligerence in South Asia for all of the last fifty-odd years.

One of them, the Islamic, said Huntington, is the most conflict-prone on the planet. "Islam," he observed, "has bloody borders."[4]

Huntington's critics have bitterly assailed his thesis for having endowed religion-based civilizations with far greater vitality and cohesion than they deserved at the same time that it breezily understated both the hold on power retained by sovereign state entities as well as the tenacity and continuing appeal of modernity and secularism.[5] Cropping up in critical assessments of his thesis with particular insistence, however, has been the charge that he attached disproportionate importance to the signs of imminent struggle emerging *between* civilizations to the neglect of immediate struggle already present *within* them—that in depicting acute regional conflicts as materializing along suprastatal and semimythic civilizational fault lines, in other words, he grievously underplayed the tangible interests of physically-existent state and substate entities.[6] These accusations illustrate a point of great importance to the discussion of religion's role in the Kashmir dispute: Even if observers uniformly concede that Kashmir's straddling of an especially deep and tricornered civilizational fault line[7] has contributed in some way to the Kashmir dispute's complexity as well as, presumably, to its bloodiness, there will still remain ample space for fundamental disagreement over the precise nature and scale of its impact. Kashmir's multicivilizational configuration offers, in fact, a rare opportunity to probe the merits not only of Huntington's placement—or misplacement—of fault lines in the South Asian context but of his critics' complaints.

This chapter's central task, then, is the critical examination of the portentous debate over religion's role in the Kashmir dispute. One of its goals is to frame the analysis of religion's role in a way that adds conceptual clarity to the discussion. Some of what is included here, in other words, is meant not so much to settle an issue as to put it in language that facilitates dispassionate consideration of it. A more important goal, however, derives from my personal conviction that the Kashmir dispute is as much a struggle over religious identity—more precisely, over the *interpretation* and *representation* of religious identity—as it is over anything else. By this I mean that discussion of religion's role in this dispute, whether concerned with the origin, conduct, or solution of it, is in some respects as much a weapon in the arsenals of the contending sides as are the armed forces patrolling the Line of Control. I hope to identify, in the course of this chapter, some of the more important ways in which this interpretative weapon has been deployed in discussions of Kashmir. Beyond that, I hope to establish that its widespread deployment has resulted both in the routine inflation, deflation, and/or distortion of religion's role in the dispute and, inevitably, in the profound impairment of our understanding of it.

The discussion in this chapter focuses largely, though not exclusively, on developments from about 1990 onwards. We deal with the religious issue here deliberately as an instance of *internationalized* identity politics, in which not only India and Pakistan—and the political struggles going on within and between them nowadays over the religious content of their national identities—but a variety of other nearby or more distant global players, obviously including Afghanistan and the United States, are implicated. We make unapologetic use here of Huntington's imaginative terminology, but without incurring any automatic indebtedness to the particular arguments he used this terminology to convey. We revisit his thesis, for the most part sympathetically, I should note, in the concluding section of this chapter. Discussion here focuses on three dimensions of religion's role in the Kashmir dispute: First, the salience of religious identity in the Kashmiri cultural tradition; second, the role of religious identity in motivating the contemporary upsurge in Kashmiri Muslim separatism; and third, the nature and magnitude of religion's role in shaping Pakistani and Indian state strategies in present-day Kashmir. Our discussion of the interrelationship of religious identity and the Kashmir dispute begins with a look at the state of Jammu and Kashmir's ethno-religious cultural composition.

Faultline Politics I—Religion in Kashmiri Identity

Raju Thomas reminds us in a recent book that Kashmir has a "three-in-one" identity problem: Are Kashmiris, he asks, to be understood as Indians, Muslims, or simply Kashmiris? "The answer," he says,

> is they are all three depending on which characteristic is being attributed to Kashmiris at any given time, and this would determine whether they are part of India, Pakistan or a separate nation. In Kashmir, we may identify its basic secular "Indian" character because its peoples are mainly Hindu descendants and have been influenced by the more secular Hindu tradition over the centuries; or we may identify Kashmir's basic "Islamic" character since the majority of its population is Muslim and therefore may perceive closer religious and emotional links with Pakistan; or its essential "Kashmiri" character that draws together Valley Muslims, Dogra Hindus, Kashmiri Hindu Pandits and Ladakhi Buddhists in a self-perception of an independent nation that is often referred to as the "Kashmiriyat."[8]

Thomas's perceptive comment points at two basic truths about Kashmir. The most obvious is that it has a highly fragmented cultural fabric: Its inhabitants mirror in their microcosmic setting the extraordinary cultural pluralism that characterizes the South Asian region as a whole. The second is that the fragments, unlike the precut pieces in a two-dimensional jigsaw puzzle, can be abstractly assembled in more than one way: Kashmir's cultural pluralism lends itself, in other words, to any of several rival interpretations—or, as Thomas implies, to all of them simultaneously. These rival interpretations or representations of Kashmir's cultural pluralism embody deeply conflictive assumptions, both about the nature of Kashmiri cultural identity considered as a whole, as well as about the relationship to this identity of religion in particular. The first of these two truths draws us to consider the specific ethnographic configuration—the spatial and numerical distribution of distinct ethno-linguistic and religious identities—that prevails in Kashmir. The second focuses our attention directly on the salience of religion in Kashmiri culture, specifically on the cultural tradition of *kashmiriyat* and the controversy that surrounds it.

Kashmir's Ethno-Religious Diversity

When at the end of the Anglo-Sikh War (1845–46) the British colonial authorities rewarded Gulab Singh, their Jammu-based Dogra Rajput ally against the Sikhs, with the cession of all the territory between the Beas and Indus rivers, they did not pause to worry about the potential consequences of the arbitrary grouping and political transfer of the territory's ethnically polyglot population. Their decision, which produced the core of the Dogra Hindu principality that was to endure until 1947, had, in fact, momentous consequences: It joined under one political roof peoples with widely differing religious, religious-sectarian, ethno-linguistic, caste, and historical backgrounds, but in relatively segregated sociogeographic circumstances that left their separate identities still largely intact a century later.

No systematic census enumeration of Jammu and Kashmir—of either its Indian- or Pakistan-controlled portions*—has been conducted

---

*Indian-controlled Kashmir (formally, Jammu and Kashmir State) today consists of three main divisions: the Kashmir Valley, Jammu, and Ladakh. The Pakistan-controlled sector is divided into two parts: Azad (Free) Jammu and Kashmir, customarily called Azad Kashmir, and the far larger but lightly populated Northern Areas. The Chinese control the largely uninhabited Aksai Chin region in northeastern Ladakh.

Figure 3.1

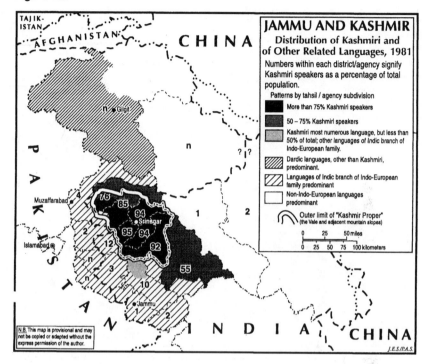

since 1981. Accurate ethnographic breakdowns of its present population are further handicapped by the intrusion upon earlier census operations of a certain amount of subjective (partisan) reckoning of group
sizes, by inconsistencies over time in the ethnic designations of the
peoples being counted, as well as by the occurrence of in- and out-
migrations, including—as in the case of the Kashmiri Pandits (Hindu
Brahmins) in the early years of the 1990s—those induced to some extent by deliberate campaigns of "ethnic cleansing." But while the arbitrary inflation and deflation of relative group proportions of the
population remains, on both sides of the LOC, a favorite political pas-
time, the fact persists that Kashmir "presents a classic case of linguistic
and ethno-religious diversity."[9]

Figures 3.1 and 3.2, based on the recent and careful estimates of the
University of Minnesota–based geographer, Joseph E. Schwartzberg, depict the distribution in Kashmir of languages and religions. They mirror
the polylinguistic and polyreligious character of Kashmir's population.

Figure 3.2

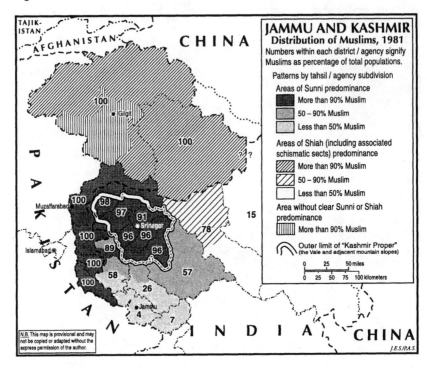

They also mirror, regionwise, the highly asymmetrical distribution of both language and religion.

As for the linguistic dimension, the strong dominance in the Valley of Kashmir of Kashmiri, the most widely spoken language of the Dardic branch of the Indo-European language family,* is matched by its light representation or near absence in Azad Kashmir, the Northern Areas, Ladakh, and Jammu. In those areas, it contends for cultural space with Dogri (a dialect of Punjabi), Gujri, Balti, Pahari, Tibetan, Potohari, Burushaski, and other languages and dialects. Thus, while Kashmiri-speakers commanded a bit over 52 percent of the Indian-controlled sector's population in the 1981 census, they would inevitably plummet to a distinctly minority status were the overwhelmingly non-Kashmiri-speaking Azad Kashmir population added to the equation.[10]

---

*The exact position of the Dardic group of languages in relation to the Indo-European language family remains a subject of debate among linguists.

Table 3.1

Population and Religion, Jammu and Kashmir State (1981)

Region	Population	Muslim (%)	Hindu (%)	Other (%)
Kashmir Valley	3,134,904 (52.36%)	94.96	04.59	00.05
Jammu	2,718,113 (45.40%)	29.60	66.25	04.15
Ladakh	134,372 (02.24%)	46.04	02.66	51.30
Totals	5,987,389	64.19	32.24	03.57

Source: Census of India, 1981.

Much the same picture presents itself when the area's religious diversity is examined. As can be seen in Figure 3.2, the Pakistan-controlled sectors of Kashmir are inhabited almost exclusively by Muslims (nearly 100 percent); and Muslim demographic dominance of the Indian-controlled Valley of Kashmir is nearly as complete (since the exodus from the Valley of between 100,000 and 150,000 Hindu Pandits following the outbreak of separatist violence in the early part of the 1990s, even more so today than at the time of the 1981 census). But when one's gaze is widened beyond the Valley in the Indian-held portion of the state, a very different picture comes into view. The total population of this portion in 2000 has been estimated at around 9.45 million.[11] Of this figure, judging from the 1981 census (see Table 3.1), Muslims constitute roughly 64 percent, Hindus 32 percent, with Buddhists and Sikhs making up most of the remainder. Once again, the regional disproportions magnify the diversity: in primarily Hindu Jammu, non-Muslims represent 70.4 percent of the population, and in primarily Buddhist Ladakh, non-Muslims represent 53.96 percent of the total.[12]

When one takes into account sectarian, caste, or other subgroup identities, even these figures further dissolve. For instance, between the Dogra Hindus of Jammu and the Hindu Pandits now dwelling as refugees among them, there are profound cultural (and political) differences, and some of the animosity that marks Sunni-Shi'a sectarian relations elsewhere in the Islamic world is also detectable in Kashmir. Schwartzberg estimates that Sunnis are solidly entrenched (over 90 percent) among the Muslims of the Valley, Jammu, and Azad Kashmir.[13] But there are important Shi'a majorities in Baltistan—in both its Pakistan-held (Baltistan Agency of the Northern Areas) and Indian-held (Kargil district of Ladakh) portions—as well as a large (and politically troublesome) Shi'a representation in the Gilgit Agency of Pakistan's Northern Areas.

Kashmir's ethno-religious diversity lends itself, as was suggested earlier, to a considerable variety of inventive (and, not infrequently, mutually exclusive) interpretations. Hindu spokesmen for the persistent autonomy movement in Kashmir state's Jammu division, for instance, are apt to emphasize the cultural differences and yawning political divide between Jammu and the Valley. Stalwarts of Kashmiri Muslim separatism, on the other hand, determined to curb any territorial hemorrhaging from the Greater Kashmir of their political imagination, are just as likely to underscore the state's fundamental cultural unity.[14] The character of this interpretative or representational rivalry over the "real" nature of Kashmiri cultural identity shows up with particular clarity in the ongoing debate over the role in this identity of *kashmiriyat*. The discussion turns now to this debate.

The Culture of Kashmiriyat

The concept of *kashmiriyat* (meaning being Kashmiri, or Kashmiri-ness) is generally understood to represent the commonly shared cultural traits of all the peoples of Kashmir, whatever their religious, linguistic, or political affiliations. Said to be rooted deep in the history of the area, it is described as the irreducible element of Kashmiri culture—its "essence"— the part that lends this culture its interior coherence and vitality as well as its distinctiveness from the surrounding and exterior South Asian cultural traditions. Claimed in particular for Kashmiri cultural identity under this rubric is a strong penchant for religious syncretism and tolerance (and corresponding disinclination for religious fanaticism and zealotry). Riyaz Punjabi's description of Kashmiri ethnicity is characteristic. "Hindus, Muslims, Sikhs, Buddhists and even Christians," he observes,

> have contributed to the emergence of this ethnicity. The traditions followed by Kashmiri Muslims, the indigenous methods of practicing their faith, and following the customs, . . . makes them distinct from their co-religionists elsewhere.

The same is true, he points out, of

the Hindus of Kashmir, . . . [who] have developed their own indigenous philosophies, devised their own symbols, and created their own traditions, [making] them markedly distinct from the preponderant majority of their co-religionists in the subcontinent.

"The lineage of Kashmiri people," he says,

had given them distinctive looks; the fusion and assimilation of varied faiths and cultures had resulted in their particular and specific ethnicity. The land, the climate, the geography shaped the evolution of their particular ethnic profile. A common language bound them closer into a distinct cultural grouping. In case religion is taken to be the main ingredient of ethnicity, then the Kashmiri people had evolved their indigenous religious practices by assimilating the religious practices of varied religions; and *Rishis* [holy men] had put a final seal to this mutual understanding long ago.[15]

For the more secular-minded of Kashmiri Muslim separatists, this "mutual understanding" is no mere pious principle. On the contrary, sustaining the legitimacy of a claim to a *united* Kashmir—that is, to either the autonomy or independence of a Kashmiri territorial entity *that does not entail the state's repartition along lines of ethno-religious identity*—can hardly be accomplished without it.

Indian commentators on *kashmiriyat*, whether of Hindu or Muslim background, commonly judge *kashmiriyat* to be currently in sharp, even precipitous, decline. The reasons they give for the decline show predictable differences. Reflecting a politically moderate and secular Kashmiri Muslim point of view, Punjabi, a Srinagar-born Muslim academic at the University of Kashmir, distributes blame evenhandedly among both Hindus and Muslims. Kashmiri Pandits, he explains,

who had laid the foundation of this ethnicity [*kashmiriyat*] and played the pivotal role in developing the identity of Kashmir, started identifying themselves with the larger Hindu religious majority of India. For various political and economic reasons, they abandoned their indigenous beliefs and traditions, and started merging with the traditions and beliefs of India's majority religious community.

Reacting to the pressures of Islamic fundamentalism coming from Pakistan as well as to those of Hindu nationalism coming from India, Kashmiri Muslims appear also, he says, to be "diluting the ethnicity of Kashmir.

They appear to have been led to a course where the religious edge of Kashmiri Identity in its exclusive form is getting more and more sharpened to the detriment of the Kashmiriyat."[16]

In contrast, K. Warikoo, a Srinagar-born Hindu Pandit and a member of the Jawaharlal Nehru University faculty, attributes the decline almost exclusively to the calculated policy of the state of Jammu and Kashmir's Kashmiri Muslim bureaucracy and political leadership. He points in particular to the state's systematic patronage of Urdu, which he considers the South Asian region's foremost symbol of Muslim cultural identity, and its simultaneous efforts to curb the teaching of Kashmiri and other local mother tongues. The "government's policy towards local mother tongues," he observes,

> including Kashmiri, reflects the political dynamics of Muslim majoritarianism, in which supra-national religious ethnicity has been artificially superimposed over the linguistic ethnicity. This has been done with the object of bringing Kashmiri Muslims closer to the Muslim *Ummah* in the subcontinent, and particularly with the adjoining Islamic State of Pakistan. This task has been carried forward by numerous Islamic political, social and cultural institutions . . . and the *madrassahs* or even public schools run by these organisations, all of which have been preaching and promoting Islamic world view both in political, social and cultural affairs. With the result a firm ideological base has been prepared to mold the political and cultural views of Kashmiri Muslims on religious lines rather than ethno-linguistic/cultural basis, thereby negating the indigenous secular and composite cultural heritage.[17]

The primacy given to Islam over language, declares Warikoo, has consolidated "the religious divide between Kashmiri Muslims and Hindus who otherwise inherit same language, habitat and way of life. True spirit of Kashmiriat can be restored only after giving rightful place to the indigenous Kashmiri language and culture."[18]

The actual content of this "true spirit" of *kashmiriyat* is itself far from uncontroversial. The conventional view, visible in the comment of Riyaz Punjabi quoted above, is that *kashmiriyat* sprang from the cultural marriage in fourteenth-century Kashmir of unorthodox and mystical branches of both Islam (Sufism) and Hinduism (Shaivism). The offspring of this union, it is argued, while unquestionably having a religious content, was remarkably secular, or at least secular in tone, and fundamentally differentiated Kashmiris—Hindus and Muslims alike—from their religious counterparts elsewhere in the subcontinent.[19]

Colliding with this interpretation is the more recent (and identity-conflating) Hindu nationalist thesis, visible in the Hindu counterattack upon the alleged contemporary hijacking by Muslims of the state's cultural heritage, that this heritage owes more to its Hindu than its Islamic ancestry, that its Islamic components, to the extent they are present, are relatively late (and not infrequently unwholesome) historical additions, and that, at bottom, Kashmiris are Indians. Observe, for instance, how the journalist and erstwhile Rashtriya Swayamsevak Sangh (RSS) organizational activist Narender Sehgal frames the issue. What is today called *kashmiriyat*, he writes,

> is not, in any case, different from Indianness. Kashmiriyat has no independent existence. Those who harbour the idea of regional nationalism by dividing the Indian culture in Kashmiriyat, Panjabiyat, Assamiyat, Bangla, Tamiliayan etc., have been responsible for the shrinking of the geographical area of India which was once a vast country. . . . That is why Kashmiriyat is not a product of any one religion. This Kashmiriyat is not the one that was born 600 years ago. Let those, who while taking arms in their hands to disturb the conception of Kashmiriyat, watch carefully and realise which blood runs in their veins. The blood is of their Hindu ancestors. Those very ancestors who watered Kashmiriyat with their blood. It is that very blood. The sects and cults of snake worship. Shaivites, Buddhists, Vaishnavas, Sufis and Rishis have, like flowers, bloomed on the soil of Kashmir lending fragrance to Kashmiriyat. Everyone has a share in Kashmiriyat. And this Kashmiriyat is part of that Indian culture whose strange form has been shaped by the kind God with His hands.[20]

Emphasizing *kashmiriyat's* Hindu origins (brushing aside its Muslim and Buddhist antecedents, in other words), lends historical weight, of course, to the demand by some refugee Kashmiri Pandit organizations, in particular Panun Kashmir, founded in 1991, that an autonomous enclave—Panun Kashmir (Our Kashmir)—be carved from the Valley and placed under Pandit administration. Its creation would provide a secure homeland to which the displaced population of Pandits could be repatriated and in which it could be rehabilitated, at the same time that it assured preservation of *kashmiriyat*, of the heart and soul of which, as Pandits tend to see it, their Hindu ancestors are the aboriginal founders.[21] Panun Kashmir's advocates envision an entity of about 8,400 square kilometers—or about 4 percent of the total area of pre-partition Jammu and Kashmir. It would embrace the northern part of the Valley and, according to one skeptical geographer, would mean setting aside almost half the area of the entire Valley—including its fabled capital city of Srinagar—for 5 percent of the state's total population.[22] Meeting the relatively small Pandit minority's culturally aggressive requirements in this way has no appeal at all, of course, to the Valley's Muslims, now running close to 100 percent of its total population. From the Pandits' point of view, however, the religious exclusivism and extremism they insist is mounting among militant elements of the Kashmiri Muslims prevents the Pandits' return to the Valley under any other circumstances.

Western scholarship, bred in recent decades on a strong diet of postmodern skepticism for the so-called Orientalist discourse or tradition of scholarship—a key to which was the tendency to radically distill or "essentialize" non-Occidental cultures, to represent in exaggerated terms, in other words, their uniformity and durability[23]—almost inevitably calls into question the grander claims made on behalf of *kashmiriyat's* coherence, endurance, and intercommunity appeal. In the face of Kashmir's multifaceted and undeniable diversity, such claims inevitably give the appearance at least of romanticism, if not of politically motivated construction. Schwartzberg, who otherwise concedes the persistent and pervasive power of *kashmiriyat's* transcommunal (Hindu-Muslim) reach, strongly implies that this reach does not likely extend far beyond that of the Kashmiri language. "Although one cannot objectively map the extent of the area over which kashmiriyat may be said to be the dominant cultural complex," he observes, "one can map the area in which the Kashmiri language, the vehicle through which the sentiment of kashmiriyat is transmitted, is dominant. . . . The area of strong Kashmiri dominance corresponds remarkably well with that of Kashmir proper [the Valley and the Muslim-majority areas of Jammu]."[24]

It seems, however, that even a *kashmiriyat* of these relatively modest dimensions may not square with the empirical realities of Kashmir. In fact, there are persuasive reasons for doubting, even if not for peremptorily dismissing, the notion that the cultural fusion, mutual understanding, and tolerance implied by *kashmiriyat* were *ever* dominant in Kashmiri society—even *within* the Kashmiri-speaking language community. Indian sociologist T. N. Madan's study some years ago of the sociocultural identity of Muslims and Hindus of rural Kashmir observed, for instance, that while at the practical level of everyday living Muslims and Hindu Pandits were mutually dependent and accustomed to pragmatic accommodation of one another, at the ideological level there was "complete mutual exclusion. . . ." Muslims excluded Pandits on grounds of monotheistic Islam-based moral abhorrence, while Pandits excluded Muslims on grounds of caste Hinduism-based ritual impurity. Villagers sharply differentiated Muslim from Hindu identity. Far from demonstrating exemplary religious syncretism and mutual understanding, each side viewed the other as inferior. Common Pandit stereotypes of Muslims included "low born," "dirty," "polluted," "unprincipled," "omnivorous," and "lustful." Muslims reciprocated with equally derogatory stereotypes of Pandits, including "faithless," "double-dealer," "mean," "cowardly," "corrupt," and "dirty." "Kashmiri rural society," Madan concluded, "when subjectively defined, comprises two social orders, not one."[25]

Kashmiriyat, it turns out, has in practice a relatively elastic and obviously controversial meaning. Its historical origins, cultural contents, and territorial breadth are all contested. So, too, are the forces said to be shaping and reshaping it in the contemporary period. This unavoidable finding renders problematic, of course, the definition of Kashmiri separatism. While it may be perfectly clear, as Madan says, that Kashmiri separatism is against pan-Indian secular nationalism,[26] precisely what inspires it—pan-Kashmiri ethnic nationalism, Islamic fundamentalism, or a hybrid somewhere midway between the two—is much less clear. A closer look at what motivates the separatist movement itself is required.

Faultline Politics II—Religion in Kashmiri Separatism

We observed above that ethno-religious identity is widely conceded to loom large across the landscape of the Kashmir dispute. We noted, however, that the exact content of Kashmiri identity and, in particular, the capacity of its alleged *kashmiriyat* core to appeal across the religious, sectarian, linguistic, and regional boundaries of the state's ethnographically diverse population, are subjects of intense and ongoing controversy. The focus of much of this controversy in recent years has been the motivations and objectives of the Kashmiri Muslim separatist movement—in particular, the question of the extent to which Islamic faith, especially its radical, extremist, or "fundamentalist" strain, has fastened its grip on this movement. Tied up in this controversy, of course, is the burning question about the *indigenous* character of this movement—about its dependency, in other words, on non-Kashmiri coreligionist state and nonstate organizations for both moral inspiration and material support. Tied up in it also, of course, is the question of its *legitimacy*—of the rightfulness of the Kashmiri Muslim militants' claims to self-determination, in other words, whether their claim is to complete independence or simply the conduct of a free and multi-optional plebiscite.

In what follows, we examine a number of alternative understandings of the motivational roots of Kashmiri separatism. We divide these understandings into two main categories—those ascribing separatism primarily to *secular* (political, social, and economic) forces and those ascribing it primarily, or at least prominently, to *religious* (cultural, communal, or fundamentalist) ones. We subject each of these understandings to critical scrutiny. Our immediate objectives are (1) to identify the several ways in which religious identity is customarily dealt with in scholarly treatments of the subject of Kashmiri separatism, and (2) to take note of the manner in which initial assumptions in regard to religious identity powerfully and differentially affect the content of scholarly argument over Kashmir.

Debating Separatism's Roots: Secular Forces

The accent in a number of studies of Kashmiri separatism has been on secular forces, for the most part relating to political and socioeconomic developments *within* India. In these studies, the role of religion is muted.

Political Mobilization and Institutional Decay

One such study is that of Sumit Ganguly, *The Crisis in Kashmir.* In it, he identifies "four broad categories" of argument adduced so far to explain the onset of the separatism. Only three clearly qualify as more or less coherent arguments.[27] The first of these emphasizes external agency, namely Pakistan's sponsorship of terrorism in Kashmir—"that Pakistan has engaged in a systematic strategy of infusing Islamic fundamentalist ideology into the Kashmir valley since the late 1970s."[28] The second and third (in most respects simply opposite sides of the same coin) emphasize internal agencies—the Indian state (its misrule, repression, and denial of Kashmiri self-determination) is the second, the Kashmiri nationalist movement ("the emergence of ethnic subnationalism in Kashmir and its challenge to the Indian state") the third. Without entirely dismissing any of these three categories of explanation, Ganguly proposes that the best explanation of the origins of the secessionist insurgency in Kashmir is to be found in a structural dichotomy—"the increase in political mobilization [of Kashmiris] against a background of institutional decay [in India at large]."[29]

Ganguly's "political mobilization and institutional decay" thesis draws heavily upon the corpus of nation-building and political development literature produced in the United States during the 1960s and 1970s under the auspices of the Social Science Research Council and, in particular, upon the work of Harvard scholar Samuel P. Huntington. In brief, Ganguly argues that India's post-independence national policies and programs (affecting education and literacy, exposure to both print and electronic media, and economic development) eventually were translated into political mobilization—meaning heightened consciousness of political rights and privileges, as well as of the forces affecting societies undergoing modernization and of the means for addressing them—"on a historically unprecedented scale across India and in Kashmir particularly." This potentially explosive phenomenon ran up against a parallel (and equally volatile) development in India—"deinstitutionalization," which Ganguly defines as the gradual weakening of the legal and administrative procedures inherited at independence, the decline of parliamentary norms, and the promotion of an increasingly populist and unstable brand of politics.[30] Dating roughly to the mid-1960s, according to Ganguly, deinstitutionalization incapacitated the machinery of Indian government at exactly the moment when political mobilization had begun to produce a critical mass of politically alert and demanding Kashmiri citizens. Denied since independence the development of an honest political opposition, they naturally sought relief from massive electoral malpractice, corruption, and deceit via extra-institutional (and ultimately violent) devices. The insurgency in Kashmir, suggests Ganguly, is thus "the result of a fundamental paradox of Indian democracy: Kashmir represents both the mobilizational success and, simultaneously, the institutional failure of Indian democracy."[31]

As Ganguly interprets it, the political mobilization of Kashmiris took place on the basis of ethno-religious identities more for adventitious reasons than because these identities were in some predetermined way bound to collide both with one another and with Indian national identity. These reasons include the fact that the state happened to be administratively subdivided into religious-majority districts; that the Kashmiri Muslims, both geographically and culturally isolated from the mainstream of Indian Islam, had acquired an exceptionally localistic and parochial view of their position in India; that no other viable means for the expression of discontent was available; and, finally, that Pakistan sensed the opportunity, thus offered up to it by India, to exaggerate and exploit ethno-religious differences to its own strategic advantage.[32] This way of looking at Kashmiri separatism strips it, of course, not only of the glamour and moral superiority that might attach to a "true" (indigenous, progressive, and ideologically motivated) movement of national liberation and self-determination, but also of intrinsic durability and historical inevitability—both qualities that the separatists routinely claim for their movement.

Ganguly thus departs in very substantial ways from the other categories of explanation identified by him. Unlike them, his scheme moves to center stage certain structural forces—some of them "global" socioeconomic forces (widened education, for example) stemming from rapid modernization, others of them pertaining to broad institutional trends (the decline of the Congress party's dominance, for instance) in Indian politics. Unlike them also, the forces he points to are as often socially positive (advancing literacy, for example) as negative (the decline in parliamentary norms, for instance). These forces, moreover, are essentially transient phenomena, dysfunctional byproducts of barely escapable but yet for the most part temporary structural disjunctions, and thus are amenable to enlightened policy management and reform. No radical surgery (grant of plebiscite, autonomy, or independence, for instance) is needed, in other words. Ganguly's argument, we should note here, does allow into the explanation of Kashmiri separatism a major role for Pakistan; but, for him, it is not determinative.

What distinguishes Ganguly's argument also, at least from some of the alternatives, is that his explanation places relatively modest weight on the factor of cultural identity. In his hands, this factor makes its way into the equation of separatism, to be sure, but more by default than by any intrinsic virtue of its own. For Ganguly, cultural identity (including religious identity) *complicates* the Kashmir problem but does not *define* it. It should certainly not be the basis for *resolving* it. The Kashmiri insurgents' claim to self-determination, he says,

> is itself problematic. The vast majority of the insurgents would not extend the privilege of self-determination to members of other communities. Despite the many malfeasances of the Indian state, the best hope for the redressal of the grievances of all minorities remains within the ambit of a secular, democratic, and federal Indian polity.[33]

Betrayal of Democracy

Another study that accents secular forces is that of Sumantra Bose, *The Challenge in Kashmir: Democracy, Self-Determination and a Just Peace.* In this book, Bose pronounces the Kashmir problem overwhelmingly a product of India's own political failures.

Five main arguments are woven through the book. The first is that Kashmiri secessionist impulses, which finally turned violent in 1989, were prompted very largely by India's denial of democracy to the people of Kashmir. Taking issue in particular with those who have laid the blame for the insurgency on Pakistani sponsorship, Bose contends that the secessionist urge "can be explained . . . by one factor alone: the Indian state's consistent policy of denying democracy. . . ."[34] His second argument is that the repressive counterinsurgency practices of Indian security forces in Kashmir, including such things as routine cordon-and-search operations, arbitrary detention of thousands of youths, extended curfews in major towns and cities, looting, rape, and torture, far from being aberrations "are integral components, or at least inevitable extensions, of a *systematic policy.*"[35] A third argument is that Pakistan's intervention in Kashmir, "dogmatically irredentist" and "virulently communal" in content, has been largely counterproductive. Far from having won Kashmiris to the brotherhood of Islam, it has seriously alienated them. They are now, according to Bose, unambiguously and unequivocally committed to independence from *both* India and Pakistan.[36]

A fourth argument Bose makes is that the Kashmiri separatist movement, while obviously dependent on "a deeply-felt collective Muslim identity,"[37] is essentially noncommunal in inspiration. It is true, he concedes, that the mosque has emerged over the course of the Kashmiris' struggle as a focal point of popular mobilization and resistance to Indian rule; but that, he says, is due to "the total absence of any alternative channels of collective action and protest."[38] Kashmiri identity, he maintains, is syncretic and fundamentally tolerant, and it has not been submerged in Islam. Warning against interpretations of the Kashmir struggle that cast it as a civilizational faultline conflict, Bose insists that it is not at all a product of an underlying Hindu-Muslim animosity.

Fifth and last, Bose contends that the solution to the Kashmir imbroglio has to be sought, at one level, in the renewal of Indian democracy and, at another, in the "skillful renegotiation and complex redefinition of the concept and practice of state-sovereignty in South Asia."[39] In practical terms, he endorses strengthened autonomy for Kashmir within the Indian Union.

There are some obvious differences in the arguments of Bose and Ganguly. While both assign to developments in India the major share of responsibility for the separatist insurrection in Kashmir, their readings of Indian democracy diverge substantially. Ganguly hails post independence India's "success with democratic institution-building" and praises Jawaharlal Nehru for recognizing "the vital importance of the federal system in India" and for playing "a critical role in nurturing democratic political institutions and practices." As he sees it, the process of deinstitutionalization, which would eventually have such disastrous consequences in Kashmir, had its roots largely in the 1960s and coincided with the rule of Nehru's successors, Indira Gandhi and Rajiv Gandhi.[40] Bose, in contrast, unleashes a broad and far less equivocal assault on the very foundations of Indian democracy. The "coercive homogenisation and assimilation" of Kashmir began, according to him, almost immediately following the state's accession to India, and Nehru, far from being a visionary democrat, led in fashioning a Kashmir policy reeking of "profound condescension and almost imperial arrogance. . . ." Indeed, "the origins of the Indian state's anti-democratic and ultimately futile and destructive Kashmir policy," according to Bose, "are to be found squarely in the Nehru period."[41]

The arguments of Bose and Ganguly are more nearly alike when it comes to the matter of religious identity. Both accept uncritically the conventional representation of Kashmiri culture—kashmiriyat—as uniquely tolerant and syncretic. Both also locate the most poisonous species of communalism—of politically charged religious identity, in other words—on the Pakistan side of the border. For them both, moreover, Kashmir is a political, not a cultural problem: it most certainly is not, for either of these authors, an arena for "the clash of civilizations."

The most consequential similarity in their arguments, however, is that the solution for both lies essentially in the rejuvenation of Indian secular democracy. Religious identity, whether as a cause of the Kashmir conflict or a component of its resolution, is central to the analysis of neither. Neither, moreover, gives any consideration to the possibility that rejuvenated democracy itself—even in the unlikely event that the extraordinarily corrupt and cynical practices of the past could somehow be ruled out—might have to share the role of villain. They seem unaware that majoritarian communalism has a well-established record in

Jammu and Kashmir, including that of the present National Conference government in Srinagar,[42] and that political democracy, even in its most chaste and honorable form, has few good defenses against it.[43]

Debating Separatism's Roots: Religious Forces

Among the major alternatives to the kinds of explanations given by Bose and Ganguly are those placing greater weight on cultural, specifically religious, identity. They do so, however, in radically different ways, reflecting not only their advocates' general understanding of religious identity in the South Asian milieu but how each of them ties this understanding to the particular circumstances of religion's linkage with political separatism in Kashmir. In this discussion, we categorize these religion-weighted theses under three headings—Religious Radicalism: Holy War and Sponsored Terrorism, Majoritarian Communalism, and Submergence of Subnational Identity.

Jammu and Kashmir's own religious diversity, we observed earlier, inevitably helped to define religion's linkage with the political separatist movement that surfaced in the Indian-controlled section of the state in the waning months of 1988 by setting some rather severe cultural limits to it. After all, the movement appealed to and drew its support almost exclusively from the Kashmiri Muslim (*Sunni* Muslim) community, and, for most of the next decade, its direct impact was limited geographically largely to the Kashmiri Muslim-dominated Valley (an area encompassing about 10 percent of the entire pre-partition princely state of Jammu and Kashmir). The state's large non-Muslim population (Hindu, Buddhist, and Sikh) was, for the most part, either indifferent or downright hostile to the movement. The debate we examine here over the movement's linkage with religion ranges well beyond the "given" of the state's ethno-religious settlement patterns, however, focusing instead on rival interpretations of the way in which religious extremism, in both its Islamic and Hindu forms, has intersected with Kashmiri separatism.

Religious Radicalism: Holy War and Sponsored Terrorism

A large body of opinion has developed in South Asia in which a heavy accent in the explanation of Kashmiri separatism has been placed on religious radicalism, in particular Islamic—more accurately *pan*-Islamic—radicalism. Common to those sharing this opinion is the belief that

Islamic radicalism in Kashmir is culturally subversive, at odds with *kashmiriat* and the Sufi religious traditions of the Kashmiris, and externally driven—orchestrated ideologically and organizationally for the most part by neighboring Pakistan. As Yoginder Sikand puts it, the radical Islamic rhetoric that has captured the popular imagination in Kashmir recently "to a considerable extent, represents an external agenda that is being sought to be imposed on Kashmir, and one that seems at odds, in several respects, with the internal conditions in Kashmir itself."[44]

Only in the last decade or so has this point of view attracted much attention among observers of Kashmir. This may be the result, at least in part, of the relatively late emergence in Pakistan of conscious efforts to Islamicize its domestic and foreign policies. Until its defeat in the 1972 war with India, Pakistan had held itself somewhat aloof from the Islamic world to its west and, to a large extent, had soft-pedaled the Islamic component of its formal national identity. The defeat itself, with its painful reminder of the severe practical limits to the Two Nation Theory promoted by Pakistan in the 1940s, did not lead immediately to Pakistan's unconditional public embrace of Islamic politics. In fact, not until the political upheavals of the late 1970s—the toppling of the Bhutto regime by the Pakistan army in 1977 and the even more jarring Iranian Revolution of 1978—did Pakistan's neighborhood (and Pakistan itself) begin the systematic shredding of its hitherto largely secular political orientation. And not until the last years of the 1980s, when the mass mobilization of Kashmiri Muslims behind separatism began to develop into a serious matter for India, was much attention paid either to the impact of political Islam upon the evolution of contemporary Kashmiri identity. Up until then, Pakistani prospects for winning Kashmiris en masse to Pakistan's side in the Kashmir dispute, whether on the grounds of fraternal religious identity or anything else, had, in fact, seemed pretty meager. There had been no visible expression of mass Kashmiri Muslim disappointment when Pakistan's first bid to win Kashmir by wresting it forcefully from India ended in a stalemate in early 1949. And the Pakistanis, no less than the Indians, viewed the Pakistan army's disastrously unsuccessful project, code-named Operation Gibraltar, in late summer 1965 to enlist Kashmiri Muslim support for its guerrilla raid on Indian forces in the Valley as a misadventure—the product of a profoundly unrealistic reading of Kashmiri Muslim sentiments.[45]

The so-called Islamic resurgence of the last several decades has recast in basic ways the role of Islam in the politics of the South Asian region.[46] Inevitably, it has also magnified the Islamic ideological "presence" in the separatist milieu of Kashmiri politics. This milieu bristles now not only with the familiar rhetoric of Islamic militancy but also with the pan-Islamic organizational trafficking (in money, arms, and armed men, for instance) that gives militancy its teeth. With equal inevitability, of course, the appearance of the Islamic resurgence in Kashmir has opened the door wide to allegations of sponsored terrorism leveled, in particular, against Pakistan.

Significant variations have developed within the religious radicalism school of thought. On one side is the "hard" perspective, which we label the Sponsored Terrorism thesis, that Kashmiri separatism itself is for the most part a foreign import, cynically disguised in Islamic dress by its Pakistani paymasters. This perspective highlights the violent, terrorist, and nonindigenous character of the separatist movement.

The most detailed, authoritative, and influential expression of this point of view to appear on the Indian scene in the 1990s was that of Malhotra Jagmohan, twice appointed governor of the State of Jammu and Kashmir and more recently elected to the Indian parliament under the banner of the Bharatiya Janata Party. In his book *My Frozen Turbulence in Kashmir*, first published in 1991, Jagmohan narrates an explanation of India's dilemma in Kashmir that rests very heavily on a theory of Pakistan-directed Islamic conspiracy—a theory we took note of in Chapter 1.[47] When he arrived back in Srinagar in January 1990 for his second tour of duty as governor, Jagmohan says that he found an entirely transformed political situation: In the short interval since the end of his first tour as governor in July 1989, Pakistan-backed terrorist organizations—as many as forty-four of them were then active, he reports—had gained a stranglehold on virtually the entire Valley. "The people," he writes,

> had been asked to surrender their passports because they described the passport-holders as Indians. The shopkeepers were ordered to paint their hoardings green, hoist flags, write slogans and observe "hartals" whenever calls in this regard were given. [The terrorists'] "diktat" was law, and the punishment was stoning, arson or even a bullet.
>
> The public were also instructed not to pay taxes. They were only too happy to obey. The State machinery was incapable, and even unwilling, to collect even routine taxes like entertainment tax and excise duty. . . .[48]

Practically all organized sectors of society in the Valley, he says, had been infiltrated by terrorists and subverted; this included the police, the state bureaucracies, the hospital administration, the courts, the bar associations, and the press.[49] The groundwork for this virtual takeover of the Valley by subversive Islamic elements was laid, he argues, years earlier. In spite of his repeated warnings, he says, both the State and federal governments had permitted the steady and sinister efforts of these elements to displace the tolerant brand of traditional Kashmiri Islam in the minds of Kashmiris and to plant in its place the seeds of Islamic fanaticism. He quotes a poem, for instance, that had been prescribed for use at the Class III level in the 150 schools and *madrasahs* run by the government-tolerated Jama'at-i-Islami organization:

> Little children, be very calm,
> I will tell you what is Islam.
> You may be few and without army.
> But you must fight for Islam.[50]

Jagmohan describes Pakistan's direct aiding and abetting of this subversion of the Valley after 1989 as "frenzied." It

> provided not only moral, political and propaganda support to the subversionists in the Valley, as it itself admitted, but also actively helped them in training in guerrilla warfare and techniques of contemporary terrorism. Batches after batches of the Kashmiri youth were trained in POK and Pakistan. Sophisticated weapons and finances were made available. A strong underground network for motivation, recruitment and guidance was set up. . . . An overall strategy was also worked out to ensure that in the long run Kashmir fell like a ripe apple in the lap of Pakistan. The operation was largely conceived, controlled, and directed by the Inter Services Intelligence of Pakistan, which virtually functioned as a "state within a state."[51]

Jagmohan strives to document his account of Pakistan's role in the subversion of Kashmir with a lengthy description of the Pakistan army's so-called Operation Topac, a multiphased master plan for covert action, supposedly hatched in April 1988 by the military dictator Zia-ul Haq. The basic objective of this plan, Jagmohan avers,

> was to make Kashmir a part of Pakistan. What Pakistan could not achieve through the wars of 1947–48, 1965 and 1971 had to be achieved through an amalgam of subterfuge, subversion, force and religious fundamentalism.[52]

Jagmohan acknowledges at the end of his discussion that Operation Topac's actual authorship has been questioned in some quarters and that the possibility exists that it was hatched by Indian rather than by Pakistani intelligence. Who hatched it, he insists, is "immaterial" since the pattern of Pakistani subversion described in it was real enough.[53] Numerous other Indian writers have reported the Operation without any such disclaimer at all.[54] This compulsion to report as fact any allegation concerning Pakistan's subversive activity in Kashmir is itself revealing. The sponsored-terrorism argument is apparently so tempting that, even when confronted with evidence of its possible inflation by Indian intelligence (itself an obvious attempt at subterfuge), even fictionalized accounts of it continue to be given wide circulation.

The sponsored-terrorism argument runs up against the obvious criticism, as Sumit Ganguly puts it, of being "both incomplete and self-serving." On the one hand, it lets the Indian state off the hook for precipitating the crisis, while, on the other, it

> grossly exaggerates Pakistan's role in fomenting the insurgency. Pakistan's part in aiding the insurgency is incontrovertible; the insurgents have derived the bulk of their weaponry as well as much of their training from Pakistani sources. Their grievances against the Indian state, however, are not of Pakistan's making. Pakistan has simply exploited the existing discontent within a segment of Kashmir's population.[55]

The distinction Ganguly makes has acquired even greater importance in light of President Pervez Musharraf's crackdown on religious militancy in Pakistan in the wake of 11 September and the war on terrorism. Candidly acknowledging that Islam in Pakistan had been "undermined" by religious extremism, Musharraf took a number of unprecedented steps in late 2001 that appeared designed to meet Indian demands that Islamabad rein in anti-Indian militancy in Kashmir.[56] These steps—including the arrest of top leaders of militant groups active in Kashmir—Indians inevitably invoked to support their contention that New Delhi had been right all along about Pakistan's sponsorship of terrorism. If widely accepted, that contention, as we noted at an earlier point in this book, could conflate Kashmiri separatism entirely with terrorism and leave it without any moral claim at all on the world community. It is thus a matter of considerable importance to note that Pakistan, when it comes to the roots of Kashmiri militancy, has more often than not—by Indian as well as by foreign observers—been acquitted of major responsibility for the initial eruption of the separatist insurgency.

In this context, it is important to note also that the Kashmiri separatists in the Valley never wholly acceded to Pakistan's leadership of the separatist movement. Indeed, Pakistan's popularity among the Valley's Kashmiris had in the final years of the twentieth century seemed to most observers to be in fairly sharp decline. There had been for some time much discussion of the apparently widening public rift that had developed not only among the leaders of the Kashmiri dissidents' political umbrella organization—the All Parties Hurriyat (Freedom) Conference (APHC)—but also among the armed militant groups themselves over the separatist movement's ultimate political loyalty. On one side of the argument in the APHC, for instance, was Syed Ali Shah Geelani, the Jama'at-i-Islami chief in the Valley and for long an outspoken defender of Pakistan, whose insistence both on Pakistan's inclusion in any dialogue process undertaken with the Indian government as well as on the limitation of the Kashmiris' right of self-determination to a choice of accession to either India or Pakistan (that it did not extend, in other words, to the right to choose complete independence of both) was apparently not shared by the APHC's other leaders.[57] Among non-APHC leaders on the other side of the issue, by the way, was Shabir Ahmad Shah, whose Democratic Freedom Party, founded in 1998, took a position placing far higher priority on the independence of Kashmir than on the unity of the Islamic *ummah*.[58]

Viewed objectively, the sponsored-terrorism argument does have the merit of recognizing not only the potential importance of religious identity in the Pakistan-Kashmir equation but also the potential for that equation to bear a significant element of cross-border subversion and terrorism. Pakistan is, after all, formally designated an *Islamic* republic; and its government's deliberate sponsorship in recent decades of a host of Islamic revivalist measures, affecting practically every branch of Pakistani society, has increasingly given this designation more than ritual significance. In both symbolic and substantive terms, Pakistan constitutes, in fact, an indispensable geographic *cum* political link between Kashmir and the rest of the Islamic world. No small part of Kashmiri separatism's material (including military) and ideological connection with Islam, let there be no doubt, carries a "made in Pakistan" label; and this label, though of private as well as governmental manufacture, definitely incorporates some measure of Islamic zealotry as well as of terrorism. None of this, of course, establishes unambiguously either that religion supplies the *primary*, much less the *only*, motivation for Pakistan's Kashmir policy or that the Islamic religious bond between Pakistanis and their Kashmiri co-ethnics actually weighs very heavily upon this policy's execution. Neither, for that matter, does it provide a satisfactory set of criteria for determining when separatist militancy actually crosses the line into terrorist activity. These particular reservations certainly complicate, even if they do not rule out, the sponsored-terrorism argument. We return to them when we look at Pakistani state strategy in Kashmir from a different angle at a later point in this chapter.

On the other side of the religious radicalism school of thought is the "soft" perspective, which we label, for convenience sake, the Holy War thesis. The Indian scholar Yoginder Sikand has articulated this thesis most perspicaciously.[59] Like the sponsored-terrorism thesis, this thesis grants prominence both to Islamic radicalism as well as to Pakistan's commanding role in its cross-border orchestration. It does so, however, without demonizing either the militant organizations or their Pakistani patrons. It acknowledges their role in promoting violence, but without either recklessly conflating separatism with terrorism or excusing India of its own major part in the promotion of violence. It maintains that Islamist rhetoric has only limited appeal to Kashmiris, yet it recognizes that it has acquired the appeal it has in no small part by virtue of Indian, not Pakistani, actions. "The increasing salience of the Islamist element within the Kashmiri struggle," writes Sikand,

> can also be seen, in a crucial sense, as a response to the escalation in anti-Muslim violence in India, and the increasing threat to Muslim community identity at the hands of chauvinist Hindu groups in league with the Indian state. . . . The growing insecurity of Muslim life and identity in India had as a natural consequence the assertion of an Islamic identity in Kashmir. To make matters more complicated [there] was the sheer brutality of the Indian army response to the Kashmiri struggle, which was seen by many, by both Kashmiri Muslims as well as Indian Hindus, in purely religious terms.[60]

In short, while the Holy War thesis concedes, like the sponsored-terrorism thesis, that Pakistani militants virtually hijacked Kashmiri separatism for their own—pan-Islamic, non-Kashmiri nationalist—purposes, it doesn't conclude from this either that Kashmiri separatism is a fabrication of Pakistani intelligence services or that it is without a just cause.

Majoritarian Communalism

Between the radicalization of pan-Islamic identity, postulated, for example, in the writings of Jagmohan and Sikand, and the erosion of political democracy, argued by both Bose and Ganguly, there is ample space remaining for still other understandings of Kashmiri Muslim separatism. Absent thus far from all but Sikand's analysis, for instance, is an explanation that gives serious attention, even if not exclusive emphasis, to the interplay in the Kashmir conflict of religious identities in *Indian* society. Islamic communalism, in some cases in its most demonized and terrorist-overlain form, crops up conspicuously in all of the arguments we have already examined; but its converse—Hindu communalism—is practically absent in two of them (Jagmohan, Ganguly); and in a third (Bose) it is portrayed almost solely as a relatively discrete and politically *peripheral* phenomenon associated with the Hindu nationalist Bharatiya Janata Party and its ideological fellow travelers—the so-called *sangh parivar.* Omitted from all but Sikand's analysis is the possibility that, for India as well as for Pakistan, religious identity operates powerfully in the political mainstream—that for the alleged majoritarian communalism of Pakistan, in other words, there may exist an equally paramount Indian analogue.[61]

Ayesha Jalal considers Kashmir in relation to the theme of majoritarian (Hindu) communalism in her controversial study, *Democracy and Authoritarianism in South Asia.*[62] In this comparative examination of the political development of India, Pakistan, and Bangladesh, Jalal unveils a biting critique of South Asian–style democracy, which, in her treatment of it, retains few if any redeeming qualities. She rejects the "general scholarly view," visible in Ganguly's discussion of democratic deinstitutionalization, that the roots of democracy's failures in India are relatively recent. For Jalal, Indian democracy has always been more formal than substantive, and far more than institutional atrophy is at fault. She argues that it was independent India and Pakistan's joint failure to replace what she labels "the bureaucratic authoritarianism inherent in the colonial state structure" that must be held mainly responsible for the sordid postindependence political records of both states.[63]

Distinguishing Jalal's review of the Kashmir problem from most other discussions of it is her placement of Hindu communalism high on the list of the most important factors accounting for the Kashmiri Muslims' drift toward separatism. Already apparent in New Delhi's Kashmir policy in the initial phases of the Kashmir dispute, she observes, Hindu communalism rose by the 1980s to be a dominant, even if only implicit, theme in it. While Hindu right-wing parties from Jammu and northern India were themselves directly responsible for giving "a saffron colouring to the politics of the state," the Congress Party–led center's "throttling of democratic aspirations in the valley" went hand-in-hand with "an invidious policy of turning a blind eye to, if not actually provoking," these efforts. "Majoritarian communalism, after all," she writes, "has been since the early 1980s New Delhi's favourite ideological weapon against movements of regional dissidence."[64] Highlighted in Jalal's account is the steady decline of India's increasingly formalistic secularism in the face of the calculated deployment by India's ostensibly secular leaders of an at least implicitly Hindu communal card. While she concedes that separatism in Kashmir has multiple roots, and that these include "the repeated denial of the political as well as the economic and social rights of citizenship," Jalal asserts that it was the *combination* of these "with the inversion of secularism to promote a crude form of Hindu communalism that [prompted Kashmiris] to agitate for complete independence from India."[65]

Jalal's version of the Kashmir problem's roots, in sharp contrast with Jagmohan's, focuses almost exclusively on developments *internal* to India. Scarcely anything is said, in fact, about its *international* (meaning Pakistan-sponsored) aspect. The burden of her argument is to cast the Kashmiri separatist uprising beginning in the late 1980s as a *popular* movement, fueled by *Indian* waywardness. Pakistan's complicity is acknowledged, but Jalal's brief reference to it clearly seeks to move the spotlight elsewhere. "Seeing India's troubles as gifts from abroad," she observes,

> is a standard line of defence. But in the past Kashmir has led to military confrontations between India and Pakistan without a widespread popular revolt against the union. So Pakistan's new found prowess in masterminding the recent Kashmiri revolt, even if conceivable, cannot be an adequate explanation for the unprecedented developments that have activated a people, long the butt of criticism for expecting others to fight their battles.[66]

Jalal's comment risks misconstruing the actual religious dynamic of the Kashmir dispute: Religious identity clearly makes its way into this dispute along a number of paths, not all of them originating in India and not all of them a product of New Delhi's ruthless sponsorship of Hindu communalism. Much more noteworthy, however, is the contribution her version of events makes to solving the puzzle of religious identity in the Kashmir dispute. Framing the issue of religion's role in Kashmir as Jalal has done it corrects the barefaced lopsidedness of the sponsored-terror-ism argument, as expressed by Jagmohan. It also offers necessary amend-ment to the heedlessly secularist arguments, like those of Ganguly and Bose, for whom matters of religious identity—especially on the Indian side of the border—are considered merely accessory to the fact of demo-cratic decline. Jalal's discussion compels us to recognize that the threat of religious militancy runs in more than one direction, that ostensibly secular institutions may mask religious motivations, and that when it comes to the Kashmiri Muslims, in particular, their religious identity may serve them no less as shield than as sword.

Submergence of Subnational Identity

Self-consciously approaching the subject of Kashmir from a postmodernist point of view, Navnita Chadha Behera provides a me-ticulously researched, theoretically sophisticated, and elaborately drawn discussion of the relationship between political violence and Kashmiri cultural identity.[67] She develops themes consistent in at least certain respects with the arguments of some of the other writers we've exam-ined (most notably Bose, Sikand, and Jalal); but in focusing directly upon the matter of identity, in both its religious and ethnic forms, and in mounting an argument that India's nationalist discourse, centrist ideol-ogy, unitary political institutions, and interventionist strategies bear most of the responsibility for the emergence of Kashmiri political alienation and separatism, she makes the most persuasive case yet for an under-standing of the Kashmir dispute that is based squarely on *culture*, in-cluding its *religious* derivatives, and the *clash* of cultures.

Behera's argument runs as follows:

- Hindu and Muslim identities in precolonial India were heterodox and flexible, only loosely bordered, and lacked a strong sense of "self" and "other." Hindu-Muslim group rivalry, as such, did not exist.
- The colonial era brought with it to India a much-strengthened sense of collective identity, orthodoxy, and territoriality, greatly reinforced by census enumeration and development of the vernacular lan-guages. Of particular importance, "it forced individuals and com-

munities to choose *one* aspect of their identity, in this case religion, over all others by prioritizing them in ascending order."[68]

- The colonial era also introduced India to a new form of political authority—the highly centralized, unitary, sovereign state—and thereby created a fundamental disconnect between the modern Indian state and the complex cultural mosaic of traditional Indian society. The logic of the modern nation-state drives it to identify itself with only one cultural identity and to deny political space to all others. At bottom, it is inherently intolerant.
- Nehru's vision of modern India was secular and pluralist; but his unquestioning acceptance of the European model of statehood contradicted his vision and created a paradox: Conceptually secular and pluralist, he was driven nevertheless to construct a strong state, a prerequisite for which was the cultural unification of India in a manner "which did not fit the pluralities and diversity of Indian society."[69]
- In independent India, subnational identities soon found themselves viewed with suspicion and their political claims subordinated to the centralizing Indian state.
- With the Indian state seeming to adopt a majoritarian or even sectarian character, these subnational identities (including, of course, that of the Kashmiri Muslims), threatened with marginalization or worse, naturally turned to violence.

One additional component of Behera's argument needs to be noted. Much of her book, in fact, targets not merely the majoritarian-inclined central state but the similarly inclined subnational identities who, in seeking to recover their own political space, "merely reproduce the hierarchical social and political conditions they seek to escape, and in its turn the state with all its instrumentalities provides the rationale for further fragmentation of identities."[70] In developing this point, Behera conducts a searching analysis of the contending subnational identities of Jammu and Kashmir State and of the undoubtedly majoritarian (hence, further fragmenting) Sunni Muslim and Kashmiri-speaking impulses of its National Conference government. Her study is thus unique in the attention paid not only to the clash between national and subnational cultural identities but also to the clash among rival subnational cultural identities (Hindu, Muslim, Buddhist) *within* Jammu and Kashmir. Behera thus recognizes (like Jalal and Sikand) that religion's entry into the Kashmir dispute can come from *Indian* state-building strategies, driven at least in part by majoritarian Hindu communalism, as readily as it can come from Pakistan's. She also recognizes, and dwells at length upon, the fact that *Muslim* majoritarian communalism welded to the state-building strategy of Jammu and Kashmir's own local Muslim rulers can spawn its own destructive and fragmenting species of religious politics. She reminds us, in other words, that in the multilevel politics of Kashmir, their religious identity may serve Kashmiri Muslims no less as sword than as shield.

Notable in Behera's study is that it poses the problem of religious identity in regard to Kashmir in a way that avoids crude stereotypes of religious fanaticism, whether Hindu or Muslim, and that steers examination of the roots of discord in Kashmir in a direction where dispassionate and impartial discussion of the issues has at least some prospect of survival. That is not a small accomplishment. For our immediate purposes, however, her study signals the importance of religious identity in the state-building strategies of India and Pakistan. India, no less than Pakistan, is actively engaged in attempts to shape or, at least, to sustain religious identities in Kashmir. The reasons for India's engagement in this process, like those of Pakistan, require clearer definition. Needed, then, is closer inspection of the role of religious identity in the state strategies toward Kashmir of both India and Pakistan.

Faultline Politics III—Religion in State Strategies Toward Kashmir

Shifting the focus from separatism's roots to the state strategies of India and Pakistan enables us to reconsider, from a sharply different angle, the manner in which religious identity gains entry into the Kashmir dispute. We are concerned here, once again, not merely with seeking to define the Kashmir strategies of India and Pakistan, in both their declared and undeclared forms, but with taking careful note of how differences in the representation or depiction of these strategies lend themselves to radically different understandings of religion's role in the dispute. We begin with Pakistan.

Religion in Pakistan's State Strategy

Pakistan's *declared* policy on Kashmir, modified but never abandoned over five decades, has had the following objectives:

- to promote the notion, formally acknowledged in United Nations Security Council resolutions of 13 August 1948 and 5 January 1949, that the state of Jammu and Kashmir has been disputed territory continuously since the end of British rule over the subcontinent and that this standing cannot be unilaterally discarded by either party;
- to insist that resolution of the dispute can be achieved only by securing the right of self-determination for the Kashmiri people via conduct of a free and impartial plebiscite;
- to confine interpretation of the proposed plebiscite to a strictly bifold choice of permanent accession to either Pakistan or India, thus denying a potential third option of independence for both; and
- to champion the necessity for continued international involvement in the Kashmir dispute, whether in the form of mediation, peacekeeping, or plebiscite administration.

In the foreground among these objectives has been Pakistan's overt activity to secure the Kashmiris' alleged right of self-determination through conduct of an internationally supervised plebiscite. Exclusion from that right of a third—independence—option implies rather strongly, however, that Pakistan, like India, covets Kashmir for itself and that its policy is, therefore, more territorially irredentist than politically liberationist in motivation. The ideological basis for the irredentist sentiment—the belief that Pakistan must somehow "recover" or "redeem" territory lost to it in 1947—is, of course, the so-called Two Nation Theory. This is the idea, espoused by Pakistan's founding fathers in the years preceding partition and independence, that British India's Muslim and Hindu confessional groups constituted separate nations, destined to claim fully independent states of their own. In effect, it conflated *religious* identity with *national* identity, thus denying alternative claims to Kashmir based either on secular or ethno-linguistic grounds. In this idea lie practically irrefutable grounds, of course, for the contention that Islamic religious identity—and not merely concern for the unalloyed self-determination of Kashmiris—stands presently among the determinants of Pakistan's Kashmir policy. The separatist uprising now in its second decade, since its heterogeneous mix of motivations challenges the claims to Kashmir of *both* India and Pakistan, has put Pakistan's policy, along with India's, under severest scrutiny.[71] For the Indians, in the meanwhile, Pakistan's covert and *undeclared* policy of material aid to the uprising has clinched the case for the irredentist motivation.

Pakistan: External National Homeland State?

Islamic religious identity is clearly implicated in Pakistan's Kashmir policy, in both its declared and undeclared forms. In its declared form, religious identity supplies what Pakistanis insist was the legitimate, principled basis for British India's partition in 1947 and that continues to warrant the conduct of a plebiscite embodying the right of self-determination. When it comes to the undeclared form of Pakistan's Kashmir policy, religious identity is more a practical instrument of statecraft—a convenient means, in other words, both for mobilizing popular support (among Kashmiris and Pakistanis) as well as for undermining the adversary's hold on coveted territory. Beyond that, however, the picture we have of religious identity's relationship to policy remains disappointingly murky. Is it yet possible to discern an alternative and perhaps more satisfying way to characterize religion's salience in this policy?

The first point to be made here is that Pakistan's policy on Kashmir, declared and undeclared, is consistent in its main parts with the definition of what Rogers Brubaker calls an "external national homeland" state. The nationalisms of such states, he avers,

> assert states' right—indeed their obligation—to monitor the condition, promote the welfare, support the activities and institutions, assert the rights, and protect the interests of "their" ethnonational kin in other states. Such claims are typically made when the ethnonational kin in question are seen as threatened by the nationalizing (and thereby, from the point of view of the ethnonational kin, de-nationalizing) policies and practices of the state in which they live. . . . A state becomes an external national "homeland" when cultural or political elites construe certain residents and citizens of other states as co-nationals, as fellow members of a single transborder nation, and when they assert that this shared nationhood makes the state responsible, in some sense, not only for its own citizens but also for ethnic co-nationals who live in other states and possess other citizenships.[72]

As Brubaker employs the concept, the "homeland" need not be the actual (recent or ancestral) homeland of the targeted national minority. Neither is it necessary that the minority think of the external state in any way as its homeland. What *is* required, according to him, is only that the external state *act* like a homeland.[73] Now, the homeland state's actions need not involve the threat or use of force, and they may not be, in the strict sense, irredentist—that is, as in Pakistan's case, where it is the self-determination of Kashmiris via plebiscite that is ostensibly sought, they need not be aimed specifically at the physical recovery of lands or peoples considered to have been stranded under alien rule. But, according to Brubaker, neither force nor irredentism is excluded from the practical repertoire of the homeland state; and, what is more, the *host* state of the targeted national minority, engaged in what Brubaker calls a "representational struggle" both with the minority and the homeland adversary, is virtually bound to depict the actions of the minority itself "as actually or potentially disloyal," and those of the homeland state "as actually or potentially irredentist."[74]

It has been Pakistan's fate, in a way, to have awakened to its own fragile independence in 1947 predestined to play the part of external homeland and, thus, to have been allotted both the opportunities and representational liabilities implied by that. In staking at the outset a moral claim to "ownership" of Kashmir by virtue of its Muslim demographic majority, Pakistan's founders bequeathed to subsequent Pakistani leaders a vision of Pakistan as an "incomplete" state and of Kashmir as the "unfinished business" of partition. Pakistani inheritors of this vision have been free, of course, to play the part of external homeland in any number of ways, involving many different levels and kinds of moral and material support for their Kashmiri coreligionists. But their freedom has been constrained, it is only reasonable to assume, by the compulsions stemming from performance of the role itself—that is, from engagement in the generally triangular struggle that exists among Pakistan, India, and the Kashmiri Muslim national minority. Seen from this angle, the infusion of religious identity into Pakistan's Kashmir strategy responds, at least in part, to a structural imperative for the existence of which Pakistan is not solely responsible. The alleged Islamic fundamentalist conspiracy at work in Kashmir, to put it more crudely, is not entirely a home brew.

In seeking to portray in the most accurate terms possible the linkage that exists today between Pakistan and Kashmiri separatism, we are thus faced with the need to move our examination very cautiously through what Brubaker terms an "arena of struggle"—the nexus of a highly conflictive set of relationships that binds India, Pakistan, and the various peoples of Kashmir in a continuous, often ruthless, and high-stakes contest in which what often matters most is which side's representation of the contest wins the larger or more influential audience. These competing representations are mined with semantic explosives: One side's "terrorists," reconfigured by the other, mutate at the blink of an eye into "freedom-fighters"; what the one describes as "planned genocide" and "inhuman atrocity" is, in the other's view, the wholly justified and pragmatic response to criminal, religiously fanatic, and foreign-backed insurgency; and even the appropriateness of employing the word "dispute" when speaking of Kashmir is itself in contention!

A second point is that it would be a serious mistake to think that Pakistan's external homeland strategy, assuming, of course, we agree this fairly describes Pakistan's approach to Kashmir, ruled out any substantial future changes either in its objectives in regard to Kashmir or in the means for achieving them. Conceded by practically all analysts of the Kashmir problem, including most Indians, is that the content of Pakistan's Kashmir policy has, in fact, varied enormously over the years. So, too, has the religious content of that policy. The reason for this is that the merger of Islamic religious identity with Pakistan's Kashmir policy is not now and has never been a simple, straightforward, or isolated process. It has taken place in an international environment of intense triadic struggle, involving India and the Kashmiris along with Pakistan, where each side, to return again to Brubaker's language, engages in continuous "reciprocal interfield monitoring"[75]—a watch on the competing interpretations, representations, and misrepresentations of the other two—that periodically requires both active and reactive policy adjustments. It has also taken place, it is exceedingly important to recognize, in an environment of intense struggle among competing interpretations and points of view *within* the homeland state—within Pakistan, in other words. In this dynamic and complex kind of situation, religion's role in Pakistan's Kashmir policy has always necessarily been fixed, not simply in compliance with some abstract moral imperative or reified notion of Islamic identity, but rather in relation to changing religious *and* secular circumstances both internal and external to Pakistan.

Pakistan's Kashmir Policy: Revisionist Voices

In spite of Kashmir's transparent Islamic connection with Pakistan, the fact is that there is not today and has never been in Pakistan a uniform view of Kashmir's importance to Pakistan. Pakistanis have, in fact, never ceased to question either the actual validity of their country's bond with Kashmir or the requirement of their continuing sacrifice on Kashmir's

behalf. Indeed, nothing approximating unconditional societal endorsement of Pakistan's Kashmir policy has ever been achieved. Sharp disagreement over the proper course of action for Pakistan to pursue in
regard to Kashmir surfaced in Pakistan, in fact, even before Kashmir's
accession to India at the end of October 1947. When preparations got
under way in Pakistan during that month to lay forcible claim to the
state by transporting several thousand armed Pashtun tribal raiders from
the North West Frontier Province to the state border, there was marked
reluctance in some quarters of the civil bureaucracy and within the upper ranks of the Pakistan army to lend support to the proposed invasion.
In a book published in 1983, A. H. Suharwardy, a retired Pakistani civil
servant, complained bitterly, for instance, that "[t]he story of tribal invasion was not one merely of bad planning but of no planning at all."
Volunteers, he said, "met discouragement almost at every step from the
Pakistan Army as well as [from] many high-placed Muslim civil officers. . . . [T]he attitude of many senior Pakistani officers was not only
unhelpful but also enigmatic." The attitude, in particular, of the defense
secretary at the time, Iskandar Mirza, "was one of active opposition to
any interference in the Kashmir State. . . . Many senior officers of the
Pakistan Army . . . neither bothered nor helped in the least."[76] Mirza,
who later (1955–1958) served as president of Pakistan, made no secret
of his lack of sympathy for the objectives of the tribal invasion.[77] The
Pakistan army command, even after Kashmir's accession to India and in
a period when the army's involvement in Kashmir was gradually deepening, clearly remained of two minds about it. Conceding that Pakistani
denials of involvement in Kashmir in the period immediately before and
after accession could not stand up to scrutiny, Ayesha Jalal, quoting
Western diplomatic sources, argues nevertheless that the "more revealing" fact was

> the reluctance of the Pakistani army command to commit itself firmly
> in the Kashmir war. It instead wanted a cease fire and until that could be
> negotiated wished the tribesmen "good luck." Pakistani officers not in-
> volved in the fighting in Kashmir were of the view that the tribesmen
> were "doing well against the Indian Army" and that so long as they
> stuck to the tactics deployed against British troops they would "cause
> continual embarrassment and a steady toll of casualties." *These atti-
> tudes mark the beginnings of a split within the Pakistani army com-
> mand: between those who wanted a direct involvement in Kashmir and
> those who opposed such a course.*[78]

The deep division of opinion over Kashmir visible within the Pakistan bureaucracy and army command in the earliest moments of the Kashmir dispute survived the First India-Pakistan War (1947–1949) to become almost immediately thereafter an explosive ingredient of domestic and foreign policy debate in Pakistan. Soon after General Mohammad Ayub Khan's appointment as commander-in-chief of the Pakistan army in January 1951, the division surfaced, in spectacular fashion, in the so-called Rawalpindi Conspiracy—an alleged plot to overthrow the central government of Pakistan. The government, acting on the recommendation of Ayub and Secretary of Defense Mirza, announced detection of the plot in March 1951. Following an eighteen-month closed trial, the proceedings of which have never been released, fifteen of the accused (eleven military officers and four civilians) were sentenced to prison. Included among them and the alleged ringleader was the chief of general staff Major General Akbar Khan, a celebrated war hero who as a colonel in 1947 had fought in Kashmir under the pseudonym "General Tariq." At the time of the arrest, responsibility for the planned coup was laid at the doorstep of international communism. Later it was given an internal—and less sinister—emphasis. In his autobiography, Ayub Khan, who by the time of its writing had earned the distinction of having himself been a key figure in the overthrow of Pakistan's constitutional government, conveniently wrote the Rawalpindi Conspiracy off largely (and vaguely) as a product of discontent with a civilian-led government "which failed to discharge its functions properly."[79] All of the military men among the accused, however, not only Akbar Khan, were veterans of the fighting in Kashmir; and widespread at the time of the trial was the belief that they were crushed for differing with the government over its Kashmir policy.[80] The government had accepted the cease-fire arranged by the United Nations. Some believe that Ayub Khan, who had never served in Kashmir, was selected for the post of commander-in-chief partly because of his sympathy for the government's "moderate" Kashmir policy.[81] The coconspirators, in contrast, seem to have favored resumption of the war with India and viewed the government's caution as a betrayal of principle. While some aspects of the Rawalpindi Conspiracy remain shrouded in mystery, it clearly appears to have been, at least in part, "a tussle," as Jalal puts it, "between two divergent perspectives on the Kashmir dispute within the Pakistani defence establishment."[82]

Only once since the Rawalpindi Conspiracy case has dissent over

Kashmir policy erupted again in Pakistan in an equally dramatic fashion.* The occasion was the signing in the Soviet Union on 10 January 1966 by Ayub Khan (by then president of Pakistan) of the Tashkent Declaration, formally ending the second India-Pakistan war. Having been fed for some time a diet of central government commentary on that conflict dilating both the sinister intentions of the Indian foe and the unprecedented military triumphs of the Pakistani armed forces, the Pakistani public was simply not prepared for the pallid results of the Soviet-mediated talks. The declaration itself said almost nothing about Kashmir, except to note that it had been discussed and that each side had put forth its respective position. Ayub's politically ambitious foreign minister at the time, Zulfikar Ali Bhutto, having already won considerable public acclaim for his seemingly more resolute stand against India, quit the cabinet "and published a statement in which he said that the Tashkent Declaration was not an end in itself and that the slate would not be sponged clean until the people of Kashmir had exercised their right of self-determination."[83] Government propaganda organs struggled to put the best face possible on the "spirit of Tashkent"; however, as the British historian Herbert Feldman remarked, "feeling against [Ayub] was harsh, particularly in the armed forces and among those who had lost menfolk in the fighting." Public protests, violent demonstrations, and riots occurred in a number of Pakistani cities. Several people were killed in police firings and hundreds, mainly students, were arrested. Reportedly, fourteen Pakistani Navy officers were eventually sentenced to life imprisonment in consequence of their opposition to the Tashkent Declaration.[84]

The infrequency during the past fifty odd years in Pakistan of major flare-ups of public dissent directed specifically against the government's Kashmir policy cannot be taken as a reliable index of public (elite or mass) support of it. Long stretches of martial or quasi martial law have ensured that whatever dissent existed within ruling groups at any particular time over this quintessentially sensitive matter would be muted and, for the most part, concealed from public view. Mass opinion has had few unregulated outlets and was always subject to government orchestration. Media suppression has been the rule, and there has never been in Pakistan a tradition of autonomous parliamentary investigation

---

*There were signs early in 2002 that the extraordinary pressures Pakistan was facing both from India and the United States to end its support of armed militancy in Kashmir might result in a public showdown over Kashmir policy.

and oversight to serve as a check on the government of the day's version of the facts. Indeed, for practically the entire span of Pakistan's national life, open dissent from the government's declared Kashmir policy has risked exposing the dissenter to embarrassing rebuke or even to the charge of treason.

Nevertheless, evidence gathered from the author's interviews in recent years with a substantial sampling of senior Pakistani opinion leaders provides strong grounds for the judgment that, whether or not there existed in the past anything approaching a Pakistani consensus on the subject of Kashmir, no such consensus exists now.*

To be sure, Pakistan's Kashmir policy was described by some of the author's interlocutors, especially those of the older, partition-era generation, as nearly sacrosanct. A number of them gave vent, in fact, to patriotic rhetoric that clearly implied that anyone who deviated sharply from this policy was disloyal or at least badly misled. One individual, a retired senior military officer, went so far as to insist in a fairly well-attended forum that any Pakistani known to have deviated in this manner would be (*should* be was implied) lynched! Striking, however, was the nearly universal tendency of most informants, including some at the highest levels of government, to allow for serious revision—in a few instances the wholesale discard—of the official position on Kashmir.**

One of the milder but most widely shared of these revisionist views, one that had the support of informants representative of virtually every point on the ideological compass, pertained to the plebiscite. A unitary

---

*The basis for the assessment of current Pakistani public opinion given here rests, in part, on my four research visits to Pakistan, totaling about four months in the field, between November 1996 and December 1997. During the course of these visits, I interviewed or held formal discussions on the subject of Kashmir, often in seminar format, with over 140 individuals (senior-level diplomats, army officers, government officials, political leaders, journalists, academics, and professional analysts) in five urban centers (Islamabad, Rawalpindi, Lahore, Karachi, and Sialkot) and in Azad Kashmir. Two of these visits I undertook as a member of an independent study team commissioned by the Kashmir Study Group. Most of the interviews and discussions during these two visits were accomplished jointly with one or more other members of the study team. Apart from the author, the team consisted of former ambassador Howard B. Schaffer, Dr. Joseph E. Schwartzberg, Dr. Ainslie T. Embree, and Dr. Charles H. Kennedy. The team's co-authored report on its spring 1997 visits to both India and Pakistan was privately printed and distributed in October 1997 with the title *1947–1997: The Kashmir Dispute at Fifty: Charting Paths to Peace*.

**To ensure promised anonymity, the identities of the author's informants have been concealed.

plebiscite embracing all regions of the state of Jammu and Kashmir, as had been envisioned in the original UN Security Council resolutions, now struck practically everyone as impractical. Higher government officials, in particular, seemed to consider it essentially a dead issue. In its place many of the author's respondents, including some influential persons notorious for extremely conservative opinions on the Kashmir question, expressed approval for regional or even district-level plebiscites that would allow Kashmiri Muslim sentiment in the Valley to be separately registered and, potentially, justify breakup of the state along ethnoreligious lines. This would amount to resurrecting something akin to the "regional plebiscites" proposal, never formally accepted by Pakistan, made by UN mediator Sir Owen Dixon in 1950.[85] This proposition is probably less revisionist than appears on the surface, however, since the government of Pakistan, according to comments made to the author by an official of the Foreign Office, had itself already moved quietly in that direction. On 18 January 1994, he said, Islamabad had presented the government of India with an unofficial "nonpaper"—one of two such documents conveyed to Indian leaders at the time detailing proposed Pakistani terms for resuming talks with India—dealing with modalities for holding a plebiscite. One of its paragraphs, he said, expressed Pakistan's willingness to consider new and innovative methods to ascertain the will of the people. This meant, he observed, that the method of measuring the popular will was negotiable.[86]

Unquestionably radical, however, was the suggestion, made by a surprising number of very senior—both retired and active—members of Pakistan's bureaucratic and political establishment (albeit by a small minority of the author's interlocutors), that the whole idea of a plebiscite might well be jettisoned and, instead, that the LOC be endorsed as the permanent international boundary between Pakistan and India. This proposal has the status of conventional wisdom on the Indian side, of course; but in the contemporary Pakistani political milieu, it bordered on heresy. If its appeal were to spread, Pakistan's homeland strategy would obviously soon be in tatters.

Admittedly, the author's informants displayed varying degrees of firmness and enthusiasm for the LOC option. A prominent leader of an opposition political party put the most bluntly favorable reading on it: If Punjab and Bengal could be divided at partition in 1947, he asked, why couldn't Kashmir be divided now at the LOC? Why should a small fraction of the region's population, he added, hold a billion hostage?[87] A key member of the ruling Pakistan Muslim League party offered the tantalizing speculation that perhaps "down the road"— and provided India met other conditions—he too could see the LOC as a permanent border between India and Pakistan.[88] A retired army general, on the other hand, took a rather more equivocal position: Pakistan could not get the whole of Kashmir, he conceded, but the Valley had to be granted self-determination. "Maybe," he said, "Pakistan can have the Valley. But one must be realistic." Getting the Valley would be "*very* difficult." At the same time, the Valley's retention by India *on India's present terms*, he observed, was out of the question. Some kind of autonomy for Kashmir was possible, however. The Valley could aspire to *maximum* autonomy in some sort of loose federation. Kashmir as a whole should have a "special status."[89] Taking this last point a step further, a senior-serving diplomat among the author's Pakistani informants indicated that even Pakistan's traditional interpretation of the plebiscite—that it should offer the people of Kashmir the strictly bi-fold choice of permanent accession of the state to either Pakistan or India—was up for reconsideration. The third option of independence, he averred, was being given serious attention in Pakistan *at the highest level.*[90]

Variations notwithstanding, the Pakistanis interviewed by the author evinced as a group surprising willingness to rethink Pakistan's longstanding official position on Jammu and Kashmir and, where necessary, to shed or at least remodel those aspects of it that had proven unproductive. Uncompromising resistance to any and all changes to Pakistan's Kashmir policy, in other words, had few takers. For many of those interviewed, apparently, the precise nature of the bonds of Islamic religious identity between Pakistan and the Kashmiri Muslims were negotiable (as, indeed, was the Two Nation Theory itself).

The above opinions were drawn from a relatively modest sampling of a tiny, policy-oriented, and, for the most part, sophisticated elite class. The opinions of this class on the subject of Kashmir obviously may diverge from those of ordinary Pakistanis, who for the most part are likely to have a less secular outlook on life and whose exposure to ideas on Kashmir differing from the government line may well be quite limited. As often as not, however, the author's interlocutors reported a growing *convergence* between elite and mass opinion on the subject of Kashmir. Many expressed the view, in fact, that the principal trend in Pakistani mass opinion about Kashmir, far from being blind hostility for India, was sharply declining interest in Kashmir. Many Pakistanis, commented a prominent member of the legal profession, were starting to feel that their *own* future was jeopardized by continuing confrontation with India over Kashmir. The conventional emphasis on Kashmir's liberation, he said, was "not as resolute as it used to be."[91] Pakistani interest in Kashmir has diminished, claimed a prominent journalist. At Kashmir-related events, one saw only small audiences and television coverage was modest. "There is almost no public support for the Kashmir cause," he asserted, "*anywhere* in Pakistan." What support for it there was existed only in small pockets in a few urban centers such as Lahore. Pakistani youth as a class, he said, were not interested. Kashmir, he claimed, had not been a key issue in either the 1990 or 1993 elections, nor had it figured much in the 1997 elections. Pakistanis, he declared, were amenable to change over Kashmir.[92] Agreeing with that sentiment, a prominent opposition political leader observed that there is not as large a body of Pakistanis thinking emotively about Kashmir today as there was twenty years ago. There was awareness now of its cost to the economy, he said, and that there was need for bold India-Pakistan initiatives.[93]

Claimed by several respondents was the existence of significant *regional* variations in public outlook on Kashmir. Among Sindhis, stated a senior journalist, echoing others, Kashmir was probably not an issue. At the popular level, he suggested, it probably wasn't much of an issue either in Baluchistan or the North West Frontier Province. Even in the southern Punjab, he added, there was little interest in Kashmir. It was only in northeastern Punjab, especially urban Punjab (and most especially Lahore) where substantial consciousness about Kashmir existed. Lahore was the media center of Pakistan. Residing there were many ethnic Kashmiris. It was a religiously conservative city—and the powerful media organs in Lahore were in the hands of religious and political conservatives. That, he said, was what had kept the Kashmir issue alive.[94]

An Azad Kashmir political figure offered the ironic observation that even in Azad Kashmir support for the Kashmiri Muslim cause on the Indian side of the LOC was far from unqualified. Many Azad Kashmiris, he claimed, favored keeping a fairly low profile in the current difficulties in the Valley. The right-wing Jama'at-i-Islami forces and some youths, he said, did put stress on Azad Kashmir's unity with the Valley. But generally, he insisted, the people of Azad Kashmir were not very enthusiastic about assisting their coreligionists in the Valley if that meant risking themselves.[95]

It would be a serious mistake, I believe, to interpret these somewhat startling observations as evidence that the Pakistan government was on the verge of abdicating its long-standing claim to Kashmir. Heard in Pakistan with considerable frequency, in fact, was the sentiment that normalization of relations with India, no matter what compulsions Pakistan faced, would not translate into any such behavior. Pakistan is "not prepared to yield an inch," declared a retired member of Pakistan's foreign affairs bureaucracy, echoing many of the author's respondents. "Pakistan, for the sake of peace, doesn't have to yield an inch on its Kashmir position." Pakistan, he insisted, will not acquiesce to India's occupation of Kashmir; but it will not go to war. "We are not so down and out that we have to surrender. . . . We are not under that kind of compulsion."[96] It would be just as mistaken, however, to dismiss these observations as the frivolous ruminations of a tiny and unrepresentative minority. They are clearly more than that. They are, in fact, a formidable challenge to the assertion of Pakistan's corporate indivisibility and unswerving commitment to the cause of Kashmir's liberation from Hindu rule. At a minimum, they suggest to us that no examination of the prospects for extricating India and Pakistan from the grip of their dispute over Kashmir should be allowed that attributes Pakistani reticence to compromise to a uniform and mulishly unbending public opinion.

Observe here that the existence in Pakistan of a division of opinion in regard to Kashmir does not rule out the possibility that compromise-minded Pakistanis are finding themselves, in the circumstances prevailing in early 2002, increasingly marginalized—threatened, on the one hand, by domestic Islamic zealots still wedded to the objective of "talibanizing" Pakistan and, on the other, by anti-Indian xenophobes frightened by India's threatening military posture. The war on terrorism, so far anyway, does not appear to have added visibly to religious extremism's appeal in Pakistan, at least not outside of heavily Pashtun-settled areas adjacent to the border with Afghanistan. It has, however, brought India and Pakistan uncomfortably close to the brink of war, a development that could easily precipitate a domestic political crisis. In any event, when it comes to the matter of compromise, the state of public opinion in Pakistan is only one part of a very complex equation in which Indian state strategy also plays a far from insignificant role.

Religion in India's State Strategy

Pakistan's strategy on Kashmir, I argued above, seems to fit reasonably well the stance embodied in Brubaker's model of the external national homeland state. Such a state, to recall our earlier discussion, asserts its responsibility to monitor the conditions, protect the interests, and promote the welfare of ethnonational kin in other states. It justifies its action on grounds of shared nationhood, in particular, when the alleged conationals are deemed threatened by the nationalizing strategy of the host state.

We need now to decide how best to characterize *India's* strategy on Kashmir, especially the manner in which religious identity is incorporated in it.

India: Nationalizing or Supranational State?

One obvious option at hand, already implied, perhaps, in Jalal's depiction of India's "majoritarian communalism," is to apply to India the stance outlined in Brubaker's model of the nationalizing state. "Characteristic of this stance, or set of stances," according to Brubaker,

> is the tendency to see the state as an "unrealized" nation-state, as a state destined to be a nation-state, the state of and for a particular nation, but not yet in fact a nation-state (at least not to a sufficient degree); and the concomitant disposition to remedy this perceived defect, to make the state what it is properly and legitimately destined to be, by promoting the language, culture, demographic position, economic flourishing, or political hegemony of the nominally state-bearing nation.[97]

It is not necessary, explains Brubaker, that the state's nationalizing stance be expressly avowed or articulated. It is enough, he says,

> if policies, practices, symbols, events, officials, organizations, even "the state" as a whole are *perceived* as nationalizing by representatives of the national minority or external national "homeland," even if this characterization is repudiated by persons claiming to speak for the state [emphasis in original].[98]

Neither is it necessary, Brubaker observes, that the nationalizing state pursue a fixed or univocal set of policies or practices. The nationalizing state should be thought of, he suggests, in terms of a dynamically changing field of differentiated and competitive positions or stances adopted by different organizations, parties, movements, or individual figures within and around the state, competing to inflect state policy in a particular direction, and seeking, in various and often mutually antagonistic ways, to make the state a "real" nation-state, the state of and for a particular nation.[99]

Ethnocultural heterogeneity is characteristic of the nationalizing state, says Brubaker, even if it is not an absolute requirement. Also characteristic of such a state, he observes, is the existence in it of a "core nation" or nationality that is understood to "own" the polity and for the promotion of whose specific interests a variety of remedial and partly compensatory actions is believed essential.

The real-world cases that form the basis for Brubaker's model are drawn from the new states of Eastern Europe and the Near East that emerged from the collapse of the Ottoman, Habsburg, and Romanov empires in the second decade of the twentieth century. The comparability of these cases with postcolonial India is, of course, debatable. India clearly shares ethnocultural heterogeneity with them, but scholars of India are deeply divided on the extent to which (or even whether) India is bound to reproduce the West's historical experience—to follow the same developmental trajectory, in other words—of state- and nation-building. At issue is not only the question of whether India even has a core nation to claim ownership of the polity, but also whether Indian state strategies toward peripheral national minorities, such as the Kashmiri Muslims, bear much resemblance to their Western antecedents.[100]

One of the most comprehensive efforts thus far to build a case for India's *divergence* from Western models in this regard, and thus to supply us with another way to look at the India-Kashmir equation, is to be found in Maya Chadda's study of the nexus of separatism and state security strategy in India.[101] In this study, Chadda urges the conception of India as a *supra*national state attempting to manage a complex system of interlocking internal and external power balances through use of a strategy that she calls "relational control." The supranational state, in Chadda's formulation of it, is a relatively impartial or *custodial* entity: it is the instrument or captive of no particular "core" nation. Insofar as any of India's historical "nations" are concerned, the supranational state is, in a sense, "above identity." Its goal is not to "realize" the destiny of any particular subgroup of the polity; rather, it is to guide the modernization of the whole. Relational control, she says, does involve a search for some degree of overarching power but it does not presuppose hegemonism or outward expansionism as inherent state motivation. It is a unique strategy, aimed at the consolidation of the modernizing state but modeled after the "layered order" of the historical Indian state.[102]

The strategy of relational control, says Chadda, has three objectives:

1. To establish influence over the structure of interaction between players, that is, to have some capacity to set the "rules of the game" in conflict and cooperation.
2. To exercise, if possible, a degree of control over the actions of its neighbors, or at least to control the consequences flowing from such actions, if these are seen to be adverse to India's nation-building enterprise.
3. To acquire a degree of leverage over cultural orientation and ideology in the region.[103]

In combination, these objectives are intended "to insulate [India's] nation-building project from any destabilizing development in neighboring countries." Such a development might include, for instance, "threats to the cultural identity of specific ethnocommunities or transborder ethnic conflicts [that] could destabilize the interlocking balance within India. To maintain its own independence and internal stability, India thus recognized the value of having neutral neighboring countries."[104]

Chadda concedes that relational control has a "family resemblance" to hegemony since, like hegemony, "it underlines influence over the policies of a neighbor." According to her, however, it differs fundamentally from hegemony in a number of ways. One is in its purpose. Hegemony, she says, is intrinsically expansionist. Relational control, in contrast, does not presuppose "the existence of homogenized nation-states with hard frontiers of the European variety that translate growing economic or military strength into an extension of influence beyond these frontiers." It does incorporate the elements of unequal power and coercion; but "it does not pre-suppose an European-type nation-state (as the destiny of third world states) and looks at once in both directions, internal and external."[105]

A second way in which relational controls differs from hegemony, she argues, lies in the fact that relational control is not confined to relations between two states. It encompasses relations between a state and nonstate actors (resistance groups, ethnonationalities, opposition parties, and the like); between nonstate actors themselves (e.g., two or more ethnonationalities within a state); or between elements of a transborder ethnonationality that owes allegiance to two or more states.[106]

Relational control, Chadda explains, means a kind of "graded influence, from the ethnolinguistic federal units of the core to the faint strictures implied by bilateralism at the periphery." In developing it, she observes, India's postindependence leadership "recreated in its essentials something similar to the Mandala (meaning concentric circles) system of the Mauryan state."[107] Nehru, she argues, abstracted from the historical record of that pre-Christian era state a number of principles for use in governing modern India. These included, on the one hand, the state's autonomy of the social order—its ability to rise above particular social interests and to retain substantial freedom in the exercise of domestic and foreign policy—and, on the other, the state's creation of "a universal order that transcended specific ideologies and beliefs but did not seek to eliminate or merge them." This "tolerant and inclusive" order accommodated separate caste and religious communities so that "each maintained its distinctive identity but derived it, in large part, through reference to the whole."[108]

When it comes to India's actual application of relational control to Kashmir, Chadda takes the position that this strategy was quite successful—at least up until the 1980s. Contrary to the claims of Kashmiri nationalists, she says, continuing turmoil and protest were not characteristic of New Delhi's relations with Kashmir. In fact, there were lengthy stretches of "relative calm and cooperation."[109] The strategy eventually failed, she admits, "because of the erosion of interlocking balances and New Delhi's failure to democratically integrate the J&K within the Indian union."[110] For the most part, however, responsibility for these developments, she claims, lay not in Indian hands. "What made Mrs. Gandhi throw democratic norms overboard in Kashmir [in the early 1980s]," she avers,

was its status as a disputed territory, Pakistan's never-ending claims to it on the grounds of religion, and the close military cooperation that had developed between Pakistan and the United States. In the face of these unsettling developments, New Delhi simply had to have control over the J&K.[111]

Applied to India, the nationalizing and supranational state models discussed here obviously lead to radically differing interpretations of the Indian state and, in particular, of state strategy toward Kashmir. The nationalizing model suggests the deliberate dilation or extension of an exclusive Indian (Hindu) core identity, by force or otherwise, so that it includes and subsumes all the indigenous ethno-religious identities of the former princely state. The supranational model suggests a relatively benign, inclusive, equilibrium-focused, and state-guided transition to a democratic and secular unity.

In at least one major respect, however, these two models bear a remarkable resemblance: They both incorporate as a norm of state behavior the coercive integration of peripheral ethno-religious minorities. In the case of the nationalizing state, the coercion arises from the core nation's presupposed "ownership" of the state and its efforts to translate this ownership into the creation of a more homogeneous and, thus, "true" nation-state; it is bluntly and unapologetically assimilationist, in other words, at least in its long-term objectives. In the case of the supranational state, the coercion arises from the state's structurally induced power-balancing or equilibrating function and its efforts "to shield the interlocking internal balance from rude exogenous shocks";[112] it, too, is assimilationist, in other words, but only contingently and unintentionally. This means that while motivations may differ, the end result—the more or less compulsory cultural conversion of minorities—does not.

Chadda dismisses this coercive dimension of the supranational state as relatively secondary. While the historical nationalizing states discussed by Brubaker indulged often in the systematic and relatively unrestrained mistreatment of national minorities, Chadda's portrait of the Indian supranational state's behavior toward its minorities, while allowing for the state's misbehavior, clearly relegates it to the background. It surfaces, she claims, mainly when the supranational state consistently mismanages the system of interlocking balances—as the Indian state did, she claims, during the nine years in the decade of the 1980s when India was ruled by Indira Gandhi and then her son Rajiv Gandhi. As a rule, she says, brute force is the "last resort" of the supranational state.[113]

From the standpoint of the Kashmiri Muslims or their Pakistani coreligionists, however, relational control inevitably carries strong symptoms of cultural hegemonism—the involuntary reorientation of "subject peoples," in other words, to the cultural practice and ethos of northern India's Hindi (and Hindu) heartland. The process or dynamic of relational control, whatever it is labeled, is unambiguously and explicitly integrative. As Chadda defines it, the "supranational State must transform historically formed perceptions and patterns among the nesting nations in the service of modern statehood." And this, she says, "gives rise to fluidity in the identity formation driven by constant negotiations." Inherent in relational control also, she adds, is conflict between the supranational state and the nesting ethnonations

> over control of the pace and direction of modernization . . . . As the nesting nations become more politicized, the demands of their elites become more insistent, sometimes aggressively so. The problem for the supranational State then becomes one of maintaining its independence and its capacity to give an overall lead to the State in the face of insistent demands for regional autonomy. In contrast to the first type of conflict, a permanent condition to be found at all stages of the development of the modern state, the second becomes more acute as modernization progresses.[114]

From whatever vantage point and with whatever policy inflection, in other words, relational control clearly involves the *state-led transformation of Kashmiri identity.*

Chadda's discussion of the concept of relational control ascribes to Indian state strategy, especially in the Nehruvian period, a virtually culture-blind and altruistic motivation. Self-aggrandizing nationalism—*Hindu* nationalism, for instance—enters into strategy, from her point of view, only when the rational mechanism of relational control is neglected or misused (as, for instance, during the rule of Indira Gandhi and Rajiv Gandhi). The strategy itself, since it is not driven by nationalism, has no dark side. The effect of this, I think, is to hand India what comes perilously close to a strategic blank check to deal both with neighboring states, such as Pakistan, and with any of the "nesting ethnonations," such as the Kashmiri Muslims. The supranational state simply has no choice, Chadda claims, when it comes to selecting means for maintaining a stable equilibrium of interlocking (internal and external) balances: The occasionally coercive measures it takes are forced upon it, in other words, by the role it plays as overarching central balancer. Power projections are not aimed at dominance, she says, but at the restoration of relational control.[115] That these measures *resemble* hegemonism, Chadda acknowledges; but since seemingly hegemonic impurities among the state's motives find themselves categorized (and, thus, implicitly neutralized) under the heading of relational control, the resemblance gets swept aside, replaced by the claim that the intended purpose of these measures is the quite modest (nonexpansionist and reflexive) one of safeguarding the supranational state's essential autonomy—its ability to govern free of the curse of cultural (especially religious) identity, in other words, and without becoming mired in ethnonational rivalries triggered by the stresses and strains of modernization.

* * *

All of the arguments that we have surveyed in this chapter in relation to Kashmiri cultural identity, separatist motivation, and state strategy have conceded a role in the Kashmir dispute to religious identity. Observed in this survey, however, has been enormous variation both in the portrayal of the role religious identity plays in the dispute and in the overall importance assigned to it. This result was hardly unexpected: It has been one of the main burdens of this chapter, after all, to delineate the ways in which the interpretation of religion's role in the dispute has been deployed as a weapon in the relentless struggle to shape public (national and international) understanding of this dispute. This interpretative struggle, as was suggested in the introduction to this chapter, is not merely an incidental offshoot of the Kashmir dispute—the altogether forgettable spawn, so to speak, of the "chattering classes." On the contrary, it is an integral part of the Kashmir dispute—the part that furnishes it, in fact, with most of its moral as well as a good part of its political significance. How we plot the intersection of religious identity with the dispute over Kashmir determines, to no small extent, where we stand in regard to the dispute as a whole. When It comes to Kashmir, in other words, religion—even when its impact is being most strenuously denied—simply can't be bypassed: It counts a lot.

In the discussion of *kashmiriyat*, for example, we found champions of Kashmiri culture's vaunted religious tolerance and syncretism among both the secular- and religious-minded as well as on both sides of the Hindu-Muslim communal divide. Some of them, however, claimed that the origin of this remarkable cultural ethos lay in Kashmir's Hindu, not in its Islamic past. Most saw this tolerant ethos presently in great jeopardy, albeit the threat, for some, stemmed from radicalized Islam, for others, from radicalized Hinduism, and for still others, from both of these. At least one (Madan), finding deeply rooted Hindu-Muslim animosity and invidious prejudice more abundant in a Kashmiri village than tolerance, implicitly questioned whether *kashmiriyat's* alleged tolerance and syncretism were not entirely fictional imaginings. A finding, on the one hand, that Kashmiri tolerance has its roots primarily in Hinduism lends weight, obviously, to the characterization of Islamic *in*tolerance as the main culprit in Kashmir—a characterization that can be converted, as we saw, into a demand for a Hindu Pandit homeland or, in any event, demonized to the political advantage of the officially secular (Indian) side. A finding, on the other hand, that this tradition of tolerance and religious syncretism was in large part fable, while hardly enough to force assent to Huntington's fault-line thesis, would have to be reckoned a point in its favor.

When it came to the contemporary roots of Kashmiri Muslim separatism, we saw the same kind of representational contest enacted. On the one hand were analyses giving heavy weight among mobilizing variables to cultural identity—in two cases (Jagmohan and Sikand) placing the accent largely on Pakistan-driven Islamic extremism, in another (Jalal) shifting the accent to majoritarian Hindu communalism, in still another (Behera) dividing the accent between Hindu and Kashmiri Muslim majoritarian communalism. On the other hand were analyses that focused almost exclusively on noncultural variables, in Ganguly's case emphasizing about equally both the decay of political institutions and socioeconomic modernization, in Bose's case giving almost exclusive explanatory power to democratic decline. Five of these six particular observers, it may be noted, placed primary or at least equal responsibility for the outbreak of militant violence in Kashmir on India, but only two of them (Ganguly and Bose) appeared to think that domestically orchestrated democratic reforms (less corrupt elections or bolstered federalism, for instance) would be an adequate antidote to the current malaise. With the possible exception of Jagmohan, whose affiliation with the Bharatiya Janata Party obviously suggests a Hindu majoritarian orientation, we encountered in this section of the discussion no unambiguously religious, or religion-favoring, point of view. Absent, in particular, was a voice directly representing the Kashmiri Muslims, whatever might be its ideological perspective. Had one been included, the range of possible motivations would undoubtedly have been extended even further. Nevertheless, it hardly bears mention that the interpretative differences cited here are still simply colossal, and the consequences of choosing one over the other as a guide to private action or public policy can hardly be overstated.

Note, too, that the discussion of Indian state strategy, while focusing for the most part on Maya Chadda's provocative argument, sought to establish that the conceptual design selected for viewing state response to ethno-religious heterogeneity, far from being a choice from among equally neutral analytical instruments, would very likely bear the marks of a fundamental philosophical or ideological commitment. In Chadda's case, this meant that the Indian state's unique and unavoidable strategic balancing mechanism, which she labeled relational control, forced the subordination of religious and other cultural identities to the "culture-blind" requirements of the mechanism itself. The policy implications of such a model, I went to some lengths to point out, are considerable.

At the end of the discussion, however, it must be conceded that a definitive judgment in regard to the weight of religious identity in the Kashmir dispute remains elusive. On the one hand, we are presented with a wealth of reasons for believing that we downgrade the subject of religious identity in the discussion of Kashmir at the peril of our under-standing of it, but on the other, we recognize that we are yet well short of a satisfactory answer from anyone as to its actual material impact on the Kashmir dispute. Conspicuously absent from current accounts, for instance, is reliable and comprehensive data on individual Kashmiri re-ligious orientations and sentiments—data we would need even to begin to generalize confidently about the contemporary political mobilization of religious groups and subgroups in Kashmir. To assemble even pre-liminary data on such topics would clearly require a wide-ranging and intensive research endeavor of the sort largely ruled out under present circumstances.[116]

Thus, an unavoidable conclusion is that the conceptual models re-viewed here do not equip us very well for the main task facing us, that of nailing down either the probability or likely pace and direction of change in the political salience of religious identity to this dispute in the years ahead. Indeed, some of the most pressing questions relating to religious identity are unlikely to be addressed satisfactorily using any of the conceptual frameworks examined in this chapter. These questions include: Is either India or Pakistan—or are both of them—heading into an era of increased religious nationalism, in which the sectarian identities of the peoples of the region will play an even greater role than at present? Are the civilizational fault lines that transect Kash-mir currently deepening, in other words, so that the parties to the Kash-mir dispute will soon have even greater incentive to exploit the susceptibilities to communal rivalry and violence that presumably deepen with them? Is cultural militancy of the religious kind on its way *in* in the region? Or on the way *out?*

The most nettlesome question to emerge unanswered from the discussion so far, however, has less to do with the technical (empirical or conceptual) deficiencies of the theoretical models and arguments we reviewed than with the huge interpretative gaps that surfaced among them. Confronting us is the transparent fact that normative concerns arising from the more or less incommensurable ideological or philosophical stances of the analyst-interpreters are an invasive and insistent presence in all such discussions. Arguments grounded in secular understandings of religious identity—that such identity, for instance, inclines those embraced by it *to an exceptional extent* toward fanaticism and irrationality—are by their nature extremely difficult, if not impossible, to reconcile with those largely empathic with religious thought and behavior. Even if we were cognitively enriched about the religious affinities of Kashmiris, in other words, we might not be inclined to alter the normative path of our present arguments. This stubborn fact unquestionably complicates, if it does not entirely stymie, the mobilizing of a consensus in regard not only to explanation of the conflict's motivation and evolution but also to prescription of its management and resolution. We will have to confront this particular issue in Chapter 4.

It should be clear by now that the summary dismissal of Professor Huntington's clash of civilizations thesis is not warranted by what we now know of the Kashmir case. Contrary to what some of his critics have asserted, this thesis does not rest upon a simple-minded assumption of civilizational solidarity—that the world was grouping itself literally, in other words, into fixed, tightly knit, and uniformly hostile civilizational or religious camps. Huntington was as aware as any of us that Muslim states and groups-within-states more often warred with one another than with representatives of the world's other great religions. Enough has been said, however, to suggest that the Kashmir dispute includes a huge *religious* component. It could hardly be otherwise, since religious identity is virtually bound to figure in the working definition assigned to the dispute by interested foreign powers. The Chinese government, for example, views Kashmir at least in part through a lens tinted with its misgivings over China's chronic problem with separatist violence in the Muslim-majority Xinjiang Uighur Autonomous Region, a sprawling and lightly populated area in western

China that shares a common boundary—as well as a common religious identity—with Kashmir. For its part, the Organization of the Islamic Conference (OIC), a world body charged with the virtually impossible task of representing over fifty politically and socioeconomically diverse societies ostensibly drawn together by a common Islamic bond, has little choice but to trumpet the Kashmiri separatist cause. Indeed, the OIC can scarcely keep Kashmir *off* its agenda if even one of its members (Pakistan) wants it there.

The "world war" of sorts that began in Afghanistan in the final months of 2001 obviously cannot be reduced, any more than the Kashmir dispute, simply to a war of religions. Nevertheless, visible to all but the most obstinate of Huntington's critics (and in spite of strenuous official denials by American leaders) is the hefty element of religious clash that accompanies it. This element is virtually bound to produce ripple effects in nearby Kashmir. We noted, in this connection, the importance to Kashmiri Muslim separatists of the support extended to them not only by immediately adjacent Pakistan but also by other and more distant Muslim states, including Afghanistan. This phenomenon, which Huntington considered under the heading of civilization- or kin-country rallying[117] (and which we examined from different angles in Chapter 2 and in part II of this chapter), entails the provision by coreligionist state, interstate, or nonstate agencies of direct or indirect material aid to the Kashmiri separatists. As we have seen, this aid has taken various forms in relation to Kashmir, including territorial sanctuary, cash, propaganda, weaponry, military training, and—most provocatively, perhaps—foreign mercenary fighters from various parts of the Islamic world. Foreign mercenaries are an acknowledged staple of Muslim-based separatist movements in a number of countries. Incontrovertible proof that such fighters have wholly hijacked the Kashmiri separatist movement, as is not infrequently alleged on the Indian side, is lacking, but they have unquestionably evolved in the past few years into considerably more than a token ally of their embattled Kashmiri coreligionists. Enlisted ostensibly as "holy warriors" under the banner of the Islamic Jihad, they are an obvious symbol of the transborder appeal of pan-Islamic identity. They are simply terrorists, of course, from New Delhi's perspective, and it is in this guise, more than ever since the earthshaking developments of September 2001, that New Delhi projects their existence to the global community. Together with all the other forms of material assistance, they bear measurable witness, in any event, to the rallying phenomenon—

and, perhaps as well, to the greater or lesser power of civilizational identity in global politics.

To concede, in terms such as these, that the Kashmir dispute constitutes a global religious problem obviously falls well short of awarding it the status of an incipient "fault line war" in a coming "clash of civilizations." Granting it status of that kind would require a surrender to the Huntington model which, whether judged on the basis of its inherent theoretical robustness or the particular facts of the Kashmir case itself, would likely have to be judged premature. This does not mean, however, that the Huntington model has *no* application to the Kashmir dispute. On the contrary, to the extent that it helps to reverse the narrative tide that either entirely omitted or else underplayed the role of religious identity in this dispute, it will have made a markedly positive contribution to our understanding of it.

We carry the above concerns along with us as we continue examining the Kashmir dispute, albeit from yet another angle—that of conflict resolution. We will find that the religious identity problem leaves no angle on the dispute untouched, including this one.

4

The Problem of Conflict Resolution
The Autonomy Puzzle

One turns to the matter of resolving the separatist conflict in Kashmir with more than a little leeriness. This is due in part, of course, to the Kashmir conflict's deserved reputation for extreme complexity and intractability. Having defied resolution for over a half century, in other words, it is not unreasonable to think that it might continue its defiance indefinitely. Prescribing or even describing remedies, under the circumstances, can easily acquire the appearance at least of futility if not of naïveté. The leeriness is due in larger part, however, to nagging reservations about the project of conflict resolution itself—that its insistent advocacy might owe more to the optimism bred of intellectual dominance in the West of Enlightenment liberalism than to either what might be justified by the historical record or any realistic assessment of its actual future prospects.

Especially in the United States, the idea that intergroup conflicts, even those with centuries of bloody history behind them, can, with the requisite determination and resources applied, be made to yield to reasonable solutions has acquired the character of unassailable dogma. The partisans of this dogma are housed in academic institutions, think tanks, voluntary associations, church organizations, and the media on a scale that is impressive to behold. Equally impressive, apparently, is the influence they wield on public policy.[1] For them, nothing is more certain than that the steady accumulation of methodically acquired knowledge about intergroup conflict will lead eventually to its taming. They are enthusiastic about founding, and then funding, sizeable research-underwriting organizations like the United States Institute of Peace, a congressionally mandated and tax-supported, grant-giving body established in 1984 "to strengthen the nation's capacity to promote the peaceful resolution of international conflict . . . in the tradition of American statesmanship which seeks to limit international violence and to achieve peace based upon freedom, justice, and human dignity."[2] To those who formulate them, lofty sentiments of this kind may seem self-evident. They risk being interpreted by others, however, as self-serving and self-deluding. Benjamin Schwarz is not the only one, for instance, who suggests that "the history we hold up as a light to nations is a sanctimonious tissue of myth and self-infatuation. We get the world wrong because we get ourselves wrong. Taken without illusion, our history gives us no right to preach—but it should prepare us to understand the brutal realities of nation-building, at home and abroad."[3]

The discussion here of the Kashmir conflict, thus cautioned, will proceed deliberately unburdened of the assumptions either that resolution is probable, in any practical or immediate sense, or, even if probable, that it would likely be accomplished in substantial accord with the elevated nostrums of the liberal tradition. For our purposes, the idea of conflict resolution will be dealt with in morally neutral terms as compatible equally, on the darker side, with political domination and forceful imposition (with the "brutal realities of nation-building," in other words) and, on the lighter side, with political accommodation and compromise. The author's preference is, of course, for the latter. But it is the former, he believes, that, in the case of Kashmir, remains still the more likely.

Defining suitable ways in which to accommodate the planet's numerous disaffected ethnic minorities has generated a protracted and global —at times philosophical, at other times policy-focused—debate among scholars that shows no signs of abating. A major focal point in this debate has been ethnic self-determination—an idea or norm that has raised, as Donald Horowitz put it, "intertwined questions about patterns of ethnoterritorial politics, about the status of ethnic self-determination in philosophy, and about rights to a territorially conceived ethnic self-determination in international law."[4] Disagreement has pitted liberals, committed to individual-centered conceptions of the self, against communitarians and advocates of group rights; modernists against both postmodernists and primordialists; and proponents of integration and assimilation against stalwarts of secession.[5]

When the debate has turned to consider particular modalities of ethnic conflict reduction and management (whether, for instance, ethnic discontent is best handled by augmenting the discontented group's *voice* within the existing framework of a society's political institutions or, alternatively, by granting it the right of *exit*), attention has frequently been drawn to ethnic autonomy—a middling formula for organizing multiethnic states which, at least in principle, skirts the extremes of secession, on the one hand, or full integration, on the other.[6] There have been experiments with various forms of autonomy in dozens of countries. India has an especially impressive record.[7] In India, the oldest and longest-running case of applied autonomy happens to be Kashmir. It is far more than a problem of autonomy, of course, since the international conflict between India and Pakistan centers upon their dispute over ownership of Kashmir.

Ranking among the world's most intractable regional conflicts, the Kashmir dispute has generated a fairly massive corpus of literature recommending one or another approach to its resolution. I confess to having contributed more than once to this literature.[8] Without denigrating the value of such endeavors, it is not the aim of this chapter either to conduct a fresh inventory of proposed remedies or to add a new one to the existing stockpile. Rather I propose to examine in some detail, and as dispassionately as I can, one category of remedy—that of autonomy— whose prospects in regard to Kashmir are generally held to be superior to others and whose design and desirability are currently matters of wide-ranging debate, in India and elsewhere.

My objective will not be to advance the cause of this particular remedial model. In truth, I am not convinced that autonomy's instant realization in Kashmir would necessarily hasten the onset of the desired subcontinental "peace based upon freedom, justice, and human dignity" any more than other proposed models (including here on my list of equally doubtful models, by the way, *azadi* or complete independence of Kashmir, sought by some Kashmiri militant groups). My objective will be, instead, to undertake a critical assessment of autonomy's practical suitability in the Kashmir case—providing, on the one hand, as clear an explanation as I can both of what the autonomy model, in its various forms, might entail in terms of territorial, cultural, and political compromise, and, on the other, an accounting of its likely limitations. I maintain in this chapter that the autonomy solution, in spite of its seemingly self-evident reasonableness, has thin prospects of near-term adoption in Kashmir in any but an extremely diluted form and that these prospects are not likely to be enhanced through invention of still more creative autonomist models. As far as a "solution" to Kashmir is concerned, I contend, moreover, that it does not in any event lie in altering Kashmir's territorial or political circumstances so much as it lies in a fundamentally altered relationship between India and Pakistan. That, I conclude, means that India and Pakistan must first find a way to establish a reasonably stable and pacific modus vivendi between them *without* fundamental change to the existing, inherently ambiguous, and unresolved political-territorial status of Kashmir. As the reader may anticipate, this implies my impatience with the formally expressed demands of *both* sides in regard to Kashmir—Pakistan's for an internationally supervised plebiscite, India's (when angry) for Pakistan's complete withdrawal from the territory of pre-partition Jammu and Kashmir or (when less angry) for conversion of the Line of Control to a permanent international boundary. I endorse, instead, indefinite retention of the existing—and nominally impermanent—Line of Control. My reasoning is that until India and Pakistan (and, along with them, the assorted groups of contending Kashmiris) can learn to live more or less peacefully with that interim but by now wholly familiar arrangement, they will not be able to live amicably with any other. It is to the inescapable and not wholly undesirable "permanence of impermanence" when it comes to Kashmir, in other words, that I ultimately commit myself.

Autonomy's Global Appeal

Exactly what does ethnic "autonomy" mean? According to Yash Ghai, Public Law Professor at the University of Hong Kong, it "is a device to allow ethnic or other groups claiming a distinct identity to exercise direct control over affairs of special concern to them, while allowing the larger entity those powers which cover common interests."[9] A more methodical attempt at definition is contained in *Power Sharing and International Mediation in Ethnic Conflicts*, a 1996 publication by Timothy D. Sisk. Sisk identifies ten distinct "conflict-regulating practices" —half of them falling under the heading of "consociational" approach, the other half under the heading of "integrative" approach. A consociational power-sharing approach, he maintains, freely recognizes and represents separate ethnic groups as groups, while an integrative approach adopts practices that downplay separate ethnic group identity in favor of crosscutting individual (usually economic) interests.[10] As you can see in Table 4.1 that follows, Sisk places the practice of autonomy on the consociational side of the ledger, and he further classifies it among the "territorial divisions of power." He then comments that agreements to accommodate ethnic minority groups through grants of autonomy

> are reached between the rump government and the autonomous units over issues such as economic and foreign relations and regional commerce. Decisions on these limited issues are made jointly. Critical variables are the degree of economic interdependence, the structure of fiscal relations, and the balance of dependency.[11]

Clear from Sisk's and other discussions of the concept of autonomy is that it is a very capacious term, used by various commentators to cover a wide range of arrangements. Taking this diversity into account, Ruth Lapidoth in her study of autonomy settles on what she calls an "eclectic description" of autonomy—one that allows for different kinds of autonomy, different degrees of power transfer to the autonomous entity, and greater or lesser inclusiveness in terms of the specific powers transferred. In regard to the latter, she notes that while foreign relations and external security are ordinarily reserved for the central government, there have been instances in which the autonomous entity was granted power to enter into international agreements or to join international organizations.[12]

Writers generally distinguish between two different kinds of autonomy —territorial and personal (or cultural). The latter (nonterritorial) kind clearly has relevance in circumstances where the ethnic group is fairly small, weak, and/or territorially dispersed.[13] In our discussion of autonomy for Kashmir, it is territorial autonomy that is more relevant, and we will confine our attention to that. As for territorial autonomy, Lapidoth comments that

> a territorial political autonomy is an arrangement aimed at granting to a group that differs from the majority of the population in the state, but that constitutes the majority in a specific region, a means by which it can express its distinct identity.

Observe here once again use of the words "distinct identity," for it is political control over precisely this—the capacity, in other words, to define, protect, and promote a group's separate identity—that is gener-

Table 4.1

Conflict-Regulating Practices

	Consociational approach	Integrative approach
Territorial divisions of power	1. Granting autonomy and creating confederal arrangements	6. Creating a mixed or noncommunal federal structure
	2. Creating a polycommunal federation	7. Establishing a single inclusive unitary state
Decision rules	3. Adopting proportional representation and consensus rules in executive, legislative, and administrative decision making	8. Adopting majoritarian but integrated executive, legislative, and administrative decision making
	4. Adopting a highly proportional electoral system	9. Adopting a semimajoritarian or semiproportional electoral system
State-ethnic relations	5. Acknowledging group rights or corporate federalism	10. Adopting ethnicity-blind public policies

Source: Timothy D. Sisk, *Power Sharing and International Mediation in Ethnic Conflicts* (Washington, D.C.: United States Institute of Peace, 1996), p. 70.

ally understood to be implied by autonomy.* There are, of course, other "arrangements" in addition to territorial autonomy to secure the diffusion of power. Lapidoth identifies five of them: federal systems, decentralization, self-government, associate statehood, and self-administration.[14] She concedes that territorial autonomy has much in common with at least some of them, and, indeed, it is sometimes spoken of interchangeably with them. She notes, for instance, that the "Framework for Peace in the Middle East" (the 1978 Camp David accords between Egypt and Israel) referred to "full autonomy" for the Palestinian Arabs, whereas in subsequent negotiations the preferred term has been "self-rule" or "self-government."[15] The differences among these terms are not in all cases trivial, however, for they do not all attach the same importance to the maintenance and promotion of a distinct identity. While autonomy seems to imply less self-rule than does the term *confederalism*, for instance, it is generally understood to imply greater self-rule than *federalism*, which, as in the American case, need not cater to ethnic group identities at all. In the face of the common Indian assertion that Kashmir's separatist inclinations can be adequately satisfied within the context of a reinvigorated Indian federalism, this caveat needs to be kept in mind.

By the year 2000, the idea of ethnic autonomy had clearly gained considerable ground internationally—especially, but not only, in the West—as a legitimate device for conflict resolution. One leading analyst of ethnic conflict, Ted Robert Gurr, offered the rather startling observation, in fact, that a global consensus in regard to the handling of intergroup relations in ethnically mixed societies already existed by then, and that this consensus was paying off with a measurable diminution in ethnic warfare.[16] A major strategic shift from confrontation to accommodation, he claimed, was under way. Government repertoires of ethnic conflict management, hitherto heavily emphasizing repression, had consciously been expanded to include minority group rights and various forms of autonomy. Contrary to the conventional wisdom that represented ethnic warfare as getting worse, it was, he said, decidedly on the wane. It had peaked, according to him, in the early 1990s. "Between 1993 and the beginning of 2000," he pointed out, "the number of wars of

---

*There is the additional matter, taken note of below, whether use of such terms as "distinct" in connection with ethnic identity is conceptually misleading, i.e., that it "essentializes" identity (meaning that it falsely assumes greater group cultural homogeneity than most ethnic entities can, in fact, rightfully lay claim to).

self-determination has been halved." Most important, he suggested, was that the trend in resort to violent tactics was overwhelmingly positive. In 1999, he noted, there were 59 armed conflicts under way. Of these, "23 were de-escalating, 29 had no short-term trend, and only 7 were escalating—including Kosovo. By the late 1990s, the most common strategy among ethnic groups was not armed conflict but prosaic politics."[17]

Intellectuals, including increasing numbers of liberals, had helped pave the way to ethnic autonomy's acceptability by identifying ways to reconcile insistent demands for recognition of collective or *group* rights with the prevailing post–World War II emphasis on individual or *human* rights.[18] Lending additional weight to autonomy's acceptability were a number of concrete examples of its apparently successful incorporation in state practice, as in the 1979 Home Rule Act of the Danish parliament granting substantial self-rule to Greenland or, as recently as 1999, the concession by the United Kingdom of a separate Scottish parliament.[19] Nothing has given autonomist principles a firmer global boost in recent years, however, than the emphatic endorsement of minority group rights by the Conference on Security and Cooperation in Europe (CSCE), in 1995 renamed the Organization for Security and Cooperation in Europe (OSCE). In this respect, the CSCE/OSCE has achieved an undeniably remarkable record. According to Tim Sisk, it "has been the most proactive international organization in recognizing collective rights as an element of international law and developing compliance mechanisms." It has also, he comments, "been the most innovative international organization in seeking to promote ethnic conflict management through preventive diplomacy."[20] In the Document of the CSCE's Conference on the Human Dimension, adopted in Copenhagen in June 1990, a number of path-breaking provisions were adopted. Among them were the provisions

- that questions relating to national minorities "can only be satisfactorily resolved in a democratic political framework based on the rule of law" (Article 30);
- that "[t]o belong to a national minority is a matter of a person's individual choice and no disadvantage may arise from the exercise of such choice" (Article 32);
- that members of a minority have the right to establish their own institutions and maintain contacts among themselves within their country, as well as with members of the same group abroad (Article 32); and

- that members of a minority must be allowed to effectively participate in the public affairs of the state (Article 35).[21]

The Copenhagen document identified territorial autonomy as one mechanism for ensuring protection of these rights, but it did not give it any particular precedence. The Concluding Document of the CSCE's 1991 Conference on National Minorities went a step further, commit-ting the signatories to:

- establishing advisory and decision-making bodies in which minorities are represented, particularly on education, cultural, and religious issues;
- establishing local autonomous administrative structures in territories where minorities reside;
- embracing corporate [minority group] federalism when minorities
  are not territorially concentrated; and
- establishing permanent ethnically mixed interstate commissions
  when ethnic groups reside on different sides of an international
  frontier.[22]

At a Meeting of the Experts on National Minorities convened by the CSCE in Geneva in July 1991, the judgment was reached that "[i]ssues concerning national minorities . . . are matters of legitimate interna-tional concern and consequently do not constitute exclusively an internal affair of the respective State."[23]A judgment of this kind grants a strong warrant to a category of international action commonly spoken of nowa-days as "humanitarian intervention." It is potentially far-reaching, indeed radical, in its implications for traditional treatment of ethnic minorities under the umbrella of state sovereignty. One need hardly mention that it is in harmony neither with the more robust notions of state sovereignty that still circulate nor with the long-standing declared position of the Indian government denying any international responsibility at all in the resolution of Kashmir.

The frailties of autonomist solutions currently on display in the Balkans, in the Middle East, in India's northeast, and in Northern Ire-land suggest that Gurr's assertion of a fundamental global shift in re-spect to ethnic minorities from confrontation to accommodation, if not wholly misplaced, was at least premature. Judging from their recent record, autonomist models appear, in fact, to have little insulation against the violence-prone forces found in the world's most acute cases of ethnonationalist struggle.[24] Gurr's thesis needs to be questioned not only at the empirical level of conflict frequency, however, but also at the level of overall conceptual validity. Having directed for many years the Minorities At Risk project at the University of Maryland, Gurr has carried the methodical enumeration of ethnic minority groups to greater lengths than almost any other scholar. His doing so has unquestionably given comfort to countless students of ethnic conflict baffled by the subject's extraordinary engulfment in terminological ambiguity and dogged resistance to quantitative rigor. At the same time, however, it must be conceded that his approach approximates what the Dutch anthropologist Martijn van Beek has colorfully labeled "identity fetishism"—a conception of diversity "which relies on the relative stability and irreducibility of minority groups" and "in which the identification of the 'right' social group/culture/community and its empowerment supposedly offers the greatest guarantees of peace and prosperity for all."[25] It is precisely Gurr's fierce commitment to methodically rigorous accounting of ethnic identity, from van Beek's point of view, that compels his reductionist overstatement of the "groupness" of groups. Van Beek's own examination of Buddhist-Muslim conflict in the Ladakh region of Kashmir, where he found that political fault lines only infrequently respected formal religious community divisions, testifies to a social life in that remote part of India of far greater complexity and fluidity than Gurr's approach appears to presume. At a minimum, van Beek's study suggests the need for open-minded examination of ethnic and religious community divisions in the rest of Kashmir.[26]

Autonomy for Kashmir?

Notwithstanding the Indian government's understandable anxiety when it comes to the contemporary international push for ethnic minority rights, the application to Kashmir of the idea of ethnic autonomy inevitably arouses interest in some quarters of India as a potentially viable alternative to continued separatist violence. This shouldn't surprise us. After all, the state of Jammu and Kashmir—or, to be precise, that part of it remaining in Indian hands when a cease-fire between Indian and Pakistani forces was declared in January 1949—is no stranger to formal autonomy. It began its life under Indian rule, in fact, with substantial, even radical, autonomy. The foundation for its autonomous status was readily

apparent in the Indian government's explicit and repeated acknowledgment in the early days of its dispute with Pakistan over Kashmir of the
conditional nature of the state's accession to India[27] as well as in the
unique status granted the state in article 370 of the 1950 Indian Constitution. Those initial Indian concessions to autonomy were curbed
somewhat by the terms of the so-called Delhi Agreement reached in
July 1952 between Prime Minister Jawaharlal Nehru and the charis-
matic Kashmiri nationalist leader, Sheikh Mohammad Abdullah. In that
agreement, residual powers, in contrast with all other states of the Indian Union, were said to vest in the state of Jammu and Kashmir. The
state's autonomy suffered on other counts, however, as in the extension
to the state of the jurisdiction of the Indian Supreme Court. The Delhi
Agreement was rendered moot, in any event, in August 1953, when New
Delhi ordered Abdullah's arrest and incarceration. That event set the
stage for the massive reversal of the earlier concessions. A succession of
acts of the Indian parliament had largely nullified them within just a few
years, in fact, by fostering Kashmir's nearly complete functional (fiscal,
economic, and juridical) integration into the Indian Union. By the middle
of the 1950s, any substantive autonomy Kashmir had managed to carry
over from its earlier princely statehood had largely vanished—a victim
of New Delhi's insistence that Kashmir's accession to India was final
and irrevocable, not subject to negotiation with Pakistan or, by implica-
tion, with the Kashmiris. But no matter how far Kashmir's integration
into India may have progressed, memory remains strong, especially
among Kashmiris themselves, of the state's initial flirtation with a conspicuously strong species of autonomy.

The issue of autonomy's *contemporary* relevance to Kashmir has, in
fact, in recent years achieved a fairly noisy reemergence in India. The
immediate stimulus of its reemergence was the electoral victory in legislative elections in the state of Jammu and Kashmir in September 1996
of the National Conference (NC) party. The vehicle of Sheikh Abdullah's
rise to power in the 1940s, this is the party that ruled the state in the
early—and still relatively autonomous—days immediately after independence. It is the party that has been led in recent years by Sheikh
Abdullah's son (and, at the time of this writing, the state's chief minister), Farooq Abdullah.

Farooq had made restoration of the state's autonomy the centerpiece
of his party's 1996 campaign for office. One of his first acts upon taking
over as the state's chief minister was to appoint two state-level com-

mittees to examine the issue of Kashmir's autonomy—one, the State Autonomy Committee (SAC), entrusted with the issue's interstate or "external" aspect (the relationship between the central government and the state of Jammu and Kashmir), the other, the Regional Autonomy Committee (RAC), responsible for its intrastate or "internal" aspect (the relationships among the state's three ethno-religiously polyglot regions— Jammu, Ladakh, and Kashmir Valley). Little was heard from either of these committees until mid-April 1999, over two years later, when their reports—the *Report of the Regional Autonomy Committee* and the *Report of the State Autonomy Committee*—were finally submitted to the Jammu and Kashmir assembly. Following their submission, nearly another year passed, however, before they gained much public notice. Two events drew attention to them. One was the state cabinet's sudden decision on 19 January 2000—over three years after the two committees were appointed and prior to any formal action by the assembly itself— to endorse flatly the SAC report's recommendations and to forward them to the central government for consideration. The exclusively NC-composed cabinet's peremptory action caused an immediate uproar in the national media and drew bitter condemnation from the Jammu and Kashmir state unit of the Bharatiya Janata Party (BJP), the NC's partner in the National Democratic Alliance (NDA) coalition government at the Center.[28] The second and more explosive event was the state assembly's passage on 26 June 2000 of a resolution recording its approval of the SAC report's recommendations and demanding positive and effective steps for their implementation. A closer examination of these two reports, in particular the recommendations of the *Report of the State Autonomy Committee* focusing on extremely sensitive areas of center-state relationships, will make clear the reasons for the uproar.

The Autonomy Committees' Reports

We'll begin our examination of these two reports with the *Report of the Regional Autonomy Committee*, which, since it was focused fairly narrowly on group autonomy *within* Kashmir, initially attracted less attention (and drew less criticism) elsewhere in India. Like the SAC report, however, the RAC report's central proposals, spelled out in a fairly brief document of about thirty pages, were highly controversial. That they were likely sooner or later to meet stiff resistance, at least from some segments of the state's population, became apparent, in fact, in January

1999 with the sacking of the committee's Jammu-based Hindu chairman, Balraj Puri, and his replacement by Mohammad Shafi, the finance minister and one of Farooq's most trusted advisors. Puri, a well-known and outspokenly liberal figure in India's civil rights movement (and the only member of the RAC not also a member of Farooq's National Conference), had long since made known his opposition to any autonomy scheme that sought to redraw the map of the state along more sharply communal (meaning religious) lines and, thus, to deepen communal identities. His own draft of the committee report, rejection of which by Farooq Abdullah had precipitated his removal as chairman only months before its scheduled submission, was privately published in book form soon after his departure. In this book, he called for the state's administrative and political devolution in a manner that would preserve the state's unity and leave the present three (communally more-or-less heterogeneous) regions of Jammu, Kashmir Valley, and Ladakh essentially intact. Local autonomy was to be achieved by bolstering local (village, block, and district) self-government along the lines of India's well-established *panchayati raj* system. The object was to achieve decentralization of state power and enhanced institutional representation of ethno-linguistic minorities (the state's Gujjars, Dogras, Paharis, Ladakhis, and Kashmiri-speakers, for instance) without at the same time further entrenching the communal (again, meaning religious) identities of the three regions.[29]

In sharp contrast with Puri's patently secular and religion-averse plan, the RAC report calls for a major reorganization of the state's internal boundaries, with religious identity as the obvious, albeit strictly implicit, criterion for the exercise. It affirms the virtues of ethnic accommodation and "people's sovereignty over their own affairs", and it candidly proclaims in prefatory remarks that "the homogeneity of an identity in a geographical location should remain the basic criterion of the formation of the regions classified as autonomous."[30] It dismisses *panchayati raj* as an insufficiently effective device for ensuring intergroup equity in Jammu and Kashmir, asserting, instead, that greater equity will flow from the increased convergence of the state's internal boundaries with cultural group identities.

The RAC report is painstakingly (and, in its critics' eyes, disingenuously) drafted to define the project of redrawing internal boundaries entirely in terms of "ethnic diversity" and what it calls "ethno-cultural-linguistic groups." While it acknowledges that Jammu and Kashmir "is a pluriculture, pluri-lingual and pluri-religious state of India,"[31] it denies that religious identity either motivates the demand for restructuring the state's boundaries or seriously figures in the restructuring plan. The report manages somehow to discuss Kashmir's ethnography for thirty-odd pages, in fact, while only once employing the word *Muslim* and not even once the words *Hindu* and *Buddhist*. Nevertheless, these words could not have been far from the authors' minds as they prepared the report.

When it comes to the specifics of boundary revision, the report urges that the existing three divisions of the state be broken into eight new regions or provinces, and that these new entities be endowed with elected and suitably empowered councils. The jurisdictional end-product of the report's recommendations clearly favors the state's Muslims, especially its Sunni Muslims. Whereas under the current jurisdictional dispensation each of the state's three main religious communities (Muslim, Hindu, Buddhist) enjoys at least nominal intergroup equity by virtue of possessing majority standing in one of the state's three divisions, the proposed revision of boundaries would allot Sunni Muslims (without naming them, of course) five of the new regions or provinces, with the remaining three going one each to Shia Muslims, Buddhists, and Hindus. Since the state's sole Shia-majority district of Kargil would be awarded full regional or provincial status, wholly separated from the Buddhist-majority district of Leh, the Shia community might be among those supportive of the plan. Kargil's Shias have a long history of antagonistic political factionalism, however, and at least one section of the Shia political elite would likely favor an arrangement—a separate Ladakh province or Union Territory, for example, with separate regional or district hill councils for Leh and Kargil—that retained Ladakh's unity as a counterbalance to perceived Sunni Muslim-Jammu Hindu domination.[32] In similar fashion, the state's Buddhist community would very likely also be divided on the matter, with at least some of the political elite inclined to support a unified Ladakh. The state's Hindus, in contrast, would almost certainly be overwhelmingly opposed to the plan. The Pandits, practically all of which fled the Valley in the course of the uprising, are not even mentioned in the report. The demand of some of them for their own territorial homeland (named Panun Kashmir) carved from the Valley is conspicuous by its absence. As for the predominantly Hindu Jammu division, more than three of its present six districts (those predominantly Muslim, in other words) would be shaved off to form two new regions in the reconfiguring exercise in order to secure the RAC report's putative "ethnic" homogeneity. Since the RAC report is careful to emphasize that the new regions or provinces are intended as a *supplement* to the existing central institutions of state government, not as its *replacement*, it is clear that the report's version of autonomy, if implemented in accord with the report's design, would not represent a significant departure from the centralized manner in which power has been structured and wielded in the state during the past half century.

In the event the RAC report's main proposal is deemed unacceptable by the state government, its authors offer a second model for contemplation —one that would create elected councils at the level of the already existing fourteen districts. The numerical rankings of the state's religious communities in these districts today would ensure roughly the same political outcome as that of the first model—in other words, one favoring the state's Muslims, in particular its Sunni Muslims.

In a state where, whether fairly or unfairly, Muslim, especially Sunni Muslim, domination has been routinely targeted for criticism by the non-Muslim minorities, neither of the RAC report's recommended models would appear likely to find much favor outside the Muslim community. Both models, from the standpoint of the state's religious minorities, would result not in their enhanced group autonomy but in the further entrenchment of the state's prevailing Sunni Muslim domination.[33] While in principle the notion of breaking the state down into smaller units is unobjectionable, one is forced to agree with Navnita Chadha Behera that the RAC report "presented a distorted picture of this principle, designed to serve the narrow political ends of the ruling elite and the larger interests of the majority community."[34]

The *Report of the State Autonomy Committee* is both much lengthier (184 pages) than the RAC report and more explicitly at odds with New Delhi in its recommendations. In great detail, it narrates the history of the Center's relationship with Kashmir from partition in 1947 onwards. This history, it asserts in unusually blunt language, was one of nearly unremitting and remorseless assault by the Center on the genuinely autonomous status with which the state of Jammu and Kashmir began its career within the Indian Union. In an early chapter addressing the SAC's terms of reference, it commits itself unambiguously to "full enforcement of the historic Delhi Agreement concluded [24 July 1952] between the Prime Minister of India, Pt. Jawaharlal Nehru, and the Prime Minister (as he was then called) of the State, Sheikh Mohammed Abdullah, the two foremost architects of the State's accession to the Union of India."[35] This objective—

208 THE PROBLEM OF CONFLICT RESOLUTION

the state's return to the substantial autonomy (the "special status") promised in that agreement and already largely embodied in Article 370 of the
Constitution—pervades and guides the arguments made throughout the
report. When it comes to highlighting the Center's allegedly underhanded,
undemocratic, and unconstitutional methods for subverting what it claims
was the original intent of Article 370, the report pulls no punches. "It is
abundantly clear," its authors observe at one point,

> that from 1953 onwards, especially in [the] sixties, the process of erosion
> of the state autonomy was so rapid and on such a massive scale that [the]
> entire Article 370 of the Constitution of India which was supposed to
> guarantee and preserve the special status of the State in the Indian Union
> was emptied of its substantive content with the result that the State's ju-
> risdiction over the matters as envisaged by the Instrument of Accession
> of Oct. 1947 and the Delhi Agreement of 1952 was gradually diminished
> and systematically transferred to the Union.
> Far from enjoying a special status, as Article 370 envisaged, the State
> was put in a status inferior to that of other States.[36]

The SAC report's recommendations are numerous, highly specific, and
broad in coverage. In distilled form, they urge maximum autonomy—that
the Center's writ in the state be confined to the three subjects of defense,
foreign affairs, and communications, in other words, to what prevailed,
according to the report's authors, in the period prior to 1953. "The best
course," it concludes, "is for the President [of India] to repeal all Orders
which are not in conformity with Constitution (Application to Jammu and
Kashmir) Order 1950 and the terms of the Delhi agreement of 1952."[37] It
identifies forty-two Constitution Orders needing review in these terms.

The SAC report founds its arguments on premises fundamentally at
odds with those underlying the RAC report. While the RAC report, as
we saw, hails the centrality of cultural identity and urges reorganization
of Kashmir (implicitly, I have said) along ethno-religious or communal
lines, the SAC report plants its arguments firmly in the secular grounds
of law and constitutionality—in the undoing, in other words, of the state's
integration *in its entirety* into the Indian Union. Chief Minister Farooq
Abdullah, as Aijaz Ahmad commented in *Frontline*, in forming the two
committees seems to have

> armed himself with two reports [catering] to two different constituen-
> cies. There is the State Autonomy Committee (SAC) report which of-

fers the maximalist version of the secular demand for autonomy for Jammu and Kashmir as a whole, . . . and then there is the Regional Autonomy Committee (RAC) report advocating the re-organisation of the State into eight new 'provinces' whose boundaries are defined on ethno-religious lines.

In an effort to safeguard his eroding political position, Ahmad suggests, Farooq had sought "to play the secular card (maximum autonomy of the State as a unit) as well as the communal card (division of the State into diverse religiously defined units) all at once." This corresponded, Ahmad explains, "to the new political face of the National Conference which acts as a guardian of the secular legacy in its operations in the Valley but as a party of Muslims in Jammu and Ladakh, having developed far too limited ties of representation with non-Muslims there."[38]

Dr. Karan Singh, the son of the erstwhile Maharaja of Jammu and Kashmir and the first chairman of the SAC, had resigned his position on 31 July 1997, signaling that in regard to this committee's report, too, there was likely going to be dissent. And, indeed, the state assembly's emphatic endorsement of the report in June 2000 generated a minor political firestorm. Spokespersons of the state's Hindu and Buddhist minorities, judging that the status of Jammu and Ladakh would likely be placed in jeopardy in the new order, naturally pressed for the report's rejection. Heated debate went on in the nation's press. Resistance to the state assembly's action came not only from the ruling BJP and its Hindu nationalist allies but also from the Congress party and leftist elements of the political opposition. Amidst wild accusations against Farooq Abdullah's National Conference government of betrayal and acting on behalf of foreign interests, the BJP-led Union Cabinet on 4 July branded the state assembly's so-called autonomy resolution "unacceptable." The Cabinet's public response, while reaffirming the government's commitment to "federal harmony" and the devolution of powers to the states, asserted "that the acceptance of this resolution would set the clock back and reverse the natural process of harmonising the aspirations of the people of Jammu and Kashmir with the integrity of the nation."[39]

The stunning announcement on 24 July by the Kashmiri militant organization Hizbul Mujahideen of a three-month unilateral cease-fire swept the autonomy debate abruptly off the front pages, replacing it (only briefly, as it turned out) with the exciting prospect of a negotiated end to the violence. Autonomy's perennial appeal remained intact, however, and the question of its suitability for Jammu and Kashmir was bound to persist. At issue, in the most fundamental sense, was whether autonomy could be defined and implemented in such a way as to survive the powerful crosscurrents that multiplied and thrived in Kashmir's extraordinarily complicated and treacherous circumstances. The most optimistic reply to this question came from members of a fairly recently formed, American-based, nongovernmental organization called the Kashmir Study Group. A look at this group's detailed proposal reveals the limits of autonomy's political prospects.

Autonomy—The Way Forward?

In late 1998, Farooq Kathwari, a successful Kashmiri-American businessman and driving force behind the founding of the Kashmir Study Group in 1996, convened an unusual meeting at his farm in Livingston, New York. The meeting, spread over several days between 29 November and 2 December, brought together eight eminent men—four of them, including Kathwari, from the United States, two from India, and two from Pakistan—to consider ideas relating to a solution of the Kashmir dispute. All of Kathwari's guests had had distinguished careers—four in the diplomatic service, two in the military, and one in higher education. Three of the four South Asians had been participants together for some years in the Neemrana Dialogue, a long-running and heavily publicized effort at informal or Track II diplomacy involving, for the most part, retired Indian and Pakistani officials. A major focus of the discussions at Livingston was a paper authored by Dr. Joseph E. Schwartzberg, a noted University of Minnesota geographer, outlining his ideas in regard to a solution. That paper, considerably modified and distilled, emerged at the conclusion of the meeting as the so-called Livingston Proposal, a brief (less than two pages) and unsigned draft document entitled "Kashmir —A Way Forward," to the public circulation and discussion of which the participants in the Livingston meeting had apparently given their consent.*

---

* I have been a member of the Kashmir Study Group, presently an organization of about twenty-six members, since it was founded. I was among those invited to the Livingston meeting, but I declined to participate. Some, if not all, of the participants in the meeting have been publicly identified in the Indian and Pakistani press. Nevertheless, the present discussion respects their nominal anonymity. Important to note is that the Livingston Proposal, in conformity with the agreed ground rules governing the functioning of the Kashmir Study Group, was developed by only a portion of the group's members (a "working group") and does not necessarily represent the group's consensus position on Kashmir.

Over the past few years, the Livingston Proposal has attracted considerable attention in South Asia, especially in India, both in the press and among policymakers. Some of the published commentary on it, as we will see below, has been markedly hostile. Most interesting, however, has been the recurring speculation that this proposal had acquired surprising momentum, that it had the covert endorsement of the United States government and, moreover, that the ideas outlined in it formed the core of plans presently being promoted by key players in the ongoing dialogue over resolution of the Kashmir dispute.* These players, in the judgment of one prominent Indian writer, included the National Conference government of Farooq Abdullah (and the Regional Autonomy Commission appointed by him), influential figures in India's ruling BJP and allied organizations like the RSS, India's powerful intelligence apparatus (the Research and Analysis Wing), a number of Pakistanis (including former foreign secretary Niaz Naik) active in Track II initiatives relating to Kashmir, and even elements of Kashmiri militant organizations.[40] While one should certainly view with some skepticism the Livingston Proposal's hypothesized links to a Washington-orchestrated global conspiracy focused on Kashmir, the sustained interest generated by the proposal clearly compels us to pay attention to its contents. I reproduce the Livingston Proposal below in its entirety:

Kashmir—A Way Forward

We recommend that a portion of the former princely State of Jammu and Kashmir be reconstituted as a sovereign entity (but one without an international personality) enjoying free access to and from both India and Pakistan. The portion of the State to be so reconstituted shall be determined through an internationally supervised ascertainment of the wishes of the Kashmiri people on either side of the Line of Control. This ascertainment would follow agreement among India, Pakistan, and representatives of the Kashmiri people to move forward with this proposal. The sovereignty of the new entity would be guaranteed by India, Pakistan, and appropriate international bodies.

The new entity would have its own secular, democratic constitution, as well as its own citizenship, flag, and a legislature, which would legislate on all matters other than defense and foreign affairs. India and Pakistan would be responsible for the defense of the Kashmiri entity, which

---

*The proposal's prominence was noted in Chapter 1 in connection with the back-channel diplomacy carried on by India and Pakistan from March to July 1999.

would itself maintain police and gendarme forces for internal law and order purposes. India and Pakistan would be expected to work out financial arrangements for the Kashmiri entity, which could include a currency of its own.

Kashmiri citizenship would also entitle such citizens to acquire Indian or Pakistani passports (depending on which side of the Line of Control they live on). Alternatively, they could use entity passports subject to endorsement by India or Pakistan as appropriate.

The borders of Kashmir with India and Pakistan would remain open for the free transit of people, goods, and services in accordance with arrangements to be worked out between India, Pakistan, and the Kashmiri entity.

While the present Line of Control would remain in place until such time as both India and Pakistan decided to alter it in their mutual interest, both India and Pakistan would demilitarize the area included in the Kashmir entity, except to the extent necessary to maintain logistic support for forces outside the State that could not otherwise be effectively supplied. Neither India nor Pakistan could place troops on the other side of the Line of Control without the permission of the other state.

All displaced persons, including Kashmiri Pandits, who left any portion of the Kashmir entity, shall have the right to return to their homesteads.

The proposal represents a practical framework that could satisfy the interests of the people of Kashmir, India, and Pakistan. It would end civil strife and the tragic destruction of life and property in Kashmir. By resolving the principal issue that could lead to armed conflict between India and Pakistan, it would go far towards relaxing political tensions in South Asia. It would offer enormous economic benefits not only to Kashmir, but also to India, Pakistan, and all of the South Asian region.

Livingston, New York
December 1, 1998

Circulated fairly widely in India and Pakistan over the next several months, the initial Livingston Proposal eventually (in September 1999) appeared as a handsomely printed, oversized booklet in which, under the same title (*Kashmir—A Way Forward*), alternative forms of the proposed "sovereign entity" were spelled out in detail and carefully depicted in a series of specially prepared maps.[41]

Specifically, *Kashmir—A Way Forward* presents three alternative plans—the first calling for the creation of two sovereign Kashmiri entities, one on each side of the LOC, each having its own government, constitution, and special status vis-à-vis India and/or Pakistan; the second calling for a single Kashmiri entity, straddling the LOC, having its own government, constitution, and special status vis-à-vis both India and Pakistan; and the third calling for the creation of a Kashmiri entity on the Indian side of the LOC only, again with its own government, constitution, and special status vis-à-vis the host state. Apparently having judged the question of ethno-religious composition of an entity on the Pakistan side of the LOC, where the population is nearly 100 percent Muslim, to be unproblematic, *Kashmir—A Way Forward* suggests that the areas choosing to join a sovereign Kashmiri entity on the *Indian* side "would be those imbued with 'Kashmiriyat' (the cultural tradition of Kashmir) and/or interact extensively with Kashmiri-speaking people."[42]

Allowing for the possibility of an agreement between India and Pakistan to rationalize the LOC, *Kashmir—A Way Forward* proposes a number of territorial exchanges that might be accomplished in conjunction with creation of the sovereign entity or entities. This cartographic exercise modifies but, interestingly, does not abolish the LOC. It yields three distinct outcomes in addition to the basic three plans, for a grand total of six alternative autonomy plans. Only one of the plans (Plan C), which envisions an entity exclusively on the Indian side of the existing LOC, and which calls for no modifications to the LOC, can be implemented (in theory) without any agreement at all between India and Pakistan. Another (Plan A), which envisions two separate sovereign Kashmiri entities, one on each side of the LOC (but without any modification to the LOC), to come into being would clearly require cooperation at some level between India and Pakistan. All of the others (B, D, E, F), which call for constructing an entity or entities that either overlap the LOC and/or modify it, would obviously entail maximum cooperation between the two sides. Schematically, and taking into rough account whether minimum, maximum, or no agreement between India and Pakistan on the construction of the entity or entities is required, the plans take the forms as illustrated in Table 4.2.

On the face of it, the authors of *Kashmir—A Way Forward* would no doubt concede that chances for near-term implementation of these plans, given the parlous state of India-Pakistan relations, are extremely slight. Prospects are dismal even in the case of Plan C, which we have seen calls for creation of an autonomous Kashmiri entity solely on the Indian side of the LOC, without any modifications to the LOC (meaning, of course, that it could be accomplished, on paper at any rate, without en-

Table 4.2

Alternative Autonomy Plans Depicted in *Kashmir—A Way Forward*

Plan	Need for agreement between India and Pakistan
A. Two Kashmiri Entities (both sides of LOC)	Yes/minimum or greater
B. One Kashmiri Entity (straddling LOC)	Yes/maximum
C. One Kashmiri Entity (India-only)	No
D. Two Kashmiri Entities (both sides of modified LOC)	Yes/maximum
E. One Kashmiri Entity (straddling modified LOC)	Yes/maximum
F. One Kashmiri Entity (India-only on modified LOC)	Yes/maximum

Source: *Kashmir—A Way Forward* (Larchmont, N.Y.: Kashmir Study Group, February 2000), pp. 14–23.

tailing any agreement with Pakistan). Setting aside for the moment the existence within India itself of formidable political forces hostile to anything approximating genuine autonomy for Kashmir, the fact that Plan C takes as its starting point the dismissal of any Pakistani role in its formulation virtually assures, at a minimum, Pakistan's noncooperation with the venture and, more likely, a calculated attempt to sabotage it. Any autonomy scheme exclusive of Pakistan, one may be certain, is doomed from the start.

Admittedly, the improbability of the near-term adoption of any of these plans is not necessarily a fatal weakness of *Kashmir—A Way Forward*, which was, after all, explicitly circulated not as a *final* blueprint of a settlement but to stimulate discussion of potential options. Whether these plans will merit serious consideration at *any* time in the future, however, is far from clear.

What a number of Indian critics have alleged (and what its authors might well be reluctant to concede) is that the plans contained in *Kashmir —A Way Forward*, like the recommendations contained in the *Report of the Regional Autonomy Committee* discussed earlier, have the repartition of the state of Jammu and Kashmir along religious-communal lines (its religious homogenization, in other words) as their unspoken—but overriding—goal. All of the territories designated in these plans as "likely" or "possible" areas to opt for inclusion in the hypothetical Kashmiri state on the Indian side of the LOC have, as acknowledged by the plans' authors, Muslim majorities. Nevertheless, "enormous leaps of reason," Praveen Swami argues in a trenchant critique in *Frontline*, "are used to avoid the assertion that [the subdistricts singled out for inclusion in the entity] incorporate all the principal Muslim-majority areas of Jammu and Kashmir as it exists, or that a communal sundering is being contemplated." That the entity's intended inhabitants are somehow bound together by cultural tradition (*kashmiriyat*), by the Kashmiri language, or, in the absence of any other secular tie, at least by their "extensive [presumably economic] interaction" with one another, says Swami, is mere camouflage without basis in fact. The authors of *Kashmir—A Way Forward*, Swami observes bitingly, nowhere explore the possibility that in some areas on the fringes of the proposed entity Hindu-Muslim relationships might be closer than these areas' Muslims maintain with Muslims in the entity's core area, the Valley of Kashmir. Moreover, he wonders, "if language and culture are arguments for a sundering of the existing State, it is unclear why the [Kashmir Study Group] even considers the prospect of a single entity [Plan B, in which the entity would straddle the LOC]. Punjabi, not Kashmiri, is spoken across the LoC, and cultural traditions there have little to do with those of the valley."[43] The mere existence of these plans, he argues in another essay, has already compounded the fears of religious groups in the communally charged environment of Jammu and Kashmir. "While high-political plans for a resolution of Jammu and Kashmir's bloody war may seem conceptually attractive," he asserts, "their principal impact so far has been to deepen the conflict between religious communities. Through the State, peoples and politicians have begun to position themselves in the event of a partition, however far it might yet be in the future."[44]

Important to acknowledge in this context, of course, is that the authors of *Kashmir—A Way Forward*, in proposing that Jammu and Kashmir "be reconstituted as a sovereign entity (but one without an international personality)" do not openly or unambiguously endorse partition of the state as the best remedy against continued civil strife. The details of their alternative plans, as well as the suggestions they make in regard to open borders and free trade zones, leave room for alternative explanations. Moreover, even if we judge their plans to *approximate* partition, they may take comfort from the fact that partition as a negotiated solution to conflict in culturally divided societies has its strong corps of defenders as well as its detractors. This is so whether the conflict is rooted in religion or in any other form of ethnic identity. Indian secularists, like Praveen Swami and Balraj Puri, naturally take a different view of the communally based repartition or quasi partition of Kashmir, as is outlined in *Kashmir—A Way Forward*, than would those many Pakistanis attracted to the Two Nation Theory justification for their country's origins. Even among Western writers on the subject of identity politics, there is plenty of disagreement on this subject. For every David Laitin moved to lament the "liberal ethnic cleansing" inherent in the advocacy of partition and ethnic self-determination,[45] there is a Stephen Van Evera or Chaim Kaufmann to extol their virtues.[46]

Nevertheless, the criticisms leveled by Swami and others against the recommended plans in *Kashmir—A Way Forward* are not easily dismissed. In its self-styled pose as "a practical framework that could satisfy the interests of the people of Kashmir, India, and Pakistan," this proposal passes far too lightly over the difficulties that would certainly accompany some of the steps it suggests. One of these, coming under the heading of "desirable territorial changes," is the exchange of over 700,000 people that would admittedly be entailed in the exercise of rationalizing the LOC. In a region where the human toll incurred in an earlier effort at partition earned it a place among the worst catastrophes of the twentieth century, a proposal of this kind begs for reconsideration. Moreover, the plain fact is that all three of the plans (D, E, and F), calling for territorial changes to bring about a more rational LOC have been drained almost entirely of practicality in the face of the eruption of major fighting at Kargil not many months after the plans surfaced. With the Pakistan army having so recently and so bloodily broadcast its unwavering commitment to the belief in Kargil's considerable strategic importance, it is fanciful to suppose that Islamabad would be attracted by the notably simplistic (and militarily innocent) logic of *Kashmir—A Way Forward*. Suggested in it is a territorial swap in which India, in return for giving Pakistan a belt of land to protect its Mangla dam watershed, would gain 2,844 square miles of territory, practically all of it constituting "a protective apron of territory . . . to the north of national highway 1A, especially in the vicinity of Kargil."

The greatest flaw in *Kashmir—A Way Forward*, however, is that the proposal it puts forth focuses far too narrowly on the technically fascinating but inherently marginal ethnic and territorial aspects of the Kashmir conflict. It grants unmerited precedence to the rational and arbitrary rearrangement of peoples, sovereignties, loyalties, and boundaries in one small corner of a vast region whose political landscape is literally boiling over with discord. Arising from the contemporary convergence in South Asia of a host of demographic, environmental, socioeconomic, strategic, military, and political trends, some of them global, others distinct to the region, this discord is simply not reducible to—and cannot by any stretch of the imagination be adequately explained by or resolved solely within the context of—Kashmir. In these circumstances, the remarkably formalistic autonomy schemes outlined in *Kashmir—A Way Forward* are bound to raise serious questions not only about their practicality but also about their desirability. What may, in the tidy and multicolored cartographer's representation, look to be a sensible way to pacify Kashmir could well turn out, in practice, to leave its inhabitants no more secure from ethno-territorial conflict than they are now. The authors of *Kashmir—A Way Forward* are handcuffed, I believe, to an uncompromisingly rational and linear conception of the Kashmir dispute: They accept as established fact the highly debatable assertions, heard in many quarters, that Kashmir is the core issue between India and Pakistan (that it is the primary *cause* of their sustained animosity, in other words); that irreconcilable religious identities lie at the heart of this issue; and that, with some adroit constitutional engineering, the poisonous effects of these identities can be vanquished. This argument ignores the possibility —in my judgment the near certainty—that the Kashmir dispute today, whatever it may have represented in past years, is as much symptomatic of the broadly constituted malaise inflicting India-Pakistan relations as it is a cause of it; and, furthermore, that its solution, if indeed there is one, must be sought beyond autonomy—that is, not in Kashmir alone, perhaps not even mainly in Kashmir, and most certainly not in the device of ethnically cleansed and quasi sovereign entities. In isolation, autonomy—no matter how attractively drawn—is not a panacea. For it to work in Kashmir, there first has to be movement away from the zero-sum calculus that each country applies in its dealings with the other. The task of bringing about such a fundamental change in the way India and Pakistan perceive their security environment and Kashmir's position within it is sobering in its complexity. To the question of whether such a change is even possible—and to the implications our answer holds not only for the debate over autonomy but for the larger discussion of Kashmir's resolution—we now turn.

Beyond Autonomy

The palpable and, to no small extent, baffling ambiguity built into the range of plans offered in *Kashmir—A Way Forward* as well as into its somewhat obscure concept of "sovereign entity (but one without an international personality)" is understandable, of course, as an unavoidable adaptation to the polarized circumstances prevailing in South Asia. In this region, every readily imaginable option seems wholly unpalatable to one side or another. To promote Kashmir's undiluted sovereignty, one possessed of an international personality (meaning, presumably, full independence and membership of the United Nations), would immediately drive India into unremitting opposition—and, depending on whether Pakistani-controlled Azad Jammu and Kashmir were included or not, perhaps Pakistan as well. But to dilute the meaning of sovereignty to the point that it found favor with most Indians would just as certainly turn Pakistanis—and, very likely, many groups in Kashmir—into equally staunch opponents of the plan. Regrettably, the odds in these circumstances seem heavily weighted on the side of the status quo's indefinite extension. From such a perfect stalemate, no exit—at least not a safe, negotiated exit—seems possible.

Now I believe, in fact, that extricating India and Pakistan (and, of course, the people of Kashmir) from at least the most crippling circumstances of the status quo is both possible and—as I strove to make clear in earlier chapters—plainly urgent. Left to manage the extrication entirely on their own, however, chances are that these two rivals will fail. The record in this regard is pretty clear: Pure bilateralism, for all practical purposes, is a dead-end street when it comes to improving India-Pakistan relations. Whatever chances there are, in fact, for a peaceful and decently early extrication from the Kashmir imbroglio stand in an almost perfectly inverse relationship with exclusive reliance upon bilateral mechanisms. In the face of the widespread reticence of world leaders to intervene in regard to Kashmir, considered earlier in our discussion, this is, of course, disconcerting news. Nevertheless, if we are serious about removing Kashmir from the list of global "flashpoints," then inclusion in the formula of conflict resolution of international or multilateral components of some kind is inescapable. In the remaining pages of this chapter, I lay out both my reasons for thinking so and some thoughts about possible such components.

In laying out these reasons, I do not dismiss territorial autonomy as a potential element in a final settlement of the Kashmir dispute. I think the odds are fairly good, in fact, that autonomy, in one form or another, will eventually figure in Kashmir's political future. I think autonomy itself cannot be relied upon, however, as the principal catalyst to usher in a new future for Kashmir. If there is to be a new and peaceful future for Kashmir, it will come, I believe, as a result of measures taken in the region having very little to do with ethnic autonomy. I am going to argue, in fact, that to insist on Kashmir's umbilical linkage to positive change in India-Pakistan relations is to put the proverbial cart before the horse, that substantial progress toward a more positive relationship can be made *without* there first having been agreement upon terms for a final settlement of Kashmir and, indeed, that India and Pakistan *must* abjure a final settlement of Kashmir and agree to its indefinite shelving as a first principle in any agreement directed toward an improvement in their relationship.

Bilateralism's Infirmities

My argument *against* a bilateral and Kashmir-focused strategy of conflict resolution in South Asia follows.

1. There is a radical, dysfunctional, and, for all practical purposes, incommensurable dissimilitude in the strategic outlooks Indian and Pakistani policymakers would bring to the negotiating table.

This lack of resemblance in their outlooks does not owe its existence to any great extent, in my judgment, to differences in their "strategic culture"—that is, to culture-based and deeply rooted differences in the way their policy-making elites comprehend one another and the region's security problems. You may recall that I dwelt on this issue in the preceding chapter. There I argued that the *religious* content of the Kashmir dispute had typically been oversimplified and caricatured, and, furthermore, that it was most certainly not reducible to one side or the other's exceptional zealotry or irrationality. The problem between India and Pakistan, I went to some lengths to point out, was not one of cultural pathology.

On the contrary, the problem, as I see it, is that Indian and Pakistani policy makers are driven by the geostrategic circumstances of the South Asian region, especially by the huge and growing inequality of power that exists between the two countries, to reckon their security requirements in fundamentally different ways. India's leadership has always had Great Power aspirations; more and more, these aspirations appear to growing numbers of seasoned observers to be nearing realization. A recent article by Brookings Institution scholar Stephen P. Cohen, "India Rising," both in its title and content is symptomatic of the trend in thinking.[47] Possessing a nuclear weapons arsenal, the world's third largest armed force, the world's second largest population, the world's fifth largest economy (measured in purchasing power parity), and a functioning democracy, "Indians," says Cohen, "believe that their country has both a destiny and an obligation to play a large role on the international stage. India and China, after all, are the world's only major states that embody grand civilizations."[48]

Pakistan, in contrast, whatever may have been its earlier aspirations, is nowadays increasingly classed among the smaller Asian powers and, more worrying to Pakistanis, among the least successful of them. Indeed, writers labor strenuously, it seems, to construct the most dismal scenarios of its future.[49] These scenarios are of highly uncertain reliability, and they need to be viewed with considerable caution. The fact remains, however, that Pakistanis, from the perspective of their emerging and spectacularly turbulent geostrategic circumstances, clearly do have a great deal to worry about. Having watched their alliance with the United States get shredded at the close of the Cold War, they found themselves, in the wake of the terrorist attacks on the United States in September 2001, unceremoniously pressed back into service in the West's front line, this time against global terrorism. This stunning, albeit double-edged, reversal in Pakistan's fortunes seemed certain to put it on the receiving end once again of Washington's weapons supply pipeline. Judging from its past record, this was likely to embolden Pakistan's military leadership to try to keep pace with its eastern neighbor. That, in view of India's own arms acquisition plans, won't be easy. As an October 2000 editorial in *The Times of India* rather brutally but accurately pointed out, these plans threaten to "tilt the balance decisively against Islamabad." The editorialist, commenting on a military supply agreement cemented between New Delhi and Moscow at the close of the visit to India in October 2000 of the Russian president Vladimir Putin, pointed out with seeming satisfaction that

> [t]he deals announced [including over 300 T-90S main battle tanks and license to manufacture the formidable SU-30MKI fighter aircraft] are only the tip of the proverbial iceberg. There are scores of small-ticket items that add up to providing the Indian armed forces a tremendous punch in the coming years. In these circumstances, some countries probably need to worry, . . . [T]he view from Islamabad is bound to be bleak. There has been a distressingly triumphal air about the visits of Bill Clinton and Vlad Putin to New Delhi. The arrangements worked out with regard

to Afghanistan seem designed to undermine Pakistan's victory in that country, albeit through its Taliban proxy. But Islamabad's immediate problem is how to counter the juggernaut of high-performance tanks, fighter aircraft and submarines that the Indian armed forces are acquiring in the coming decade. . . . "[50]

In short, the end of the Cold War has brought neither "peace dividend" nor peace of mind to the South Asian region. It has, on the contrary, made unmistakably plain the enormous differences in the capabilities of India and Pakistan, elevated the importance within each of them of the armed forces, and given an enormous push in each to the acquisition of advanced weaponry, both conventional and nuclear. An arms race—between equally determined states starkly unequal in capability—is clearly in progress in South Asia. In both states, undertakings for peace have taken a back seat to preparations for war. One can hardly imagine a more inhospitable environment in which to launch serious bilateral talks over a dispute as volatile and complex as Kashmir.

2. Ideological militants, with deeply hostile and irreconcilable agendas, are well organized and politically powerful in both India and Pakistan. Their existence inhibits formation in these countries of a consensus in support of a negotiated solution to Kashmir. In neither country is there a strong and broad-based peace movement to counter their influence.

Pakistani analysts are fond of pointing out that religious nationalism has been far more successful, politically speaking, on the Indian than on the Pakistani side of the border. After all, they say, whereas the "Hindu nationalist" Bharatiya Janata Party (BJP), after winning a fourth or so of the popular vote in India's 1999 election, came into national power at the head of a coalition government, never have any of Pakistan's so-called *Islam-pasand* or religion-favoring political movements been able to command more than 6 percent or so of the popular vote in any general election, much less to form the government. Their point has some merit: Vigorous debate rages in India today over the quantum of influence exercised in BJP policy-making circles by the so-called *sangh parivar*— the "family" of right-wing Hindu nationalist organizations of which the Rashtriya Swayamsevak Sangh, founded in 1925, is the ideological parent—who supply the BJP not only with its street power but with a dedicated core of workers for mobilizing voters.[51] The "fundamentalist" streak in South Asian politics, if one can call it that, clearly is not confined to the region's Islamic societies. The incontrovertible fact remains, however, that Islamic militancy, however modest its electoral appeal may be, fills a portion of Pakistan's contemporary political canvas on a scale clearly no less than—and very likely more than—that filled in India by Hindu militancy. The word "monster" crops up frequently in discussions of its role even among those confident that Pakistan's commitment to secularism is deep and enduring. The instances of retreat from efforts to leash this monster by General Pervez Musharraf, especially during the early stretches of his tenure as Pakistan's chief executive, reinforce this interpretation.[52] Unfortunately, in both India and Pakistan extremist posturing in the cause of Kashmir has for many years served as the litmus test of national loyalty—a fact that has stripped political discourse in both of these countries of language suited to reconciliation and compromise when it comes to Kashmir. This has not stopped a number of nongovernmental organizations in both countries from organizing well-publicized peace initiatives involving hundreds of Indians and Pakistanis. It has, however, confined them thus far to a relatively marginal role in regional affairs.

Notwithstanding the organizational strength and not inconsiderable appeal of ideological militancy in both of these societies (and the parallel weakness in both of the peace movement), it deserves reemphasis that I do not mean to argue the existence in *either* of them of a monolithic structure of opinion in regard to Kashmir or India-Pakistan relations in general. When it comes to internal and external security concerns, both of these societies are home to a remarkable diversity of opinion. This point is almost always conceded about India, whose extraordinary cultural pluralism bolsters its reputation for accommodating political pluralism as well. It is much less often conceded about Pakistan, however, in regard to whose basic stance on Kashmir, as I went to some lengths to point out in Chapter 3, the claim is commonly made that there is a broad and firm societal consensus—that the intransigent public position the government takes in regard to Kashmir, in other words, is "one of the few that unites Pakistanis."[53] This claim, if true, would largely relieve Indians of an obligation to engage Pakistan in serious discussion of Kashmir. It would damage, perhaps fatally, my contention that India and Pakistan can be extricated from the status quo. After all, I have conceded that extrication requires that India *and* Pakistan agree to setting aside, at least for the time being, Kashmir's final settlement. The claim thus needs to be resisted.

3. It should require little argument to make the point that India and Pakistan, meaning the central governing bodies of each, are only two of many actors whose interests are at stake in Kashmir. The interests of other actors, whether located within the region or outside of it, and including both state (China, Russia, and Afghanistan, for example) and nonstate (to include here, of course, the various and often competing Kashmiri militant groups) actors, are bound to clash in at least some respects with those of India and Pakistan. Some of these other actors command significant resources and are certain to assert their influence in any negotiations over Kashmir's fate. Any product of bilateral agreement between India and Pakistan would obviously be subject to resistance and noncompliance by these other actors. In other words, India and Pakistan are far from free to settle the Kashmir dispute in their own terms. Bilateral negotiations, considered in this light, would be bilateral in name only.

The multiplicity of competing interests at issue in Kashmir is a weighty problem in its own right, to be sure; but it becomes even more formidable when considered against the disturbingly dark side of the Kashmir conflict. That side exhibits the disagreeable reality that this conflict has never in its entire history been solely, or even mainly, about what for convenience' sake we may label the "legitimate" grounds for conflict—the self-determination of Kashmiris or their liberation from oppressive Indian rule. Long ago, it acquired its own *raison d'être*, its own momentum, and its own stock of incentives distinct from and often in contradiction with the ideal of self-determination. These incentives have included lucrative material side-payments to some of the parties to the conflict. Beneficiaries of this kind are found in not inconsequential numbers at *all* levels and on *all* sides of the conflict—among Indian, Pakistani, and Kashmiri officials (military and civil), as among both the armed and unarmed militants themselves. However ironic or perverse it may seem, the Kashmir conflict today has its own well-established "illegitimate" grounds. Among other things, these include the fact that the conflict is the chosen career "opportunity structure" or "business" of innumerable individuals, in whose career paths killing, terror, intimidation, extortion, and cruelty are routine and necessary elements. For these individuals, autonomy holds little charm. Settlement of the Kashmir dispute on any terms, in fact, since it would deprive such individuals of their livelihood, is unlikely to come to them as welcome news. The hard fact, in other words, is that enthusiasm for a just and peaceful end of the Kashmir dispute is far from universal.[54]

Outlines of a Multilateral Strategy

India and Pakistan embark upon the new century with their relationship at a perilously low point. The unstable nuclear security environment and chances, however slight, that continued tension over Kashmir will eventually produce nuclear war or, at a minimum, lock these two states in an endless and prohibitively costly nuclear and missile arms competition rule out continued exclusive reliance on the South Asian region's meager capacity for bilateral compromise. Impassioned appeals for dialogue between India and Pakistan, though frequent, have had no tangible results. They seem even less likely to bear fruit in the face of current strategic uncertainties arising from the West's "war on terrorism." Like it or not, the extrication of India and Pakistan from their present diplomatic paralysis is virtually impossible to imagine without the direct and sustained involvement of the international community, beginning with the United States. I endorse in its entirety the prescient statement in this regard made early in 2001 in a report of The Asia Foundation Commissioned Task Force on America's Role in Asia. "The United States," it observed flatly, "can no longer afford to be a bystander in [the Kashmir and Afghan disputes], which have been allowed to spin out of control and endanger the entire region as well as Central and Southwest Asia."[55] Unfortunately, when it came to Afghanistan it took a devastating blow directly against the United States to force home the truth of this observation. One hopes that American involvement in the search for a way out of the morass in neighboring Kashmir will not have to await an equally tragic event. Precisely what form would such involvement have to take? Keeping in mind our discussion up to this point in the chapter, I believe that four principles would have to govern it:

1. *Settlement of Jammu and Kashmir's final status must be indefinitely postponed.* This means acquiescence by both India and Pakistan to the ambiguity and continued nonresolution of Kashmir's legal standing—the "permanent impermanence" I spoke of earlier. Acquiescence does not require any change, tacit or otherwise, in the official position on Kashmir of either country. It requires only that each formally and fully agree to set aside for an indefinite period its existing claim—Pakistan that there be an internationally supervised plebiscite, India that a permanent international boundary be finalized between the two (without any territorial loss to India). Postponement implies, of course, that the LOC would retain its present function as a temporary dividing line between the two sides' armed forces;

it would not be converted into a permanent international boundary. Endorsement of this principle would be a concession to the intractability of the issues involved in the Kashmir dispute; it definitely would not be the equivalent of moving the dispute to the political backburner. Kashmir would remain squarely in focus, but as an immediate problem of peacekeeping, not of ethnic self-determination. Not implied here, we should note, is any support for the naively functionalist (and not uncommonly self-serving) position some take that Kashmir will somehow vanish as an issue between India and Pakistan as commercial, cultural, and other forms of contact between them grow.

2. *The necessity for the presence in South Asia of the international peacekeeping force—the UN Military Observer Group in India and Pakistan (UNMOGIP)—authorized by the Security Council in 1949 to police the Cease-Fire Line in Jammu and Kashmir must be reaffirmed by the five permanent members of the Security Council; and the agreement of India and Pakistan to its effective deployment on both sides of the LOC must be obtained.* Effective conduct of a strengthened mission of monitoring and peacekeeping would clearly require a substantial increase in UNMOGIP's authorized manpower. It would also require the formal broadening of its operational charter. Ideally, these steps would be accompanied by the extension of UNMOGIP's deployment to the Siachen Glacier sector in the north as well as to the south along the so-called "working border" in Jammu. Peacekeeping on the LOC, in short, must no longer be a nominal and wholly ineffective enterprise.

3. *There must be a formal commitment by India and Pakistan to the establishment of a joint commission on Jammu and Kashmir responsible for the LOC's administration, liaison with UNMOGIP, prevention of violations, and oversight of such measures of demilitarization of the LOC as may be eventually agreed.* By endorsing this principle, India and Pakistan would be committing themselves to the creation of a permanent, internationally monitored, and routinely functioning instrument for the bilateral management of security cooperation in Jammu and Kashmir.

4. *Vital to the successful adoption and implementation of the above principles is the formal and simultaneous commitment by the five permanent members of the UN Security Council to formation of a suitably empowered international agency, perhaps a revived UN Commission on India and Pakistan (UNCIP II), responsible for negotiating the terms of Indian and Pakistani acceptance of these principles.*

An initial step to win Indian and Pakistani acceptance of these principles has already been taken: All remaining sanctions imposed on them since the 1998 nuclear weapons tests were lifted in September 2001. A logical next step, I believe, would be formal international recognition of India and Pakistan as nuclear weapon states. It would have to be communicated to these two states in the clearest terms possible, however, that any such concession would be made wholly contingent upon formal Indian and Pakistani acceptance and implementation of these four principles. *India and Pakistan must first demonstrate to the satisfaction of the international community, in other words, both their resolve to reduce the threat of war between them as well as to institutionalize the modalities to achieve this reduction.*

Of enormous importance in this context, however, is recognition that neither India nor Pakistan can be bullied into compliance with the West's aspirations for them—certainly not if those aspirations seem to contradict what their governments understand to be their countries' irreducible national interests. They will have to be persuaded that acceptance of the above principles *is* in the national interest. The persuasion will have to be accompanied by irresistible material inducements. One can readily imagine the forms these inducements might take. The package offered to India will naturally vary from that offered to Pakistan. A sample follows:

- Grant of permanent membership in the Security Council;
- Eased access to multilateral organizations of economic cooperation in the Asia-Pacific region, like APEC (Asia Pacific Economic Cooperation) or the ASEAN Regional Forum;
- Reduction or cancellation of debt;
- Assistance in modernizing conventional arms;
- Assistance with nuclear risk-reduction measures, including intelligence sharing with each side;[56]
- Long-term aid to social, economic, and environmental programs;
- Trade concessions;
- Capitalization of fossil, nuclear, and alternative energy projects; and
- Collaboration in scientific and technological fields.

Implied in this fairly random list of inducements is recognition that the international community (or, at least, certain of its leading members) must be prepared to pay a hefty price, whatever the currency, for

Indian and Pakistani acceptance of the outlined principles. This is only to acknowledge, let it be repeated, that India and Pakistan can neither be bullied nor exhorted into acceptance of a deal where all the costs and risks are borne by them. "The United States," observed one recent writer,

> has asked Pakistan to crack down on the militant groups and to close certain madrasahs, but America must do more than just scold. After all, the United States, along with Saudi Arabia, helped create the first international "jihad" to fight the Soviet Union during the Afghan war. "Does America expect us to send in the troops and shut the madrasahs down?" one official asks. "Jihad is a mindset. It developed over many years during the Afghan war. You can't change a mindset in 24 hours."[57]

The writer suggested that the most important contribution the United States could make to Pakistan would be to help strengthen its secular education system. Be that as it may, what is clear is that endorsement of the principles outlined above is far from being cost- or risk-free for either Pakistan or India: Domestic political frailties alone preclude either from setting aside present claims lightly.

Anticipating some of the criticisms likely to be raised against the approach suggested here, I offer the following observations in its defense:

- Pakistan's leaders would be faced with the certainty that Pakistan's material aid in support of armed militancy on the Indian side of the LOC would be deemed inconsistent with the proposed principles and, thus, would have to be terminated. Needless to add, Pakistan's current role in the international coalition against terrorism further underlines the inconsistency in its policies. In light of the strategic importance Pakistan's leaders may attach to the maintenance of guerrilla assets in Indian-controlled Jammu and Kashmir, this would unquestionably be a tough decision to make. In exchange, however, Pakistan's efforts in recent years to secure reaffirmation of the international community's responsibility to help secure a peaceful and just solution to the Kashmir dispute would be strongly rewarded, not just by formal restatement of the territory's disputed status but by international recommitment to peacekeeping (UNMOGIP) and peacemaking (UNCIP II) ventures in Kashmir. Pakistan's material links to the militants in Kashmir would be bartered away, in other words, in return for the dispute's greatly increased internationalization.

• India's leaders would be compelled to stomach the long-resisted internationalization of the Kashmir dispute and in forms (a revived UNMOGIP, for example) that would certainly be difficult to digest. Without doubt, the principles outlined in the discussion above do represent some impairment of Indian sovereignty. The prospect of an end to Pakistan's cross-border support of insurgent activity should prove extremely attractive to Indians, however, as should the deliberate omission from the principles of any provision for Kashmir's final status that might be injurious to India's present territorial status in Jammu and Kashmir.

• Kashmiri Muslims, many thousands of whom have died fighting Indian security forces during the past decade, will find little in these principles to satisfy their craving, whether it be for independence, union with Pakistan, or simply genuine autonomy within India. They would get a vastly enlarged international presence in and commitment to Kashmir, however, along with the realistic prospect that a more peaceful and secure environment would quickly be reintroduced there. The chances for eventual final status negotiations would have been sustained.

• I conceded in Chapter 2 my awareness not only that the international community has for a long time been reticent about "getting involved" in Kashmir but that many of its members, including the United States, had chosen in recent years to "take sides" with India. In this light, the principles outlined here, calling both for major international involvement *and* for evenhandedness between India and Pakistan when it comes to Kashmir, may appear no more practical or consistent with present geopolitical circumstances than those dismissed by me on precisely those grounds. I do not deny that these principles—especially in an American political environment where "de-coupling" of India and Pakistan in the forming of foreign policies along with aggressive efforts at downgrading Pakistan have amassed strong followings in the policymaking community—will be difficult to market.[58] There is a profound difference, however, between them and the approaches I've dismissed: The latter are focused almost exclusively on Kashmir and the issue of self-determination, which I have tried to argue are only one part, in my mind a relatively small part, of what ails India-Pakistan relations. The approach I've recommended may not be any easier to implement, but I would insist that it is focused on the right problem—a power imbalance and a climate of distrust of such instability and inherent danger of catastrophe that it leaves little room for the international community's continued aloofness and neglect.

• Finally, in progress as I write this are the final stages of a massive American-led assault on the terrorist infrastructure of Osama bin Laden's Al Qaeda organization and its Taliban supporters in Afghanistan. The full consequences of this assault are beyond anyone's ability to foresee. One is entitled to hope, however, that among them will be greatly increased attention not just to the problem of terrorism in South Asia but, more importantly, to the inherent instability and constant peril of India-Pakistan relations. If that is among them, then the approach outlined here, or something akin to it, will have vastly greater chances of realization.

Conclusion

We began this extended discussion of Kashmir with the seemingly out-
landish observation that the Kashmir dispute was actually not about Kashmir. At least, it was not *mainly* about Kashmir. The reason for making that
statement should by now be clear: Over the fifty-odd years that the dispute has been in the making, it has grown considerably in scale, sprouted
multiple domestic and international dimensions, and, in the process, become a dispute over much more than ownership of the subcontinent's
northernmost territories. It is today more than anything else a surrogate
battleground in a struggle for dominance of the South Asian region between two of the world's most heavily populated states. As such, it is
inevitably enmeshed very deeply not only in a broad range of security
decisions made by these two states but also in their domestic politics. The
Kashmir dispute is not, however, just between India and Pakistan. On the
contrary, it figures more or less prominently in the strategic calculations
of alliance structure that are presently preoccupying virtually all the states
of Asia. The Kashmir dispute now engages far more actors—and actors of
far greater importance and diversity of interests (at the international, national, and subnational levels)—than anyone imagined it might at its
inception. Over the past decade or so, it has acquired a major separatist
dimension apart from the territorial irredentism with which it was born.
It is an element in a far-reaching discussion of global norms of self-
determination as well as of individual and minority group rights. It is
also, one hardly needs to add, an element in an equally far-reaching and
globe-girdling discussion of religious radicalism and terrorism. The Kashmir dispute is, in short, extraordinarily multifaceted and complicated.
Standing nowadays unequivocally in both the nuclear and terrorist shad-
ows, it is also immeasurably more lethal than ever before.

It is this composite, complex, not to say menacing character of the
Kashmir dispute that explains the oddly juxtaposed and seemingly con-

tradictory preferences I expressed in Chapter 4 of this book, on the one hand for the *postponement* of the quest for its final resolution (for moving that *final status* exercise, so to speak, to the back burner), on the other hand for a simultaneous *upgrade* in international, especially American, attention to it. What I mean to plead for is recognition that the Kashmir issue today *is* vitally important, but less in its own right (whether as a territorial problem carried over from partition or a moral one stemming from the denial of Kashmiri self-determination) than for the larger context it mirrors—a politically consequential and potentially calamitous struggle among major powers for dominance in Asia. For the most part, in other words, the Kashmir dispute is best understood less as a territorial or a moral issue than as a *political* and *strategic*—indeed a *macropolitical* and *macrostrategic*—issue. One can hardly imagine a solution to it, moreover, which does not favor one political or strategic outcome (and one side) over another. This is simply to say that there is not presently at hand a neutral or "win-win" remedy. This goes for autonomy, and it applies equally to Pakistan's demand that the now wholly outmoded Security Council resolutions calling for a plebiscite be faithfully executed as to India's that the fatally flawed bilateralism enshrined in the Simla Accords be scrupulously upheld. These painful truths account for my reticence when it comes to impassioned appeals for the immediate and final resolution of Kashmir.

In arguing that the quest for final resolution of the Kashmir dispute be postponed indefinitely, I am not suggesting that the beleaguered population of Jammu and Kashmir be sacrificed on the altar of *realpolitik*—abandoned, as it were, to an unending nightmare of repression, intimidation, and terror in order not to aggravate a politically perilous situation. On the contrary, the reduction in tensions that I seek between India and Pakistan is inconceivable unless it is accompanied by a sharp, simultaneous, and negotiated reduction in the violence and brutality that have become a routine part of civil life in Kashmir. That altogether desirable change in the civil circumstances of Kashmiris doesn't require, however, a full-blown solution to Kashmir. It can be accomplished in some measure simply by scaling down insurgent and counterinsurgent activity. Such activity, we need perhaps remind ourselves, was marginal to the Kashmir dispute until the late 1980s. In principle, at least, restoring Kashmir to the civil conditions existing prior to that time can be achieved without negotiating any major change in Kashmir's current (and admittedly ambiguous) territorial and constitutional status. I expressed very early in this book, the reader may recall, my preference for an approach that honored what I called the permanence of impermanence. I believe that a positive change in the Kashmir situation will be accomplished far sooner, in fact, if it is *not* made contingent upon the successful negotiation of Kashmir's permanent final status.

Turning to the other side of my argument, the need for an upgrade in international, especially American, attention to Kashmir, we face an even more puzzling issue: In the face of my earlier admission that obstacles to foreign intervention aimed at reconciliation of India and Pakistan were formidable, what explains my persisting belief that the substantial international diplomatic investment I called for in Chapter 4 would be duly rewarded with a measurably improved security environment in South Asia? Are there substantial grounds for this belief? I think there are.

In the first place, the record of India-Pakistan relations offers convincing evidence that these two rivals are perfectly capable of negotiating workable agreements in regard to matters of extreme importance to both sides and, more importantly, *of sustaining cooperative official interaction in regard to these matters over a long period of time.* Neither state is pathologically wedded to a relationship of pure conflict. Most notable in this connection is the record they have compiled in fulfilling the negotiated commitments of the Indus Waters Treaty concluded in 1960. Acting under Article VII (5) of that treaty, Indian and Pakistani officials met in Islamabad at the end of May 2001 and planned to meet again in New Delhi at the end of May 2002 for two-day annual meetings of the Permanent Indus Commission of India and Pakistan.[1] Similar meetings have been held in one country or the other annually (engineering teams representing both sides meet more frequently, generally every two months) without a break—and regardless of war and continuous tensions in India-Pakistan relations—for four decades.[2] What accounts for this exceptional instance of interstate cooperation?

The Indus Waters Treaty was arrived at only after a lengthy, arduous, and internationally mediated negotiation founded on the core principle, formally proposed in 1954, that the only realistic basis for an agreement was acceptance of a quantitative "division of the waters" of the Indus basin between the two countries. This meant granting India and Pakistan permanent and exclusive use of the waters of three rivers each— Pakistan acquiring virtually exclusive use of the waters of the three western rivers (the Indus, Jhelum, and Chenab), India likewise of the three eastern rivers (the Ravi, Beas, and Sutlej).

University of Pennsylvania political scientist E. Sridharan offers a number of interlocking reasons for the acceptance and long-term success of this formula. Insofar as the agreement's initial acceptance was concerned, he suggests, a crucial provision was the one providing for continued water supply to areas in Pakistan, the lower riparian in this case and historically dependent on waters slated for allocation to India. The device to achieve this was construction of replacement canals drawing waters from the three western rivers assigned for Pakistan's use. Construction of the canals was assured by offers of assistance worth $1 billion from six friendly countries and the World Bank.[3] Instrumental in winning acceptance of the agreement, in Sridharan's view, was the fact that the negotiations were conducted between 1954 and the treaty's signing in 1960 by engineering technicians, some of them pre-partition colleagues, rather than by politicians or diplomats. That enabled a consistent focus on functional instead of political issues. It is possible, Sridharan suggests, that the treaty would not have been approved, moreover, without international mediation by the World Bank, considered neutral by both sides.[4]

Insofar as the agreement's long-term survivability was concerned, the most crucial feature of the treaty, according to Sridharan, was to be found in the core principle itself—that is, in "the technical feature . . . that divided up the waters into three rivers each to India and Pakistan for their separate and independent development, rather than joint development." That feature, he says, "was necessary for the survival of the agreement by not requiring continuing interaction for decision making and implementation over joint development of the waters by two countries at loggerheads over Kashmir."[5] Of some consequence, too, he adds, has been the incentive for India to be faithful to the treaty's provisions due to its own vulnerability as a lower riparian in the case of other important rivers with their headwaters in Nepal and China.

Naturally, the Indus Waters Treaty cannot be held up as a model for all aspects of India-Pakistan relations. Not all of them, unfortunately, can be reduced to technical questions or tidily rearranged so as to require only a minimum of government interaction and joint official decision making. The Indus Waters Treaty is clearly instructive, nevertheless, in that it speaks powerfully not only for a politically pragmatic approach to India-Pakistan relations but also, and just as importantly, for a central and positive international role. What it discounts, by inference, is the proposition that India-Pakistan relations are unalterably hostile, in some way pre programmed for myopic and unyielding animosity toward one another. That proposition, revered doctrine in some quarters it seems, should be viewed with skepticism.

In the second place, the current agenda of India-Pakistan relations clearly offers opportunities to negotiate additional workable agreements and, thus, to expand the extraordinarily narrow current foundation for bilateral cooperation. This agenda includes issues that are ripe, in fact, for application of the principles that seem to have facilitated successful negotiation of the Indus Waters Treaty. In this regard, proposed energy-sharing projects come first to mind.

The energy context, briefly summarized, is as follows: India and Pakistan are both energy-deficit states. Neither state is able to meet current, much less future, energy needs exclusively from domestic sources. In both countries, but especially in India, energy consumption is rising at a rapid rate. To meet the rising demand, both spend a large portion of their national income to purchase energy supplies from abroad. Global production may not be able to keep pace with the demand, resulting at a minimum in higher energy prices, and possibly in increased resource tension and conflict.[6] The economies of both countries have been severely impaired in the past by shortfalls in energy supplies. If the shortfalls are not corrected, the costs to both countries—economic, social, and political—are likely to be large. Significant energy relief is available to both from enhanced energy cooperation between them. At the moment, there is none.

There are, of course, major differences between India and Pakistan in regard to the specifics of energy resources. India, the world's sixth largest energy consumer, has an abundance of coal. Domestic production of coal meets over half of India's current energy demand. Pakistan, for its part, is relatively self-sufficient in natural gas, though only in the near term; and, owing to a major investment in the increase of its (mainly thermal) power-generating capacity in recent years, it currently has an oversupply of electric power. Neither country, however, meets current demand for oil from existing domestic oil supplies, and demand for oil is generally expected to grow rapidly in both of them.[7]

Discussion of enhanced energy cooperation between India and Pakistan has focused for a number of years primarily on electric power and natural gas. In regard to the former, discussions between the two governments in 2000 in regard to temporary transfer of surplus electric power from the Pakistani grid to India have so far yielded no tangible results.

Far greater importance, in any event, attaches to the potential for cooperation in regard to natural gas.

Natural gas, which in 1999 accounted for about 40 percent of Pakistan's commercial energy consumption, falls just behind oil (41.9 percent) as Pakistan's single largest source of commercial energy. In India, where it accounted in 1999 for only about 7.1 percent of total commercial energy consumption, natural gas falls well behind coal (51.5 percent) and petroleum (33.2 percent). Both countries, however, are expected to rely in the future much more heavily on environment-friendlier natural gas to meet energy requirements. In neither, unfortunately, will known domestic reserves of natural gas be sufficient to meet the expected explosive growth in demand. India's domestic natural gas output is paltry. Currently, its plans call for bridging the gas demand-supply gap in part with imports of liquid natural gas (LNG) from abroad. This will require heavy investment, apart from carriers and domestic distribution pipelines, in construction of LNG terminals. The estimated cost of setting up such terminals is $8 billion.[8] Once considered adequate for the country's needs well into the twenty-first century, Pakistan's own natural gas reserves are rapidly being depleted. Happily, India and Pakistan border natural gas rich regions: two of them (the Gulf states and Central Asia) on the west, one of them (Bangladesh) on the east. There is, thus, a seemingly attractive alternative—that of importing natural gas by pipeline—close at hand. Neither Pakistan nor India, however, currently imports natural gas supplies from any of these regional sources.

Natural gas export pipeline proposals have been surfacing with some regularity in regard to India and Pakistan for at least a decade. By early 1997, according to one writer, there were already five separate pipeline-based gas import schemes under consideration. Two of them were to serve India—one crossing the Arabian Sea from Eastern Oman to the Indian state of Gujrat, and a second originating in southern Iran, crossing the Arabian Sea, bypassing Pakistan's territorial waters, and ending in Gujrat. Three others were to serve Pakistan—one, a land-based pipeline, from Iran to Karachi; a second, sea-based, from Qatar to Karachi; and a third, land-based, from Turkmenistan through western Afghanistan to Sui in Pakistan's Baluchistan province.[9] All of them faced vexing financial and technical problems. Some of them, the Turkmenistan option not the least of these, also faced staggering political problems. Together, they gave rise to a brisk and high-stakes "pipeline diplomacy" aimed at overcoming obstacles in their path.

Not surprisingly, this diplomacy turned rather quickly to an additional option—that of constructing an India-Pakistan pipeline that would enable transmission of natural gas from fields in Qatar, Turkmenistan, or Iran entirely by technologically simple and much less expensive overland routes. Raising this option, however, just as quickly focused attention on the huge impediment to "functional" cooperation presented by the strategic rivalry between India and Pakistan. Viewed from one angle, the logic of constructing one or more land-based pipelines connecting the gas fields of Central and Southwest Asia with energy-hungry consumers in South Asia was incontrovertible. Viewed from another angle, however, the obstacles presented by its politics seemed insuperable.

Recently, prospects for overcoming these obstacles have appeared to brighten. They brightened, we should note, in part because discussion between India and Iran in regard to construction of a natural gas pipeline had turned to consider a formula reminiscent of that which had enabled long-term survival of the Indus Waters Treaty of 1960. That formula, we may recall, involved the deliberate avoidance of a requirement for "continuing interaction for decision making and implementation over joint development of the waters by two countries at loggerheads over Kashmir." In like manner, the formula for an overland (trans-Pakistan) pipeline route put forward in talks between India and Iran in June 2001 had essentially the same objective—deliberate avoidance of continuous and joint decision making by India and Pakistan. It would achieve this by stipulating that the core contractual agreement providing for regular and secure delivery of Iranian natural gas to India via the trans-Pakistan pipeline would be bilateral—*but between the supplier (Iran) and the purchaser (India), not between India and Pakistan.* As for Pakistan's transit responsibilities, these would be for Iran and its multinational oil and banking associates to iron out directly with Islamabad. Tabling of this novel formula was unlikely, by itself, to overcome Indian reticence either to mortgage its energy future to Pakistan's goodwill or to help bail Islamabad out of its present economic difficulties. Neither did it rule out the alternative—an underwater pipeline bypassing Pakistan. However, by pragmatic avoidance of any requirement for either a three-party (India, Pakistan, Iran) or two-party (India and Pakistan) accord and by adroit substitution in their place of provision for two paired bilateral agreements (Iran-India and Iran-Pakistan), the politically ingenious formula had given a clear boost to the practicality of India-Pakistan energy cooperation.[10]

Please note here that it is not my intention to exaggerate the scale of the opportunity shared energy needs seem to offer for expanding the current foundation for bilateral cooperation between India and Pakistan. The fact is that huge obstacles, even apart from the unyielding political animosity and military threat that encumber India-Pakistan relations, lie in the path of the contemplated Iran-Pakistan-India pipeline. One of them is Iran's continued designation by the U.S. Department of State as a state sponsor of terrorism—a designation not likely to help in freeing up global capital resources for the pipeline project. Another is the existence of alternative and equally attractive energy pipeline proposals, such as the project that would connect the Bangladesh natural gas fields with the huge Indian market, that might come with less political baggage. While I strongly concur with Shamila N. Chaudhury that the Iran to India natural gas pipeline "is a venture which may change the face of regional politics in South Asia," her designation of it as a "peace pipeline" with the power to transform "social and political discourse between the countries, perhaps even leading to mediation and resolution of regional conflicts," runs the substantial risk of overrating energy cooperation as a driver of interstate politics.[11] The antidote to India-Pakistan animosity will have to be far more comprehensive than a gas pipeline.

A third and final ground for my belief that substantial international (especially American) diplomatic investment in India-Pakistan relations will result in a measurably improved regional security environment is simply this: The South Asian security environment did not acquire its present shape in a political vacuum, that is, solely by decisions reached in New Delhi and Islamabad. Neither is its future shape likely to be hammered out exclusively in these two capitals. The hostility between India and Pakistan has always had—and it unquestionably has now—multiple roots, some of them extraregional. Their hostility was never in the past—and it is not now—entirely of their own making. It arose in some measure from, or was at least reinforced by, the strategic compulsions arising from the Cold War. These included powerful incentives and disincentives deliberately placed before Indian and Pakistani decision makers by their American and Soviet suitors. Without a shadow of a doubt, those who stand at the helm of global affairs today can place equally powerful incentives and disincentives before Indian and Pakistani decision makers that can either boost or depress prospects for regional security cooperation. Pretending otherwise—claiming, for instance, that the West can do nothing to improve India-Pakistan relations until India and Pakistan have themselves taken convincing *bilateral* steps in that direction—is a prescription for deepening and unending conflict.

Let us be clear about this. India's leaders for years complained bitterly that Washington's forging of a strategic anticommunist alliance with Pakistan in the early 1950s had, besides souring prospects for closer ties between India and the United States, substantially widened the rift between India and Pakistan. Whatever hopes there might have been in those years for a bilateral agreement between these two countries over Kashmir were dashed to pieces, Indian (and many Western) observers have commented countless times, on the rock of American containment policies in Asia. These observers sometimes overstated their case. In no small measure, however, they were right: Washington's insistence on giving highest priority in framing its South Asian security policies to Pakistan's inclusion in an anti-Soviet bloc of Western-led Asian rimland states inevitably impacted heavily on New Delhi's own security perceptions and, as the emergence in the latter half of the 1950s of increasingly close ties between Moscow and New Delhi attests, eventual policy choices. This is not to say that Washington's priorities were necessarily misplaced, only that they were not innocent of responsibility for the strategic trajectories Pakistani and Indian decision makers chose for their own countries.

With memory of those Cold War years still quite fresh, there is more than a little irony in the fact that in recent years it has been Pakistani leaders who have been complaining—often in much the same language—that Washington's forging of a steadily closer strategic partnership with New Delhi threatened to exact a heavy price in India-Pakistan relations. There should be no discrimination between India and Pakistan when it comes to the lifting of American sanctions, Pakistan's ambassador to Washington, Dr. Maleeha Lodhi, declared in late June 2001 at a meeting of the Pakistan American Congress, and "a balanced U.S. policy is critical to the realization of the goals of peace, stability and long-term economic development of Asia. It would encourage conflict-resolution and foster peace and cooperation." If Washington backs New Delhi's efforts at regional domination, she said, echoing several generations of Indian envoys who preceded her in the U.S. capital, this would likely "accentuate political tensions, increase diplomatic intransigence, perpetuate regional conflicts and intensify instability in the region."[12] She, like those earlier envoys, was almost certainly right.

Even greater irony appears, however, in the yet more recent fact of

Pakistan's emergence as a key player in the American-orchestrated global coalition against terrorism—a designation that began almost at once to multiply Pakistan's political leverage with the West. This designation could conceivably result in Pakistan's greater internal political stability. It could even result in conditions conducive to the negotiation of a new and more stable relationship with India. Much will depend, however, on the manner in which the coalition pursues its war against terrorism; much will also depend on the skill with which America and its allies manage their relationships with both India and Pakistan. Nothing, to be perfectly clear here, is any more important to the development of a peaceful relationship between these two states than the *external* environment now being so forcefully and fundamentally reshaped.

So it comes down to the fact that Western (especially American) strategic priorities and objectives *inevitably* have a role to play—a *determinative* role to play—in setting the agenda of India-Pakistan relations. It was so during the Cold War years. Then, the United States chose mainly to favor Pakistan. Its choice antagonized India, at times quite severely. India-Pakistan relations were not infrequently sacrificed to what were then fairly widely regarded in the United States as more important ends. As we have seen in earlier chapters, powerful voices have been calling upon the U.S. government in recent years to favor India. They have claimed that there are more important ends to be served (economic as well as political and strategic) than fostering friendlier India-Pakistan relations. Had Washington given this claim its flat endorsement and, thus, closed the book finally on nearly a half of a century of U.S.-Pakistan strategic cooperation, it would undoubtedly have antagonized Pakistan very badly. Insofar as India-Pakistan relations were concerned (or, for that matter, the resolution of Kashmir), any such definitive step would almost certainly have had immediate and negative results. The same goes for the present. In the initial moments of the West's counterterrorist campaign, equally portentous priorities have been set and equally weighty policy decisions made. The Afghanistan crisis, no less than the Cold War, is bound to unleash its own distinctive set of strategic imperatives. It is yet too early to know whether these imperatives will operate to drive India and Pakistan further apart . . . or closer together.

Deciding U.S. strategic priorities in South Asia is, of course, no simple matter. Washington has multiple interests in the region, and some of them are bound to be in conflict with one another. They cannot all be pursued at once—or with the same level of commitment. Moreover, South

Asia is only one subregion among several in the Asia-Pacific, and American policy priorities in regard to South Asia naturally have to be determined in full view of Washington's strategic aims throughout the entire Asia-Pacific region. Washington's pursuit of these aims cannot be expected to satisfy all interests—or to reward all countries—equally. By the same token, however, precisely how Washington chooses to define and then to pursue these aims will itself be a major factor in the determination of which interests are satisfied as well as of how the rewards are distributed. The fundamental questions, therefore, are: What should those aims be? And how should they be pursued?

In the last several years, Washington has been locked in a strategic debate focused squarely on these questions. Two main schools of thought have emerged in the debate. One, the *unilateralist* school, drawing primarily on a conservative reading of trends in Asian international politics, has emphasized the importance of protecting American interests in an essentially unipolar (America dominant) world by building bilateral "strategic partnerships" along conventional lines with those Asian or Eurasian states having a shared interest in containing international "rogue" states and/or China. The other, the *multilateralist* school, drawing largely on liberal understandings of trends in Asian international politics, takes the position that America's undoubted economic and military primacy in the Asia-Pacific region will be best sustained in the twenty-first century by putting at the center of Washington's plans the augmentation of existing bilateral security arrangements in the region with determinedly crafted arrangements aimed at the development of multilateral security cooperation. As one pair of authors of this school put it:

> The fundamental security challenge in the Asia-Pacific region is to transform the balance-of-power approach proposed by those who advocate a multipolar global power structure into one that instead aims to produce security communities in which disputes are not resolved by threats or the employment of force. The process will be one of building upon bilateral security relationships to form a web of regional relationships and capabilities that reinforce security for individual states, discouraging armed aggression as a way of settling disputes, and developing habits of regional military cooperation and professional military behavior.[13]

Either side in this strategic debate could take comfort from the recent Afghanistan crisis. The deployment of massive armed force, *American* armed force, at least temporarily marginalized all talk of building cooperation-inclined security communities. Overwhelming military power took center stage, reminding everyone that tending to the balance-of-power retained life-or-death importance in international relations. For the moment, at least, force was in, dialogue was out. Equally true, however, was the enormous importance the United States appeared to attach at the time to forging as large a global coalition as possible for the long-term containment of the terrorist threat. In this respect, then, multilateralism was definitely in; unilateralism, at least in so far as the *global* containment of terrorism was concerned, was seemingly out.

The Bush administration, more than its predecessor in the White House and well before the Afghanistan crisis erupted, had consciously shifted the attention of security policy makers to the Asia-Pacific region. Their attention had been drawn, in particular, to China, the only Asian power about whose capacity for challenging America for dominance in Asia a credible case can be made. Bush administration spokespersons routinely disclaimed any intention to label China an enemy.[14] An array of steps taken by the Bush administration in its early months in office seemed to many observers, however, to belie the disclaimers. If these steps did, in fact, eventually culminate in a new Sino-American Cold War, the impact on U.S. security policies in South Asia would very likely be immense. Pakistan's already close ties with Beijing would almost certainly grow closer and further cloud Islamabad's jittery relationship with Washington, and, as we have already discussed, India's attractiveness as a partner for Washington would likely be enhanced. India-Pakistan relations, in turn, would likely be among the casualties.

The most realistic conceptual benchmark upon which to base strategic thinking in regard to the Asia-Pacific region lies somewhere midway, I believe, between the multilateralist and unilateralist concepts now vying for attention. The former, in emphasizing multilateral cooperation across a broad range of what are often called "transnational" issues, tends not only to exaggerate the relative importance of those issues but also to understate the persistence of—as well as prudential necessity for—traditional (and, characteristically, more war-fighting) security orientations and practices. The latter, the unilateralist concept, in calling for an emphasis on self-help measures to guard U.S. interests, not infrequently confuses mere arrogance, pugnacity, and jingoism with realism.[15] When it comes specifically to the South Asian subregion, however, in which the primary security challenge is clearly that of replacing raw hostility between India and Pakistan with a measure of cooperative behavior suited to two nuclear-equipped neighboring powers, I have no doubt that the accent in U.S. security policy needs to be located nearer to the multilateral side of the strategic continuum—on the side, in other words, where building security cooperation between these two historic rivals is the primary, albeit not exclusive, policy objective. Putting the accent anywhere else, however strong the temptation, will do little to ensure continued American primacy in the Asia-Pacific. It will, however, add yet another impediment to the reduction of hostility between India and Pakistan. Given the price the citizens of these two states have already paid for this hostility, making sure that the accent is put where it belongs should be the overriding priority of U.S. security planners.

* * *

Two great nations, India and Pakistan, face one another today in a region shadowed menacingly both by terrorism and the onrushing Nuclear Revolution. Having far more in common with one another than either would ever admit, they enter upon the turbulent political terrain of the twenty-first century bent with a burden of fear and distrust that neither, whether acting alone or even in company with its hostile neighbor, is fully empowered to remove. If it is not soon removed, however, or at least substantially reduced, the progress made by these two countries in this new century will not escape the extraordinarily heavy economic, political, and social penalties both paid in the last. To lend a determined international hand to the removal or reduction of this burden seems, in the end, an imperative of responsible global statesmanship. One may hope that such a hand will soon be extended.

Notes

Chapter 1. The Problem of Regional Rivalry: The "Nuclearization" of the Kashmir Dispute

1. "Pakistani's Words: 'To Restore the Strategic Balance,'" *New York Times* Web service, 29 May 1998.

2. As many as 152 national governments voiced their opposition to the tests. Strobe Talbott, "Dealing with the Bomb in South Asia," *Foreign Affairs* 78:2 (March/April 1999): 110.

3. "Text on India, Pakistan Statement," *Associated Press* Web service, 4 June 1998.

4. "U.N. Urges End to Nuclear Tests," *Associated Press* Web service, 6 June 1998.

5. T. R. Reid, "G-8 Puts Pressure on India and Pakistan," *Washington Post* Web service, 13 June 1998.

6. John Ward Anderson, "Kashmir Earns a Place on Global Agenda," *Washington Post* Web service (4 June 1998).

7. "Text on India, Pakistan Statement," *Associated Press* Web service, 4 June 1998.

8. "P-5 Plays It Cool," *Hindustan Times*, 6 June 1998.

9. John Kifner, "Through Nuclear Crisis, Pakistan Publicizes Kashmir Struggle," *New York Times* Web service, 3 June 1998.

10. John F. Burns, "Some Disputes Get Settled. Then There's Kashmir," *New York Times*, 9 August 1998, p. 4.

11. "Vajpayee Cancels Pakistan's Visit," *News*, 21 September 2001.

12. For the text of the agreement, see Michael Krepon et al. (eds.), "Indo-Pak Joint Working Groups Agreement, 23 June 1997," *A Handbook of Confidence-Building Measures for Regional Security*, 3rd edition (Washington, D.C.: The Henry L. Stimson Center, March 1998), pp. 199–200.

13. Rival versions of the 23 June Joint Statement were circulated, suitably amended to lend credence to one or another side's interpretation. For an Indian version, see the July 1–15, 1997, issue of *India News*, a fortnightly publication of the Embassy of India in Washington, D.C.

14. K.K. Katyal, "PM to Take Bus to Lahore," *Hindu*, 4 February 1999.

15. K.K. Katyal, "No Ordinary Bus Ride This," *Hindu*, 15 February 1999; "Bon Voyage, Atalji," *Times of India*, 20 February 1999; Malini Parthasarathy, "U.S. Sees

Potential in Indo-Pak 'Bus Diplomacy,'" *Hindu*, 6 February 1999; and M.P. Bhandara, "Bus to Pakistan," *Dawn*, 20 February 1999.

16. Barry Bearak, "Indian Leader Visits Pakistan in a Rare Show of Friendship," *New York Times* Web service, 21 February 1999.

17. K.K. Katyal, "Symbolism and More," *Hindu*, 1 March 1999.

18. Seema Guha, "Ice Is Finally Broken," *Times of India*, 22 February 1999.

19. For the text of all three documents, see "The Lahore Declaration," *Hindu*, 22 February 1999.

20. V.R. Raghavan, "The Lahore Declaration & Security," *Hindu*, 3 March 1999.

21. Amit Baruah, "No Secret Deal on Kashmir: Sartaj Aziz," *Hindu*, 9 March 1999.

22. A.G. Noorani, "Kargil Diplomacy," *Frontline* Web service, 16:1 (31 July–13 August 1999), and "An Aborted Deal?" *Frontline* Web service, 16:18 (28 August–10 September 1999). See also Amit Baruah, "Efforts On to End Kargil Conflict: Naik," *Hindu*, 1 July 1999. Noorani's rendering of the four points of the alleged agreement reached in New Delhi on 27 June differs slightly from the portrayal of them given to the author by Naik. In Noorani's version, they were: (1) that appropriate steps were to be adopted by both sides to assure mutual respect for the LOC in accord with the 1972 Simla Accord; (2) that the Lahore dialogue process was to be immediately resumed; (3) that Islamabad was to use its influence with the intruders to bring about their disengagement; and (4) that an expeditious solution to the Kashmir dispute was to be sought within a specified time frame.

23. Amit Baruah, "Kargil Impeded Pact on Kashmir: Niaz Naik," *Hindu*, 15 September 1999.

24. For the text of his rebuttal, see "Niaz A. Naik Rebuts Remarks About Kargil Diplomacy," *News*, 17 September 1999.

25. See, for example, Hussain Haqqani, "Blaming the Army," *Nation*, 18 September 1999; the editorial "Confusion Confounded," *News*, 18 September 1999; and the editorial "Not So Secret," *Times of India*, 20 September 1999.

26. "Eviction of Intruders Complete: DGMO," *Hindu*, 27 July 1999.

27. "ISPR Refutes India Could Have Blocked Karachi Seaport," *Dawn*, 29 July 1999.

28. K. Subrahmanyam, "Kargil Balance Sheet," *Times of India*, 26 July 1999. The Indian figure was later officially changed to 519. "519 Troops Lost in Kashmir Conflict," *Dawn*, 3 December 1999. The report of the Indian-government-appointed Kargil Review Committee, released on 15 December 1999, gave the figure of 474 men killed and 1,109 wounded. *From Surprise to Reckoning* (New Delhi: Sage Publications, 2000), p. 23.

29. "Jackal's Trap," *Times of India*, 14 June 1999.

30. Two volumes that help substantially to overcome the relative paucity of official (Indian and Pakistani) disclosure in regard to Kargil are: Ashok Krishna and P.R. Chari (eds.), *Kargil: The Tables Turned* (New Delhi: Manohar, 2001); and Kargil Review Committee, *From Surprise to Reckoning*, cited above.

31. See, for instance, the article "Pakistan's Debt Burden to Reach Point of No Return Next Year," *Nation*, 5 August 1999.

32. An editorial in *Dawn*, Pakistan's leading daily newspaper and a frequent and outspoken advocate of greater cooperation with India, set the tone in an essay entitled "Stepping Beyond the Symbolic." The Indian prime minister's visit to Lahore (the editorial commented on the day of Vajpayee's arrival) was to be welcomed as an

opportunity "to set the ball rolling for a new era of detente in South Asia." If the meeting did not produce results more tangible than the pomp and spectacle on exhibit at Lahore, however, "no one," it observed, "should be surprised if the glory of this day turns quickly to dust and disappointment." *Dawn*, 20 February 1999.

33. See, for instance, Seema Guha, "A New Dawn Breaks Over Lahore," *Times of India*, 21 February 1999.

34. V.R. Raghavan, "A Turning Point in Kashmir," *Frontline* Web service, 16:12 (5–18 June 1999).

35. On the above points, see also P.R. Chari, "Some Preliminary Observations," in *Kargil: The Tables Turned*, Krishna and Chari (eds.), pp. 16–17.

36. See Chari, "Some Preliminary Observations," p. 17. See also Balraj Puri, "Kargil in the Perspective of Indo-Pak Conflicts," *Mainstream* (31 July 1999), p. 2.

37. Robert G. Wirsing, *India, Pakistan, and the Kashmir Dispute* (New York: St. Martin's Press, 1994), pp. 150–52.

38. Dinesh Kumar, "India Lost Tracts Along LoC to Pak Army 15 Years Ago," *Times of India*, 1 July 1999.

39. "Leghari Questions Kargil 'Adventure,'" *Dawn*, 2 August 1999.

40. *From Surprise to Reckoning*, pp. 89–90.

41. Ibid., pp. 90–91.

42. Ibid., pp. 91–92.

43. For additional speculation on Pakistan's motivations in undertaking the Kargil operation, see various authors in *Kargil: The Tables Turned*.

44. In a National Assembly debate, Pakistan's foreign minister offered two objectives for the Kargil operation—one, which he claimed emerged only during the course of the operation, was to internationalize the Kashmir dispute; the other, originating from the freedom-fighters themselves, was to demonstrate their mounting ability to occupy and hold territory. "Kashmir Issue Internationalised After Failure of Covert Agreement," *News*, 14 August 1999.

45. The Indians claim that the conversation, which appears to have occurred between Musharraf, then in Beijing, and a key deputy in Pakistan on the day following the downing near Kargil of an Indian Air Force Mi-17 helicopter with Stinger missiles, reveals the heavy hand of the Pakistan army in the conduct of the Kargil operation. Portions of the surreptitiously recorded conversation were made available on *Times of India* Web service, in both print and audio form, for weeks thereafter. For what is described as the complete verbatim record of two nearly back-to-back conversations between Musharraf and his deputy, see Appendix 10 in *Kargil: The Tables Turned*, pp. 315–20. In the wake of Prime Minister Nawaz Sharif's overthrow by the Pakistan army in October 1999, unconfirmed and possibly apocryphal reports surfaced that the army's own intelligence apparatus—the Inter-Service Intelligence Directorate (ISI)—had made the telephonic intercept and had quietly conveyed a recording of it to Nawaz Sharif, by then already at odds with Chief of Army Staff General Pervez Musharraf. Allegedly, Sharif passed the recording (doctored, according to some accounts), while fighting still raged at Kargil, via secret channels to the Indian government. See "Was Kargil Tape Doctored?" *Times of India*, 2 December 1999. For a careful discussion (from the Indian point of view) of the numbers and composition of the intruding forces, see *From Surprise to Reckoning*, pp. 96–98, 102–4.

46. M.P. Bhandara, "On the Edge of the Precipice," *Dawn*, 21 July 1999.

47. Jaswant Singh, "Kargil and Beyond," speech given at the India International

Centre in New Delhi on 20 July 1999, text reproduced by the Embassy of India Web service.

48. This is the argument implicit in the post-Kargil position expounded, for instance, by the Pakistani Foreign Minister Sartaj Aziz, who has claimed repeatedly that Pakistan achieved its aims at Kargil by forcing the Kashmir issue to the top of the global agenda. "Objectives in Kargil Achieved: Sartaj," *Dawn*, 30 July 1999. See also "Opposition Criticized: Kargil Pullout Was Part of Operation," *Dawn*, 16 August 1999.

49. "Mushahid Likens Kargil Operation with Palestinian Intifada," *Nation*, 7 August 1999.

50. For a labored and ultimately unconvincing argument that Nawaz Sharif was fully informed by army headquarters in advance of the Kargil operation, see D. Suba Chandran, "Why Kargil? Pakistan's Objectives and Motivation," in *Kargil: The Tables Turned*, pp. 24–30. See also Inder Malhotra, "Row Over Niaz Naik 'Revelations,'" *Hindu*, 22 September 1999.

51. Maleeha Lodhi, "Anatomy of a Debacle," *Newsline* (July 1999). Lodhi's observations were echoed at the time by (then) ex-Foreign Minister Abdul Sattar, who wrote in an unusually blunt article that the Pakistan government's "shallow and myopic policies are manifest in pendulum swings from childish bus diplomacy to the Kargil gamble, from glorifying bilateral negotiations in the pompous Lahore declaration to self-deceiving claims in inducting American interest in resolving Kashmir." Abdul Sattar, "Harvest of Folly," *News*, 15 July 1999. Following the military coup on 12 October of that year, Sattar was drawn from retirement by General Pervez Musharraf and reappointed Pakistan's foreign minister.

52. See my discussion of this in Wirsing, *India, Pakistan, and the Kashmir Dispute*, pp. 208–10.

53. In correspondence with the author, 20 December 2000.

54. *From Surprise to Reckoning*, p. 102.

55. Praful Bidwai, "New Delhi's Draft Nuclear Doctrine Could Ignite Arms Race," *Dawn*, 23 August 1999.

56. Amit Baruah, "Any Weapon Will Be Used, Threatens Pak," *Hindu*, 1 June 1999.

57. John Lancaster, "Kashmir Crisis Was Defused on Brink of War," *Washington Post* Web service, 26 July 1999. British Minister for Foreign and Commonwealth Affairs Peter Hain reportedly made much the same claim, suggesting in a newspaper interview in London in late November that the British government had evidence that India and Pakistan had, in fact, come "very close" to a nuclear exchange over Kashmir during the Kargil crisis. Hain disclosed no details. "Peter Hain's Disclosure: Pakistan, India Came Close to Nuclear Exchange," *Dawn*, 30 November 1999.

58. "India Denies Post Report," *Times of India*, 28 July 1999.

59. See, for instance, Ramesh Chandran, "Clinton's Intervention Averted Indo-Pak War: Post," *Times of India*, 27 July 1999; and the editorial, "Post-facto Rationalisation?" *Nation*, 28 July 1999.

60. Bruce O. Riedel, "American Diplomacy and the 1999 Kargil Summit at Blair House," *Policy Paper Series 2002* (Philadelphia: Center for the Advanced Study of India (CASI) website, May 2002). See also: Alan Sipress and Thomas E. Ricks, "Report: India, Pakistan Were Near Nuclear War in '99," *Washington Post*, 15 May 2002, p. A1.

61. Devin T. Hagerty, *The Consequences of Nuclear Proliferation: Lessons from South Asia* (Cambridge: MIT Press, 1998).

62. Ibid., p. 112.

63. Ibid., p. 163.

64. Ibid., p. 3.

65. Ibid., p. 7.

66. Rodney W. Jones and Mark G. McDonough, *Tracking Nuclear Proliferation: A Guide in Maps and Charts, 1998* (Washington, D.C.: Carnegie Endowment for International Peace, 1998), p. 138.

67. Rodney W. Jones, *Minimum Nuclear Deterrence Postures in South Asia: An Overview* (Washington, D.C.: Defense Threat Reduction Agency Final Report, 1 October 2001), pp. 37–38. About the objectivity of open-source public debate over nuclear weapons in India and Pakistan, Jones cautions [p. 6] that

> official Indian and Pakistani statements about nuclear capacity or defense posture are laden with political and public relations content, omit mention of strategic and operational issues, and reveal little about nuclear stability objectives. The repeated assertion of "minimum nuclear deterrence" itself is vague and not verifiable. The same must be said of any "no-first use" pledge. The mere fact that there seems to be a vibrant, open debate among defense experts and media figures in South Asia should not be confused by Western analysts with local military transparency or analytical objectivity—in either country.

68. Claims that Pakistan had actually achieved ballistic missile superiority over India cropped up fairly regularly in the latter months of 2000. One widely read Indian military analyst declared, for instance, that India was beginning to look "miltarily powerless and vulnerable." Pravin K. Sawhney, "Pakistan Scores Over India in Ballistic Missile Race," *Jane's Intelligence Review*, Asia Section, 12:11 (1 November 2000).

69. Rodney W. Jones, "Pakistan's Nuclear Posture," *Dawn*, 14 and 15 September 1999. Indian press commentary, though commonly critical of the timing of the document's release by the BJP-led interim government on the eve of national elections, was generally approving of its contents. For some harshly critical Indian commentary, see V.R. Raghavan, "A Debatable Nuclear Doctrine," *Hindu*, 24 August 1999; and Praful Bidwai, "New Delhi's Draft Nuclear Doctrine Could Ignite Arms Race," *Dawn*, 23 August 1999. For the Draft Report itself, see the Embassy of India Web service.

70. Ashley J. Tellis, *India's Emerging Nuclear Doctrine: Exemplifying the Lessons of the Nuclear Revolution*, 12:2 *NBR Analysis* (Seattle: The National Bureau of Asian Research, May 2001), pp. 5–6. (Emphasis in original.)

71. Ibid., p. 19.

72. Ibid., p. 22.

73. Ibid., p. 21.

74. Ibid., p. 34. Tellis comments that "the exaggerated Indian emphasis on nuclear weapons as political rather than military instruments must . . . be seen as a solution that derives from more than simply a specific strategic problematic: its viability ultimately is ensured by the fact that it tolerates the possession of such weapons only so long as possession itself is grounded in the rationale that nuclear weapons cannot be treated as weapons *per se* and used as such." The draft nuclear report, he

notes, begins with a quite unique preamble that "sings the praises of universal nuclear disarmament," while ending with an appeal for, among other things, early achieve-ment of a nuclear-weapon-free world (p. 35).

75. Ibid., p. 104.

76. Ibid., p. 106.

77. George Perkovich's conclusions about India's motivations for going nuclear are consistent in most respects with Tellis's point of view. For Perkovich, as for Tellis, India's motivations are overwhelmingly political, rather than military, and are fundamentally defensive and nonaggressive in character. See Perkovich, *India's Nuclear Bomb* (Berke-ley: University of California Press, 1999), pp. 444–68. For a sympathetic review of Tellis's study, see Sumit Ganguly, "Behind India's Bomb: The Politics and Strategy of Nuclear Deterrence," *Foreign Affairs* 80:5 (September/October 2001): 136–42.

78. Stephen P. Cohen, *India: Emerging Power* (Washington, D.C.: Brookings Institution Press, 2001), p. 189.

79. Ibid. p. 186.

80. Ashley J. Tellis, *Stability in South Asia*, Documented Briefing (Santa Monica: RAND Corporation, 1997), p. 51.

81. Ernest W. Lefever, "Reality vs. Utopia," *Foreign Affairs*, 79:6 (November/December 2000): 167.

82. Celia W. Dugger, "India and Pakistan Add to War Footing," *New York Times* Web service, 28 December 2001. Arguing that "New Delhi has had few options other than nuclear brinkmanship to force Islamabad to modify its unacceptable behavior," the prominent Indian analyst C. Raja Mohan conceded, nevertheless, that "brinkmanship is clearly a high risk strategy that would force India to con-front rather difficult choices in the near future if Pakistan does not agree to crack down on the sources of terrorism on its soil." "India's Coercive Diplomacy," *Hindu*, 31 December 2001.

83. Kathy Gannon, "Pakistan Tests 2nd Nuclear Missile," *Washington Post* Web service, 26 May 2002.

84. "Brinkmanship, With Nukes," *Washington Post*, 26 May 2002, p. B6.

85. For a somewhat dated but able exposition of the argument "that India and Pakistan's nuclear capabilities have not created strategic stability, do not reduce or eliminate factors that contributed to past conflicts, and therefore neither explain the absence of war over the past decade nor why war is currently unlikely," see Neil Joeck, *Maintaining Nuclear Stability in South Asia*, Adelphi Paper 312 (London: The International Institute for Strategic Studies, 1997).

86. "Permanent Troops Likely for Kargil," *Times of India*, 1 August 1999.

87. Barry Bearak, "India, a Nuclear Power, Raises Military Spending 28 Per-cent," *New York Times* Web service, 1 March 2000.

88. See, for instance, Talbott, "Dealing with the Bomb in South Asia."

89. "India Sets Terms for Talks," *Hindu*, 14 July 1999.

90. A.G. Noorani, "From Ceasefire to Dialogue," *Frontline* Web service, 17:25 (9–22 December 2000).

91. The BJP-led government had made a fairly hefty political and diplomatic investment in the dialogue process. Its initiative, which enjoyed wider popular sup-port than many had anticipated, was applauded by practically every major political party in the country. In fact, within days of parliament's dissolution, the caretaker government of Atal Behari Vajpayee, apparently banking on the popularity of the

initiative, proposed to Pakistan that the "two plus six" dialogue process, originally scheduled for May, be resumed in June. The Conduct of parallel expert-level talks focusing on nuclear issues, outlined in the Lahore Memorandum of Understanding, was also suggested. The Pakistan government, whose Kargil operation by that time was already under way, indicated its determination to continue dialogue with India; but, taking note of the difficulty of carrying on substantive talks in the context of India's fluid political situation, it signaled unwillingness to resume any but technical-level talks until a new government had taken over in New Delhi.

92. Pamela Constable, "Brief Taste of Peace Leaves Kashmiris Wishing for More," *Washington Post*, 20 August 2000, p. A16.

93. Pamela Constable, "India Announces One-Month Cease-Fire in Kashmir; Unilateral Move Aimed at Opening Talks With Rebel Groups," *Washington Post*, 20 November 2000, p. A11.

94. For a sampling, see Pran Chopra, "Changes in Kashmir," *Hindu*, 7 November 2000; K.K. Katyal, "Scope for Creative Diplomacy in Ties with Pakistan," *Hindu*, 13 October 2000; and Aijaz Ahmad, "Ceasefire as Smokescreen," *Frontline* Web service, 17:19 (16–29 September 2000).

95. Pamela Constable, "India Tests Pakistan, Woos Kashmiri Rebels," *Washington Post*, 24 November 2000, p. A47.

96. B. Muralidhar Reddy, "Pak. Orders 'Maximum Restraint' Along LoC," *Hindu*, 3 December 2000.

97. "Pakistan Makes Kashmir Peace Offer," *New York Times* Web service, 4 December 2000.

98. Noorani, "From Ceasefire to Dialogue."

99. Harish Khare, "Ceasefire in J&K Extended," *Hindu*, 22 February 2001.

100. See "Vajpayee's Opening Remark at Indo-Pak Summit," *Hindustan Times*, 16 July 2001.

101. "Musharraf Blames 'Hardliners' for Summit Failure," *Hindu*, 27 July 2001.

102. See, among numerous other commentaries on the summit's conclusion, Pamela Constable, "India, Pakistan Can't Reach Deal," *Washington Post* Web service, 16 July 2001; Vinod Sharma and Udayan Namboodiri, "Talks Fail," *Hindustan Times*, 16 July 2001; Jyoti Malhotra, "They Broke the Ice, Then Froze," *Indian Express*, 17 July 2001; "Summit Between India and Pakistan Ends Without Deal," *New York Times* Web service, 16 July 2001; and Harish Khare, "Agra: A Failure Foretold," *Hindu*, 18 July 2001.

103. See Atul Aneja, "Reconstructing the Agra Summit," *Hindu*, 27 July 2001; and Barry Bearak and Celia W. Dugger, "On Kashmir, India and Pakistan Are Stuck on Semantics," *New York Times* Web service, 22 July 2001.

104. P.R. Chari, "Staging Summits," *Hindu*, 28 July 2001.

105. "Vajpayee Cancels Pakistan Visit," *News*, 21 September 2001.

106. Complaining about the "designs of our neighboring country," Musharraf catalogued New Delhi's anti-Pakistan tactics in unusually undiplomatic language, including a demand that the Indians "lay off" their hostile propaganda. See "Text of President's Address," BBC Web service, 20 September 2001.

107. Atul Aneja, "India, Russia Firm Up Presence in Kabul," *Hindu*, 28 November 2001; Michael R. Gordon, "Foreign Diplomats Jockey for Position in Kabul," *New York Times* Web service, 2 December 2001; and "India Stepping Up Engagement of Afghanistan," *Hindu*, 11 December 2001.

108. Reports of Pakistan's continued aid to the Taliban surfaced a month following Pakistan's formal agreement with Washington to end its support of them. Douglas Frantz, "Pakistan Ended Aid to Taliban Only Hesitantly," *New York Times* Web service, 8 December 2001.

109. The quotation is from an address by Dr. Maleeha Lodhi, Pakistan's ambassador to the United States, to the Pakistani American Congress, 27 June 2001, Washington, D.C. Copy supplied to the author by the Embassy of Pakistan.

110. American editorial page commentary on Pakistan was extraordinarily blunt. See, for example, Nicholas D. Kristof, "Our Friends the Terrorists," *New York Times* Web service, 21 December 2001; "The Pressure Rises in Pakistan," *New York Times* Web service, 20 December 2001; and "On to Pakistan," *Washington Post* Web service, 20 December 2001.

111. John F. Burns, "Pakistan Is Reported to Have Arrested Militant Leader," *New York Times* Web service, 31 December 2001.

112. C. Raja Mohan, "India's Coercive Diplomacy," *Hindu*, 31 December 2001.

113. Atul Aneja, "India Recalls Envoy to Pak," *Hindu*, 22 December 1901, p. 1; Celia W. Dugger, "India Weighs Using Troops in Kashmir," *New York Times* Web service, 23 December 2001; Neelesh Misra, "Indian Prime Minister Won't Pull Back Troops," *Washington Post* Web service, 29 December 2001; and Rajiv Chandrasekaran and Rama Lakshmi, "New Delhi Lays Blame on Pakistani Group," *Washington Post*, 29 December 2001, p. A1.

114. Chip Cummins, "U.S. Worries Pakistan-India Tension May Hurt War Effort in Afghanistan," *Wall Street Journal* Web service, 28 December 2001; and Edward Cody, "As Forces Mass Along Line of Control, Anti-Terror Campaign May Be Diluted," *Washington Post*, 28 December 2001, p. A1.

115. "Bush Blocks Lashkar Finances," *Hindu*, 22 December 2001, p. 1; John F. Burns, "Uneasy Ally in Terror War Suddenly Feels More U.S. Pressure," *New York Times* Web service, 21 December 2001; "Powell Freezes Assets of Two Groups," *New York Times* Web service, 26 December 2001.

116. "Mr. Bush's Gesture Towards India," *Hindu*, 22 December 2001.

117. John F. Burns, "Uneasy Ally in Terror War Suddenly Feels More U.S. Pressure," *New York Times* Web service, 21 December 2001.

118. See Kuldip Nayar, "The Rise of the Regional Parties," *Nation*, 15 October 1999. Though it headed a very successful coalition, the BJP itself increased its tally of seats by only one. Its share of the popular vote fell slightly.

119. On this, see, for instance, Sukumar Muralidharan, "Deadlock At Agra," *Frontline* Web service, 18:15 (21 July–3 August 2001).

120. On Najam Sethi's arrest, see Amit Baruah, "Pak. Weekly Editor Held for 'Links' with RAW," *Hindu*, 8 May 1999; "Editor's Freedom Ends at Midnight: Armed Men Beat Up Najam Sethi, Wife and Guards," *Dawn*, 8 May 1999; Rashme Sehgal, "Nawaz Sharif Out to Wrest Absolute Power: Sethi," *Times of India*, 13 May 1999; and Shaheen Sehbai, "Arrest of Journalists: US Think-tanks Caution Islamabad," *Dawn*, 13 May 1999.

121. "India-Pak. Chamber of Commerce Opened," *Hindu*, 10 April 1999.

122. "Talk, Don't Race," *Statesman*, 30 May 1998.

123. Seminar discussion, New Delhi, April 1998.

124. "Indian's Letter to Clinton on the Nuclear Testing," *New York Times* Web service, 12 May 1998.

125. See, for instance, "Pokhran Tests an Irresponsible Act: Basu," *Hindu*, 7 November 1998.

126. R. Chakrapani, "Jaswant Singh Downplays U.N. Council Resolution," *Hindu*, 11 June 1998.

127. Even some knowledgeable Pakistanis lent support to this reinterpretation. See, for example, "India's N-Plan Not Pak-centric: Munir Khan," *Indian Express*, 6 June 1998.

128. Jaswant Singh, "Against Nuclear Apartheid," *Foreign Affairs* 77:5 (September/October 1998): 49.

129. "Pakistan Seeks Mediation on Kashmir," *Associated Press* Web service, 28 June 1998.

130. Rajesh Rajagopalan, "Prospects for Peace in South Asia," *Hindu*, 26 April 1999. (Emphasis added.)

131. K. Subrahmanyam, *Indian Security Perspectives* (New Delhi: ABC Publishing House, 1982), p. 178.

132. The security implications of this fundamental difference in outlook are described with discernment, albeit one-sidedly, in the model of Indian security policy elaborated recently by Professor Maya Chadda, who, though writing from an intellectual perspective distinct from that of IDSA strategists, manages nevertheless to define Indian security policy in a way that could not but stoke insecurity across India's western border. See her *Ethnicity, Security, and Separatism in India* (New York: Columbia University Press, 1997). Chadda's views are considered in detail in Chapter 3.

133. On the CBMs proposed by India in the weeks prior to the Agra Summit, see "PM Announces Measures to Broaden Indo-Pak Ties," *Times of India*, 5 July 2001; and Pamela Constable, "Kashmiris See Light In a Crack At Border," *New York Times*, 12 July 2001, p. A21. Among the measures was the announcement that New Delhi planned to open travel checkpoints on the LOC.

134. Barbara Crossette, "India, for Better or Worse, Nears the Billion Mark," *Times of India*, 10 August 1999.

135. Iqbal Jafar, "Adrift in a Sea of Animosity," *Dawn*, 8 August 1999.

136. Ibid.

137. See, for example, K. Subrahmanyam, "Kargil Balance Sheet," *Times of India*, 26 July 1999; and Dileep Padgaonkar, "India After Kargil," *Times of India*, 23 July 1999.

138. The Pakistan side also produced quite a number of thoughtful self-examinations that arrived at quite opposite conclusions. See, for example, M.P. Bhandara, "On the Edge of the Precipice," *Dawn*, 21 July 1999; Suroosh Irfani, "On 'Diplomatic Complications,'" *News*, 21 July 1999; Shahid M. Amin, "Kargil: The Unanswered Questions," *Dawn*, 25 July 1999; the editorial, "Anniversary Reflections," *Dawn*, 14 August 1999; and Sardar Aseff Ahmad Ali, "Rising From the Ashes of Kargil," *Dawn*, 18 August 1999. ·

Chapter 2. The Problem of Global Intervention: The "Internationalization" of the Kashmir Dispute

1. The government's decision could not have been widely popular within the country's armed forces, some members of which apparently were convinced that

had Pakistan hung on until autumn the Indians would have had no alternative but to negotiate a solution of Kashmir. See Pamela Constable and Kamran Khan, "Pakistan Wary of Broad Indian War," *Washington Post*, 15 August 1999, p. A19. See also Kamran Khan, "COAS Trying to Eliminate 'Disquiet' Among Army Ranks Over Kargil Issue," *News* Web service, 5 September 1999.

2. Thomas W. Lippman, "India Hinted At Attack in Pakistan; U.S. Acts to East Tension on Kashmir," *Washington Post*, 27 June 1999, p. A26. See also Seema Guha, "Brajesh On Secret Mission," *Times of India*, 18 June 1999.

3. Lippman, "India Hinted At Attack in Pakistan," p. A26.

4. Transcript of the "Press Briefing by Senior Administration Official on President's Meeting With Prime Minister Sharif of Pakistan," Office of the Press Secretary, The White House Web service, 4 July 1999.

5. Transcript of the "Joint Statement by President Clinton and Prime Minister Sharif of Pakistan," Office of the Press Secretary, The White House Web service, 4 July 1999.

6. Transcript of the "Press Briefing by Senior Administration Official on President's Meeting With Prime Minister Sharif of Pakistan."

7. Amit Baruah, "'Accord Was Faxed to India,'" *Hindu*, 19 August 1999.

8. Maleeha Lodhi, "Anatomy of a Debacle," *Newsline* (July 1999). See also "Pakistan 'Unknowingly' Making LoC International Border," *Nation,* 28 July 1999. As noted earlier, Lodhi was appointed to a second tour as ambassador to the United States in November 1999, following the Pakistan military's overthrow of the Nawaz Sharif government.

9. Transcript of the "Press Briefing by Senior Administration Official on President's Meeting With Prime Minister Sharif of Pakistan."

10. Tanver Hussain Syed, "Surrender in Washington," *Nation*, 30 July 1999. President Clinton's unyielding insistence in the talks at Blair House on the unconditional withdrawal of Pakistani forces from Indian territory at Kargil has recently been revealingly described by Bruce O. Riedel in "American Diplomacy and the 1999 Kargil Summit at Blair House." Riedel was at the time of the meeting a senior National Security Council aide to the president, and he was present during the discussions between the president and the prime minister.

11. Amit Baruah, "The U.S. Is the Net Gainer," *Hindu* 21 August 1999. See also C. Uday Bhaskar, "In the Global Spotlight: The Strategic Relevance of Kargil," *Times of India*, 7 August 1999; and Aijaz Ahmad, "Mediation By Any Other Name," *Frontline* Web service 16:15 (17–30 July 1999).

12. C. Raja Mohan, "A Foreign Policy Consensus?" *Hindu*, 19 August 1999.

13. "Pakistan Seeks Mediation on Kashmir," *Associated Press* Web service, 28 June 1998.

14. See, for instance, Sridhar Krishnaswami, "U.S. for Indo-Pak Talks on Kashmir," *Hindu*, 11 June 1998; and "'U.S. Not Seeking Mediator's Role,'" *Hindu*, 29 July 1999.

15. "Advice and Consent," *Times of India,* 6 June 1998. See also, Chitra Subramaniam, "Blow to Pak: P-5 Denies J&K a Global Plank," *Indian Express*, 5 June 1998; and "India Renews Offer for Bilateral Talks with Pakistan," *Hindustan Times*, 8 June 1998.

16. Thomas W. Lippman, "U.S. Limits Scope of Sanctions on India, Pakistan to Minimize Hardships," *Washington Post* Web service, 19 June 1998.

17. David E. Sanger, "U.S. Allows an Exception in Supporting Loan for India," *New York Times* Web service, 26 June 1998.

18. Jane Perlez, "U.S. Sanctions on Islamabad Will Be Lifted," *New York Times* Web service, 22 September 2001.

19. For a sampling of thoughtful commentaries, see Richard Butler, "Bewitched, Bothered, and Bewildered: Repairing the Security Council," *Foreign Affairs* 78:5 (September/October 1999): 9–12; and David Calleo, "A Choice of Europes," *National Interest*, no. 63 (Spring 2001): 5–15.

20. *Jammu & Kashmir Liberation Front* Web service (Islamabad), 28 June 1998.

21. *A New U.S. Policy Toward India and Pakistan: Report of an Independent Task Force* (Washington, D.C.: Council on Foreign Relations, January 1997), p. 39.

22. For Indian commentary on the concept, see K.K. Katyal's two essays, "Primakov for 'Strategic Triangle' for Peace," *Hindu*, 22 December 1998, and "The Concept of a 'Strategic Triangle,'" *Hindu*, 28 December 1998. For two Pakistani views of it, see Afzal Mahmood, "Indo Russian Strategic Tie-Up?" *Dawn*, 27 December 1998; and Maqbool Ahmad Bhatty, "An Unlikely Triangle," *Dawn*, 29 December 1998. For an American view attaching considerable credibility to the notion of a Russian-Chinese-Indian axis, see Tyler Marshall, "Anti-NATO Axis Could Pose Threat, Experts Say," *Los Angeles Times* Web service, 27 September 1999. In January 2000, the reformulated security doctrine of the Russian government, by then under Prime Minister Vladimir Putin, identified India and China among its "allies and strategic partners." The notion of a "strategic triangle" remained, nevertheless, largely fanciful. See Vladimir Radyuhin, "Russia Names India, China as Allies," *Hindu*, 17 January 2000.

23. Sandy Gordon, "South Asia After the Cold War: Winners and Losers," *Asian Survey* 35:10 (October 1995): 894–95. Gordon is a Fellow at the Research School of Pacific and Asian Studies, Australian National University. For a related discussion, see Robert G. Wirsing, "Pakistan's Security in the 'New World Order': Going from Bad to Worse?," in *Asian Security to the Year 2000*, Dianne L. Smith (ed.) (Carlisle Barracks: Strategic Studies Institute, U. S. Army War College, December 1996), pp. 65–103.

24. See, for example, "US Soft on China Despite Nuke-aid to Pakistan, Says Think-Tank," *Times of India*, 28 August 1999. The article was commenting on a report issued by the Center for Non-Proliferation Studies of the California-based Monterey Institute of International Studies.

25. C. Raja Mohan, "U.S. Congressman for Flexibility on Sanctions," *Hindu*, 29 March 1999; and "India's Nuclear Power Status Necessary," 27 April 1999. This latter item reports on a visit to New Delhi by former U.S. secretary of state Henry Kissinger, who is said to have termed India's emergence as a nuclear power a "necessary element" in the containment of China.

26. Barbara Leitch LePoer, "The Kashmir Dispute: Recent Developments and U.S. Policy," *CRS Report for Congress* 96–730F (Washington, D.C.: Congressional Research Service, The Library of Congress, 30 August 1996), pp. 4–5.

27. See, for example, Michael Battye, "Angry India Accuses U.S. of Tilt to Pakistan," *Reuters* Wire service, 30 October 1993; and "U.S. Statement on Kashmir Kicks Off Political Storm," *United Press International* Wire service, 30 October 1993. The incident is discussed in Wirsing, *India, Pakistan, and the Kashmir Dispute*, pp. 241–42.

28. Tim Weiner and Steve LeVine, "Coup Leader Restructures Pakistan's Government," *New York Times* Web service, 18 October 1999.

29. Strobe Talbott, "Dealing with the Bomb in South Asia," *Foreign Affairs* 78:2 (March/April 1999): 120–21.

30. Sridhar Krishnaswami, "U.S. for More 'Qualitative' Ties," *Hindu*, 22 July 1999.

31. Shaheen Sehbai, "Washington Backs Nawaz on Kashmir," *Dawn*, 30 July 1999.

32. Former Pakistani Foreign Minister Agha Shahi, for instance, interpreted Daley's remarks to represent a shift from an implicit to an explicit embrace of India in U.S. policy and strategy toward South Asia and warned of "an embryonic US-India axis" in the making. "Options in the New Context," *Dawn*, 30 July 1999. See also Israrul Hague, "US Sponsored Indian Hegemony and Pakistan," *Nation*, 14 December 1999.

33. Interviews were conducted by the author as one of a five-member study team that visited four locations in Pakistan during the first half of May 1997. The team, consisting besides the author of former ambassador Howard B. Schaffer, Dr. Joseph E. Schwartzberg, Dr. Ainslie T. Embree, and Dr. Charles H. Kennedy, visited Pakistan under the auspices of a nongovernmental body, the Kashmir Study Group. The team's privately published report, *1947–1997: The Kashmir Dispute at Fifty: Charting Paths to Peace*, was released in New York by the Kashmir Study Group in October 1997.

34. Soon after Nawaz Sharif's ouster by the army in late 1999, one of Sharif's political rivals, former Pakistan president Farooq Leghari, reportedly accused Sharif and his brother Shahbaz of having secretly promised Washington not only to roll back the country's nuclear and missile programs but also to accept the LOC as Pakistan's permanent border. "Sharifs Agreed on Nuclear Rollback, Claims Leghari," *Dawn*, 8 November 1999.

35. "Text of Gen Pervez Musharraf's Speech," *Dawn*, 18 October 1999.

36. Amit Baruah, "Discuss Kashmir First: Musharraf," *Hindu*, 28 December 1999.

37. Vinay Kumar, "Militants Emboldened by Change in Pak.?" *Hindu*, 7 November 1999; and "Lashkar, Harkat Issue Fresh Threats," *Times of India*, 15 December 1999.

38. See "Statement for the Record to the Senate Foreign Relations Committee on Foreign Missile Developments and the Ballistic Missile Threat to the United States Through 2015 by Robert D. Walpole, National Intelligence Officer for Strategic and Nuclear Programs," 16 September 1999, Central Intelligence Agency Web service.

39. William J. Clinton, Report to the Congress of the United States on Weapons of Mass Destruction, 10 November 1999, Office of the Press Secretary, The White House Web service.

40. K. Subrahmanyam, "Undue Fears," *Times of India*, 13 December 1999.

41. P.R. Chari, "A Difficult Relationship," *Hindustan Times*, 26 November 1999. Chari's musings at a later date on the CTBT issue itself suggested that his own reservations about India's signing of it were fairly major. See his "Misgivings on CTBT," *Hindu*, 4 January 2000.

42. A study conducted by the United States International Trade Commission of the Glenn Amendment economic sanctions imposed on India and Pakistan following detonation of nuclear explosives in May 1998 concluded that in the case of

India's economy the sanctions "had a minimal overall impact," while in the case of Pakistan the impact was most likely "small." Testimony of Arona M. Butcher, Chief, Country and Regional Analysis Division, Office of Economics, United States International Trade Commission, to Subcommittee on Asia and the Pacific, Committee on International Relations, U.S. House of Representatives, 20 October 1999, Committee on International Relations Web service.

43. Sridhar Krishnaswami, "51 Indian Entities Off U.S. List," *Hindu*, 18 December 1999.

44. John Lancaster, "Activism Boosts India's Fortunes; Politically Vocal Immigrants Help Tilt Policy in Washington," *Washington Post*, 9 October 1999, p. A1.

45. Ramesh Chandran, "House Panel Urges Indo-US 'Strategic Partnership,'" *Times of India*, 29 October 1999.

46. C. Raja Mohan, "Sanctions: India, Pak. Must 'Show Progress,'" *Hindu*, 21 March 1999; and Sridhar Krishnaswami, "Pallone for Bill to End Sanctions Against India," *Hindu*, 9 April 1999.

47. Sridhar Krishnaswami, "Pallone Moves Legislation Against Curbs," *Hindu*, 15 May 1999.

48. "Need for Improvement in Indo-U.S. Ties," *Hindu*, 31 March 1999.

49. The Senate version of the letter, dated 21 July 1999, was supplied to the author by the office of Senator Tim Johnson of South Dakota.

50. "US Doublespeak," *Times of India*, 28 September 1999.

51. Amir Mateen, "Pakistan Gains Major Diplomatic Success at Capitol Hill," *News*, 30 September 1999. For a despairing comment on the more characteristic *absence* of such success by the pro-Pakistan lobby in the United States, see Hasan Askari Rizvi, "Lobbying Abroad for Pakistan," *Nation*, 5 September 1999.

52. Ramesh Chandran, "US Reiterates Stand: No Special Envoy for Kashmir," *Times of India*, 1 October 1999.

53. Chidanand Rajghatta, "Kargil II—A Letter War in Washington," *Indian Express*, 30 September 1999.

54. On Moynihan's withdrawal of his name, see "US Lawmakers' Move Makes Indian Lobby Panicky," *Dawn*, 30 September 1999; and Mateen, "Pakistan Gains Major Diplomatic Success at Capitol Hill."

55. Teresita C. Schaffer, Director for South Asia, Center for Strategic and International Studies, Testimony to the Subcommittee on Asia and the Pacific, House Committee on International Relations, Hearing on U.S. Relations with South Asia, 20 October 1999, Committee on International Relations Web service. In testimony on the same date to this subcommittee, Selig S. Harrison, Fellow of the Century Foundation and a Senior Scholar of the Woodrow Wilson International Center for Scholars, went a step further, condemning Pakistan's sponsorship of insurgency in Kashmir and asserting flatly that the United States should openly declare its support for the Line of Control as the permanent international boundary.

56. *After the Tests, U.S. Policy Toward India and Pakistan: Report of an Independent Task Force* (Washington, D.C.: Council on Foreign Relations, 1998), p. 10. See also the Council on Foreign Relations' earlier report, *A New U.S. Policy Toward India and Pakistan*, pp. 38–39; Selig S. Harrison and Geoffrey Kemp, *India & America, After the Cold War: Report of the Carnegie Endowment Study Group on U.S.-Indian Relations in a Changing International Environment* (Washington, D.C.: The Carnegie Endowment for International Peace, 1993), p. 34; and *South Asia and*

the United States, After the Cold War: A Study Mission Sponsored by The Asia Society (New York: The Asia Society, 1994), p. 54.

57. "Bin Laden Hand in Kashmir Terrorism—US," *Indian Express*, 23 December 1999.

58. Initially, the hijackers sought the release of only one imprisoned militant—Maulana Masood Azhar, a Pakistan-born Islamic cleric jailed in 1994. They then upped their demands to include release of thirty-six Kashmiri militants held in Indian jails plus $200 million. When these were resisted by the Indian negotiating team, the hijackers scaled back their demands to the release of three militants, including Masood Azhar.

59. "Indian Airlines Hostages Walk to Freedom," *New York Times* Web service, 31 December 1999; and Pamela Constable, "Gunmen Vanish After Freeing Indian Captives," *Washington Post* Web service, 1 January 2000.

60. See, for example, K. Subrahmanyam, "A Victory for Terrorism," *Times of India*, 1 January 2000; V. R. Raghavan, "Looking Beyond the Hijacking," *Hindu*, 4 January 2000; editorial, "Great Relief But a Heavy Price," *Hindu*, 1 January 2000; Prem Shankar Jha, "Defeat at Kandahar-I" and "Defeat at Kandahar-II," *Hindu*, 3–4 January 2000; and Harkishan Singh Surjeet, "Bungling That Proved Costly," *Hindu*, 5 January 2000.

61. Prem Shankar Jha, "Defeat at Kandahar-I," *Hindu*, 3 January 2000.

62. C. Raja Mohan, "Hijack Footprints Lead to Pakistan, Says Jaswant," *Hindu*, 2 January 2000.

63. "Declare Pak a Terrorist State—PM Tells US," *Indian Express*, 4 January 2000.

64. Hasan-Askari Rizvi, "Crisis in India-Pakistan Relations," *Nation*, 2 January 2000.

65. C. Raja Mohan, "An Unfolding Indo-U.S. Waltz?," *Hindu*, 23 December 1999.

66. For an example of this urging, see *A New U.S. Policy Toward India & Pakistan*.

67. Raymond Bonner, "With Dollars for First Lady, Group Sought President's Ear," *New York Times* Web service, 14 March 2000.

68. "India to US: Let Clinton Not Visit Pak," *Times of India*, 12 February 2000.

69. "Text of 'Vision' Statement," *Hindu*, 22 March 2000.

70. Celia W. Dugger, "In Charmed India, Clinton Wooed, and Maybe Won," *New York Times* Web service, 31 March 2000.

71. "Complete Text of President Clinton's Address to the People of Pakistan," *Dawn*, 25 March 2000.

72. Sridhar Krishnaswami, "Boom Time in Indo-U.S. Ties," *Hindu*, 26 March 2000. See also Muchkund Dubey, "Building on the Clinton Visit," *Hindu*, 22 April 2000; and C. Raja Mohan, "The Clinton Visit's Aftermath," *Hindu*, 13 April 2000.

73. Salahuddin K. Leghari, "Clinton's S. Asian Odyssey," *Dawn*, 24 April 2000.

74. "A Virtual Visit," *Times of India*, 20 March 2000. American media commentary at about the same time generally revealed similar depth of skepticism. See, for instance, Celia W. Dugger, "On Eve of Visit, Many Unresolved Issues Impede Deeper U.S-India Ties," *New York Times* Web service, 18 March 2000. For additional Indian commentary in this vein, see, for example, K.K. Katyal, "The New Beginning," *Hindu*, 10 April 2000; and John Cherian, "Bilateral Thrust," *Frontline* Web service 17:7 (1–14 April 2000).

75. "Text of India-US Joint Statement on Vajpayee's Official Visit to US," *Foreign Broadcast Information Service* Web service, 16 September 2000.

76. For a sampling of comment on the Indian prime minister's visit to Washington, see K.K. Katyal, "Summing Up a Summit," *Hindu*, 25 September 2000; J.N. Dixit, "Proof of the American Pudding," *Hindustan Times*, 26 September 2000; and Sridhar Krishnaswami, "Vajpayee's American Yatra," *Frontline* Web service 17:20 (30 September–13 October 2000). See also "The Vajpayee Visit: Defining the U.S.-Indian Relationship," A Brookings Press Briefing, The Brookings Institution Web service, 12 September 2000.

77. *Global Trends 2015: A Dialogue About the Future With Nongovernment Experts* (Washington, D.C.: National Intelligence Council, December 2000), pp. 42–43. (Emphasis added.)

78. *Proliferation: Threat and Response* (Washington, D.C.: Department of Defense, January 2001), p. 30.

79. Jim Garamone, "Intelligence Chief Details Threats Facing America," *Defense Link* (American Forces Information Service) Web service, 22 February 2001.

80. *Confirmation Hearing*, testimony of Secretary-Designate Colin L. Powell before the Senate Foreign Relations Committee, 17 January 2001 (Washington, D.C.: U.S. Department of State Web service). Powell did address the topic of South Asia at some length in the question period following his formal testimony. However, in similarly wide-ranging testimony to Congress given a few months after taking over as secretary of state, Powell again entirely omitted any reference to South Asia. *Testimony at Budget Hearing before the House International Relations Committee*, Secretary of State Colin L. Powell, 7 March 2001 (Washington, D.C.: U.S. Department of State Web service).

81. The pattern applies equally well, by the way, to India-European Union economic ties. In early 2001, trade with India represented less than 1.5 percent of the European Union's total foreign trade, and only 0.4 percent of the Union's direct private investment abroad went to India. "Ninth Heavily Debted Nation," *Hindu*, 24 February 2001.

82. *Transition 2001* (Washington, D.C.: The Rand Corporation, January 2001), pp. xiii, 45–46. The Rand Corporation report's endorsement of a "decoupling" of India and Pakistan had been urged in a discussion paper on South Asia prepared for the Transition 2001 panel by Rand analyst Ashley Tellis, who labeled his policy preference "a differentiated policy" toward India and Pakistan. See his "South Asia: U.S. Policy Choices," in *Taking Charge: A Bipartisan Report to the President Elect on Foreign Policy and National Security–Discussion Papers* (Washington, D.C.: The Rand Corporation, January 2001), pp. 83–91. In regard to Kashmir, Tellis suggested that the United States "should also clearly communicate to Pakistan's civilian and military leadership its strong preference for reconciliation over Kashmir that involves, among other things, a transformation of the current line of control (LOC) into a new international border." Tellis also advised (p. 89) that Washington make no arms sales to Pakistan, not even commercial sales, "until Pakistan ceases to challenge the territorial status quo in Kashmir by force." The only reference to Pakistan in another major think tank report prepared for the incoming Bush administration was that it was one of a handful of countries "that provide refuge or turn a blind eye to terrorists. . . ." *Navigating through Turbulence: America and the Middle East in a New Century*, Report of the Presidential Study Group (Washington, D.C.: The Wash-

ington Institute for Near East Policy, January 2001), p. 37.

83. Robert D. Blackwill, "An Action Agenda to Strengthen America's Alliances in the Asia-Pacific Region," in *America's Asian Alliances*, Robert D. Blackwill and Paul Dibb, eds. (Cambridge: MIT Press, 2000), p. 124.

84. "US Not to Shun Pakistan for India Ties: Pentagon," *News*, 23 August 2001.

85. See John F. Burns, "Pakistan Leader Defends Joining U.S. in Hunt for bin Laden," *New York Times* Web service, 20 September 2001; and Steven R. Weisman, "On the Front Lines in the Global War Against Terrorism," *New York Times* Web service, 21 September 2001.

86. See, for a small sampling, Malini Parthasarathy, "A Defining Moment for the Subcontinent?," *Hindu*, 21 September 2001; Sridhar Krishnaswami, "A Long-term U.S.-Pak Cooperation?," *Hindu*, 21 September 2001; C. Raja Mohan, "India and U.S.-Pak. Ties," *Hindu*, 21 September 2001.

87. Pamela Constable, "Pakistanis Seeking Trade-Off on Kashmir," *Washington Post*, 29 September 2001, p. A22.

88. Alan Sipress and Edward Cody, "U.S. Campaign to Extend to Kashmir: Powell Attempts to Reassure India After Strengthening Ties With Rival Pakistan," *Washington Post*, 18 October 2001, p. A24.

89. For a sympathetic view of this criticism, see Adam Garfinkle, "Weak Realpolitik: The Vicissitudes of Saudi Bashing," *National Interest* Number 67 (Spring 2002), pp. 144–50.

90. See, for instance, Chidanand Rajghatta, "Pak Losing Opinion War Over Kashmir," *Times of India*, 25 November 2001.

91. For background on Pakistan's links to Taliban-ruled Afghanistan, see Ahmed Rashid, *Taliban: Militant Islam, Oil and Fundamentalism in Central Asia* (New Haven: Yale University Press, 2000), especially pp. 183–95.

92. The congressionally mandated list issued in early October 2001 contained the names of twenty-eight groups, only one of which—the Harkat-ul-Mujahideen (at the time operating under the name Harkat-ul-Ansar)—was associated with the insurgency in Kashmir. The Harkat had been added to the list in 1998. Sridhar Krishnaswami, "J&K Outfits Not In U.S. Terrorists List," *Hindu*, 6 October 2001.

93. Indians comforted themselves with the assurance that terrorism in Kashmir would eventually be dealt with in a later phase of the global war on terrorism. See, for example, "U.S. Likely to Address Kashmir Terrorism in Phase-II: Omar," *Hindu*, 3 October 2001; and Sridhar Krishnaswami, "J&K Too On Agenda: Powell," *Hindu*, 4 October 2001. For one of many American commentaries on this issue at the time, see Jim Hoagland, "An Ally's Terrorism," *Washington Post*, 3 October 2001, p. A31. Pakistan's availability as a recruiting ground jointly for "jihadist" activities in Afghanistan and Indian Kashmir was a poorly kept secret. See, for instance, "Posters Lure Recruits to House of Martyrs," *Times*, 6 October 2001.

94. Atul Aneja, "India Recalls Envoy to Pak," *Hindu*, 22 December 2001; and Celia W. Dugger, "India Weighs Using Troops in Kashmir," *New York Times* Web service, 23 December 2001.

95. "Bush Blocks Lashkar Finances," *Hindu*, 22 December 2001; and John F. Burns, "Uneasy Ally in Terror War Suddenly Feels More U.S. Pressure," *New York Times* Web service, 21 December 2001.

96. "Mr. Bush's Gesture Towards India," *Hindu*, 22 December 2001.

97. John F. Burns, "Uneasy Ally in Terror War Suddenly Feels More U.S. Pres-

sure," *New York Times* Web service, 21 December 2001.

98. John F. Burns, "Pakistan Is Said to Order an End to Support for Militant Groups," *New York Times*, 2 January 2002, p. 1.

99. Seymour M. Hersh, "Watching the Warheads: The Risks to Pakistan's Nuclear Arsenal," *New Yorker*, 5 November 2001.

100. John F. Burns, "Pakistan Atom Experts Held Amid Fear of Leaked Secrets," *New York Times* Web service, 1 November 2001; Dennis Overbye and James Glanz, "Arrested Pakistani Atom Expert Is a Taliban Advocate," *New York Times* Web service, 2 November 2001; Douglas Frantz with David Rohde, "2 Pakistanis Linked to Papers On Anthrax Weapons," *New York Times* Web service, 28 November 2001; and Mansoor Ijaz and R. James Woolsey, "How Secure Is Pakistan's Plutonium?" *New York Times* Web service, 28 November 2001.

101. "Pakistan Is Continuing Proxy War Despite Talks, Says Advani," *Times of India* 23 October 1998; and Inder Sawhney, "Laden on His Own Won't Interfere in J&K: Officials," *Times of India*, 9 October 1998.

102. Vinay Kumar, "Militants Emboldened by Change in Pak.?" *Hindu*, 7 November 1999.

103. Kanwar Sandhu, " Security Forces Skate on J-K's Thin Ice," *Indian Express*, 7 December 1999.

104. See Appendix 4, "The Inter-Services Intelligence of Pakistan, Pakistan-sponsored Militancy in J&K and Its Nexus with Islam," in *Kargil: The Tables Turned*, Ashok Krishna and P.R. Chari, eds. (Delhi: Manohar, 2001), p. 295.

105. Yossef Bodansky, "The Hegemon's Gambit," *Defense and Foreign Affairs Strategic Policy* 28:11–12 (November–December 2000): 4.

106. Yossef Bodansky, "Islamabad's Road Warriors," *Pakistan, Kashmir and the Trans-Asian Axis* (Houston: Freeman Center for Strategic Studies, 1995).

107. Yossef Bodansky, "Pakistan's Kashmir Strategy," *Pakistan, Kashmir and the Trans-Asian Axis*. For Bodansky's most recent thinking on the region, see his *bin Laden: The Man Who Declared War on America* (New York: Random House, 2001).

108. See Sanjeev Miglani, "India Says Missile Strikes Exposed Kashmir Militants," Reuters Web service 23 August 1998), Raymond Bonner, "In Pakistan, Trying to Untie Terrorism and Creed," *New York Times* Web service (24 August 1998); Raymond Bonner and Steve LeVine, "'We Are Freedom Fighters,' Says a Leader of Militants," *New York Times* Web service, 27 August 1998.

109. "Jamaat-e-Islami Vows to Continue Aid to Kashmiris," *Times of India*, 24 October 1998; and Amit Baruah, "Hard Evidence of Pakistani 'Jihad,'" *Hindu*, 24 October 1998.

110. "Taliban Vow to Escalate Freedom Struggle in Valley," *Dawn*, 8 November 1998. See also "Pak Militant Group Plans to Strike in India: Reports," *Times of India*, 9 November 1998. For background on foreign militants in Kashmir, see Harinder Baweja, "The Hostage Crisis," *India Today* (15 September 1995): 18–25; and Victoria Schofield, *Kashmir in the Crossfire* (London: I.B. Tauris, 1996) pp. 270–73.

111. Celia W. Dugger, "India Intensifies Efforts to Tie Pakistan to Hijacking," *New York Times* Web service, 7 January 2000. For a detailed account of the hijacking episode, from an Indian point of view, see the multiauthored cover story, "Defeat at Kandahar,"*Frontline* 17:01 (8–21 January 2000).

112. Amir Zia, "Freed Rebel Vows War on India, U.S.," *Washington Post* Web

service, 6 January 2000; and "Kashmiri, Freed After Hijacking, Is Still Militant," *New York Times* Web service, 6 January 2000. Azhar later on, possibly under pressure from the Pakistan government, denied making the anti-American statements attributed to him. "Pakistan Asks Azhar to Shut Up," *Times of India*, 9 January 2000.

113. "Masood Vows to Continue Fight," *Hindu*, 11 January 2000.

114. Shireen M. Mazari, "War on Airwaves," *News*, 13 January 2000.

115. Sumantra Bose, "Kashmir at the Crossroads," *Security Dialogue* 32:1 (March 2001): 51–52. On this issue, see also Zahid Hussain, "Inside Jihad," *Newsline* Web service, 22 February 2001.

116. See, for instance, Yoginder Sikand, "Lessons of the Past: Madrasa Education in South Asia," *Himal* (November 2001); and S.V.R. Nasr, "The Rise of Sunni Militancy in Pakistan: The Changing Role of Islamism and the Ulama in Society and Politics," *Modern Asian Studies* 34:1 (2000): 139–80.

117. Nasr, "The Rise of Sunni Militancy in Pakistan," p. 142. Nasr reports an estimated total number of *madrasahs* in Pakistan today of 8,000. For additional comparative statistics on the growth, present number, and enrollments of Pakistan's *madrasahs*, see Abbas Rashid, "The Politics and Dynamics of Violent Sectarianism," www.wysiwyg://87/http://members.tripod.com/~no_nukes_sa/chapter_2.html.

118. Devesh Kapur, "Aid for Pakistan, Not Its Army," *Asian Wall Street Journal* Web service, 7 December 2001.

119. Rahul Bedi, "Kashmir Peace Talks Collapse," *Jane's Intelligence Review* Web service for Asia 12:10 (1 October 2000).

120. Jessica Stern, "Pakistan's Jihad Culture," *Foreign Affairs* 79:6 (November/December 2000): 119.

121. Kuldip Nayar, "The Taliban Lesson," *Dawn*, 1 December 2001. Another article in the same newspaper at about the same time reported an official government estimate of "more than 6,500 Madaris [*madrasahs*] functioning" in Pakistan, with "over 600,000 students" enrolled in them. Faraz Hashmi, "All Madaris to Be Registered," *Dawn*, 4 December 2001. A government estimate given only days later in the same newspaper placed the number of *madrasahs* that were to be registered at about 10,000. "Law on Code of Conduct for Madaris Under Study," *Dawn*, 14 December 2001.

122. Sumit Ganguly, "Pakistan's Never-Ending Story," *Foreign Affairs* 79:2 (March/April 2000): 6.

123. Kim Murphy, "Political Shift Stifles Islamic Anger at U.S.," *Los Angeles Times* Web service, 10 December 2001.

124. Barry Bearak, "Death to Blasphemers: Islam's Grip on Pakistan," *New York Times* Web service, 12 May 2001.

125. Pakistani President Musharraf was reported to have told a meeting of top political leaders on 31 December 2001 that he was determined "to eradicate militancy, extremism, intolerance from Pakistani society." Craig Whitlock and Rajiv Chandrasekaran, "Pakistan Detains Islamic Militants," *Washington Post*, 1 January 2002, p. A1. See also Daniel Pearl, "Pakistan Clamps Down on Islamic Militants to Avert War with India, Terror at Home," *Wall Street Journal* Web service, 2 January 2002.

126. "Pak. Epicenter of Terrorism: Jaswant," *Hindu*, 6 October 2001.

127. "The Pressure Rises in Pakistan," *New York Times* Web service, 20 December 2001; and "On to Pakistan," *Washington Post*, 20 December 2001, p. 42. See also

Douglas Frantz and Todd S. Purdum, "Pakistan Faces Increased U.S. Pressure to Curb Militants," *New York Times* Web service, 16 December 2001.

128. Sumit Ganguly, quoted in Thomas E. Ricks and Alan Sipress, "Pakistan May Hold Key to Afghan Result," *Washington Post*, 20 December 2001, p. 20.

129. Celia W. Dugger, "India Seeks International Support to Force Pakistan to Crack Down on Militants," *New York Times* Web service, 20 December 2001.

130. Sridhar Krishnaswami, "The 'Battle' of Washington: Vajpayee and Musharraf Take Their Diplomatic War to the United States," *Frontline* Web service, 18:24 (24 November–7 December 2001).

131. Chidanand Rajghatta, "US and Pak: Sleeping With the Enemy," *Times of India*, 29 November 2001.

132. Teresita Schaffer and Mandavi Mehta, "Rising India and U.S. Policy Options in Asia," *South Asia Monitor* Special Report Number 40 (Washington, D.C.: Center for Strategic & International Studies, 1 December 2001).

Chapter 3. The Problem of Religious Identity: Faultline Politics in a Disputed Territory

1. Sumantra Bose, *The Challenge in Kashmir: Democracy, Self-Determination and a Just Peace* (New Delhi: Sage Publications, 1997), p. 85.

2. See, for instance, Sumit Ganguly, *The Crisis in Kashmir: Portents of War, Hopes of Peace* (New York: Cambridge University Press, 1997), pp. 39–42; and Reeta Chowdhari Tremblay, "Kashmir: The Valley's Political Dynamics," *Contemporary South Asia* 4:1 (1995): 86.

3. See Samuel P. Huntington, "The Clash of Civilizations?" *Foreign Affairs* 72:3 (Summer 1993): 22–49. The thesis is elaborated in Huntington's later book, *The Clash of Civilizations and the Remaking of World Order* (New York: Simon & Schuster, 1996).

4. Huntington, "The Clash of Civilizations?" 35.

5. For a sampling of the critical commentaries on Huntington's original essay, see "Responses to Samuel P. Huntington's 'The Clash of Civilizations?'" in *Foreign Affairs* 72:4 (September/October 1993): 1–26.

6. Fouad Ajami, "The Summoning," *Foreign Affairs* 72:4 (September/October 1993): 9.

7. With China's maintenance since the late 1950s of at least a military presence in the northeast (Aksai Chin) corner of Kashmir, one could technically argue that a fourth one of Huntington's civilizations—the Sinic—is also represented there.

8. Raju G.C. Thomas, "Reflections on the Kashmir Problem," in *Perspectives on Kashmir: The Roots of Conflict in South Asia*, Raju G.C. Thomas (ed.) (Boulder: Westview, 1992), p. 8.

9. K. Warikoo, "Language and Politics in Jammu and Kashmir," in *Jammu, Kashmir & Ladakh: Linguistic Predicament*, P.N. Pushp and K. Warikoo (eds.) (New Delhi: Har-Anand Publications, 1996), p. 194.

10. Taking the position that the non-Kashmiri-speaking component of the Jammu and Kashmir state's population has been paid insufficient attention by observers and that it, in fact, constitutes the majority of the state's population, Balraj Puri maintains that when such borderline ethno-linguistic groups as the Gujjars and Paharis are subtracted from the putative Kashmiri-speaking population, the remaining "true"

Kashmiri speakers comprise no more than 42 percent of the state's population. "The Mosaic of Jammu and Kashmir," *Frontline* Web service 18:9 (28 April–11 May 2001).

11. Kashmir Study Group, *Kashmir: A Way Forward* (Larchmont, New York: Kashmir Study Group, February 2000), p. 8. This group's rough estimates for both Pakistani- and Indian-held areas are as follows:

Indian-held areas

Kashmir 4.70 mil., Jammu 4.55 mil., Ladakh 0.20 mil.   Total: 9.45 mil.

Pakistan-held areas

Azad Kashmir 3.10 mil., Northern Areas 1.10 mil.   Total: 4.20 mil.

Grand Total: 13.65 mil.

12. Still, three of Jammu's six districts (Doda, Poonch, Rajouri) remain today Muslim-majority areas.

13. Joseph E. Schwartzberg, "Who Are the Kashmiri People? Self-Identification as a Vehicle for Self-Determination," *Environment and Planning* 29 (Summer 1997): 2246.

14. For an example of the former, see a pair of articles by Hari Om, "Jammu Region-I: The Story of Neglect," and "Jammu Region-II: Not Too Late for Action," *Statesman*, 23 and 24 September 1996. Om has argued for many years that the Indian-controlled portion of Kashmir is a divided house, with no logic remaining to maintain it as a single political unit. He has urged its trifurcation into three autonomous regions of Kashmir, Jammu, and Ladakh. A similar argument is made by Reeta Chowdhari Tremblay, "Jammu: Autonomy Within an Autonomous Kashmir?" in *Perspectives on Kashmir*, Thomas, pp. 153–67. For a critical look at what he considers the BJP's cynical exploitation of the idea of trifurcation, see A.G. Noorani, "In Pursuit of Trifurcation," *Frontline* Web service 18:8 (14–27 April 2001).

15. Riyaz Punjabi, "Kashmir: The Bruised Identity," in *Perspectives on Kashmir*, Thomas, pp. 136–37.

16. Ibid., p. 150.

17. K. Warikoo, "Language and Politics in Jammu and Kashmir," pp. 208–9.

18. Ibid., p. 209.

19. See Punjabi, "Kashmir: The Bruised Identity," pp. 136–37. The theme of Kashmir's unique religious tolerance may also be seen, for instance, in Reeta Chowdhari Tremblay, "Kashmir: The Valley's Political Dynamics," *Contemporary South Asia* 4:1 (1995): 86–87; and in Balraj Puri, "Kashmiriyat: The Vitality of Kashmiri Identity," *Contemporary South Asia* 4:1 (1995): 60.

20. Narender Sehgal, *Converted Kashmir: Memorial of Mistakes* (Delhi: Utpal Publications, 1994), pp. 58–59. For a like-minded interpretation, see Anil Maheshwari, *Crescent Over Kashmir: Politics of Mullaism* (New Delhi: Rupa & Company, 1993), pp. 54–70.

21. "Restoration of Autonomy-Panun Kashmir viewpoint," unpublished paper

submitted by Panun Kashmir to the Committee for Greater Autonomy, Jammu, Jammu and Kashmir State, in April 1997, provided to the author by Shailendra Aima, Executive Editor, *Kashmir Sentinel.*

22. Joseph E. Schwartzberg gave the estimate in a symposium on Kashmir at the University of South Carolina in October 1994. See Vijay K. Sazawal, "A Kashmiri Perspective-II," in *Kashmir: Resolving Regional Conflict,* Wirsing (ed.), p. 61. For a detailed map of Panun Kashmir, see "Pandits Renew Homeland Demand," *Times of India,* 24 December 1993. The size of the Kashmiri Pandit population, in terms both of its proportion of the total population of the Valley in recent decades and its number worldwide, is the subject of controversy. The Panun Kashmir organization claims a worldwide total of 700,000.

23. The classic on this subject is Edward W. Said, *Orientalism* (New York: Vintage, 1979).

24. Schwartzberg, "Who Are the Kashmiri People?" 2244. About *kashmiriyat,* Schwartzberg seems to endorse the view that Kashmir's Hindu and Muslim inhabitants were historically far from hostile communities. "Kashmiris of both faiths," he writes,

> share numerous cultural traits and—until very recently—interacted closely and amicably within a wide range of social and economic contexts, even including religious observances. Unlike neighboring Jammu, Kashmir was among the few regions of India free from communal violence during the tumultuous months leading up to and following the partition that created an independent India and Pakistan. It then mattered little that the Muslims of Kashmir proper constituted an educationally and economically disadvantaged majority, while the comparatively well-educated and largely middle-class Hindus, virtually all of whom were Brahmins (known in Kashmir as Pandits) were a politically prominent elite, who, in the service of the ruling and despotic Dogra Rajput dynasty of Jammu, largely ran the State. In their common pride in kashmiriyat, Muslims and Hindus were essentially alike. (2243)

25. T.N. Madan, "Religious Ideology in a Plural Society: The Muslims and Hindus of Kashmir," *Contributions to Indian Sociology: New Series* 6 (December 1972): 130–31, 137. See also Madan's *Family and Kinship: A Study of the Pandits of Rural Kashmir,* 2d edition (New Delhi: Oxford University Press, 1989). From her recent review of the literature on Muslim-Pandit relations in Kashmir, Iffat Sanna Malik draws a number of provocative conclusions, among them (1) that, in spite of the culturally convergent tendencies of *kashmiriyat,* "differences between followers of the two religions were very apparent," (2) that, apart from a small section of Kashmiri society, "the majority of Kashmir's Muslims and Hindus followed 'mainstream' Islam and Hinduism respectively," (3) that "in terms of religious worship . . . there were few major differences between Kashmiri and non-Kashmiri Muslims" and "Kashmiri Islam thus differed little from that practiced outside the Valley," and (4) that it was not so much tolerance that accounted for the lack of religious violence in past relations between Kashmiri Muslims and Hindus, but the presence of a number of political, social, and economic circumstances   among them the pressing expedient need for Pandits to interact extensively with (and, thus, to share some cultural habits with) Muslims, since they (the Pandits) were the only Hindu caste in the

Valley of Kashmir. *Kashmir: Ethnic Conflict, International Dispute* (Karachi: Oxford University Press, 2002). See Chapter 1: Ethnic Identification in Kashmir, pp. 1–16.

26. T.N. Madan, *Modern Myths, Locked Minds: Secularism and Fundamentalism in India* (Delhi: Oxford University Press, 1997), p. 259.

27. The fourth category, which Ganguly identifies as "circumstantial accounts" (meaning "historical and narrative accounts of the insurgency"), is obviously a catchall for the essentially descriptive, atheoretical, and typically anecdotal analyses of journalists and others. Ganguly, *The Crisis in Kashmir*, pp. 19–20.

28. Ibid., p. 15.

29. Ibid., p. 21.

30. Ibid., p. 26.

31. Ibid., p. 20.

32. Ibid., pp. 39–42.

33. Ibid., p. 129.

34. Bose, *The Challenge in Kashmir*, p. 19. A recent addition to the "democratic decline" school of thought on separatism's sources in Kashmir is Sten Widmalm, "The Rise and Fall of Democracy in Jammu and Kashmir, 1975–1989," in *Community Conflicts and the State in India*, Amrita Basu and Atul Kohli (eds.) (Delhi: Oxford University Press, 1998), pp. 149–82. Widmalm argues that central interference with elective government in Jammu and Kashmir in 1983 and 1984 marked

> the beginning of a drastic decline in democracy in JK, and it is important to note that what characterizes the conflict today has little to do with what initiated the conflict. There is no evidence to support the idea that the dismissal of Farooq Abdullah was the result of ethnic antagonism or religious sentiment, or a response to demands for a separate state or accession to Pakistan—the leading themes in the conflict today. What appears to have initiated the conflict was the failure of political institutions and leaders in JK to handle pressure from an interventionist central government (p. 164).

35. Bose, *The Challenge in Kashmir*, p. 56. (Emphasis in the original.)

36. Ibid., p. 177.

37. Ibid., p. 85.

38. Ibid., p. 88.

39. Ibid., p. 106.

40. Ganguly, *The Crisis in Kashmir*, pp. 23–24.

41. Bose, *The Challenge in Kashmir*, pp. 34, 39–40.

42. Majoritarian communalism surfaces with particular vehemence in Kashmir's *interregional* politics, especially that which pits mainly Hindu Jammu against the overwhelmingly Muslim Valley. For a recent and illuminating comment (from the Jammu Hindu point of view) on both the "statistics" of the majoritarian phenomenon and the bitterness it generates, see Hari Om, "The Plight of Jammu," *Hindustan Times*, 12 March 1999.

43. For what is still by far the best theoretical exposition of the handicaps under which political democracy must operate in acutely divided multiethnic societies, see Donald L. Horowitz, *Ethnic Groups in Conflict* (Berkeley: University of California Press, 1985).

44. Yoginder Sikand, "Changing Course of Kashmiri Struggle: From National Liberation to Islamist Jihad?" *Economic and Political Weekly*, 20 January 2001, p. 227.

45. See, for instance, Mohammad Musa, *My Version: India-Pakistan War 1965* (Lahore: Wajidalis, 1983) pp. 35–45. Musa was commander-in-chief of the Pakistan army at the time of the 1965 war.

46. A recent and particularly thoughtful discussion of the Islamic revival in South Asia is T.N. Madan, *Modern Myths, Locked Minds: Secularism and Fundamentalism in India* (Delhi: Oxford University Press, 1997), pp. 106–75. For an excellent general discussion of the global phenomenon of political Islam from an outspokenly liberal point of view, see Bassam Tibi, *The Challenge of Fundamentalism: Political Islam and the New World Disorder* (Berkeley: University of California Press, 1998).

47. Malhotra Jagmohan, *My Frozen Turbulence in Kashmir*, Second edition (New Delhi: Allied Publishers, 1992).

48. Ibid., p. 374.

49. Ibid., pp. 372 93.

50. Ibid., p. 180.

51. Ibid., p. 404.

52. Ibid., p. 406.

53. Ibid., p. 410. On this issue, see my earlier comments in Robert G. Wirsing, *India, Pakistan, and the Kashmir Dispute* (New York: St. Martin's Press, 1994), pp.114–15.

54. See, for example, K.K. Nanda, *Conquering Kashmir—A Pakistani Obsession* (New Delhi: Lancers Books, 1994), pp. 303–5; Maheshwari, *Crescent Over Kashmir*, pp. 13, 51–52; and Sehgal, *Converted Kashmir*, pp. 318–26.

55. Ganguly, *The Crisis in Kashmir*, p. 16.

56. David Lamb, "Pakistan's New War on Extremism," *Los Angeles Times* Web service, 4 January 2002.

57. On this point, see Praveen Swami, "The Missing Peace Dividend," *Frontline* Web service 18: 7 (31 March–13 April 2001).

58. See press release, "'Independence is the First Option'—Shabir Shah," Jammu Kashmir Democratic Freedom Party Internet-Mail, 10 August 1998; and "Shabir Shah Presents Kashmiri Perspective Just Ahead of Indo-Pak Talks," Jammu Kashmir Democratic Freedom Party Internet-Mail, 12 October 1998. The latter transmits the contents of a JKDFP memorandum addressed to United Nations Secretary General Kofi Annan. Shabir Shah's position was akin to that of Jammu and Kashmir Liberation Front (JKLF) chairman Amanullah Khan, who from his perch in Islamabad has been an outspoken advocate of the independence option for many years. See Raja Asghar, "Kashmir Group Puts Forward Independence Formula," Kashmir Record & Research Cell, Kashmir Global Network Web service, 24 June 1998. See also "JKLF Calls Pakistan 'Occupier,'" *Dawn*, 12 October 1998.

59. The discussion here is based on one published and two draft essays by Yoginder Sikand: "Changing Course of Kashmiri Struggle," pp. 218–27; "Islamist Militancy in Kashmir: The Case of the Lashkar-i-Tayyeba"; and "The Emergence and Development of the Jama'at-i-Islami of Jammu and Kashmir [1940s–1990]." Sikand supplied the author with copies of the latter two essays.

60. Sikand, "Changing Course of Kashmiri Struggle," pp. 226–27.

61. The theme of majoritarian (Hindu) communalism is the focus of a number of recent studies, including: Achin Vanaik, *The Furies of Indian Communalism:*

Religion, Modernity and Secularization (London: Verso, 1997); David Ludden (ed.), *Contesting the Nation: Religion, Community, and the Politics of Democracy in India* (Philadelphia: University of Pennsylvania, 1996); Madan, *Modern Myths, Locked Minds*; Asma Barlas, *Democracy, Nationalism, and Communalism: The Colonial Legacy in South Asia* (Boulder: Westview Press, 1995); Peter van der Veer, *Religious Nationalism: Hindus and Muslims in India* (Berkeley: University of California Press, 1994); and Gerald James Larson, *India's Agony over Religion* (Albany: State University of New York Press, 1995). For a brief overview, see Mark Juergensmeyer, *The New Cold War? Religious Nationalism Confronts the Secular State* (Berkeley: University of California Press, 1993), pp. 81–99.

62. Ayesha Jalal, *Democracy and Authoritarianism in South Asia: A Comparative and Historical Perspective* (Cambridge: Cambridge University Press, 1995).

63. Ibid., p. 18.

64. Ibid., p. 179. "Using communalism as a counterweight to regionalism," Jalal pointed out earlier in the book (p. 95),

> was hardly a novelty in Indian politics. Deployed by the colonial state against both Indian nationalist and separatist Muslim politics, it had provided the Congress high command in 1947 with the means to cut Jinnah's and the Muslim League's demands down to size. Yet there was an important new dimension in the centre's evocation of communalism in the 1980s. Encountering implacable opposition from an array of regional forces, the political centre gave Hindu majoritarian communalism its head.

65. Ibid., p. 180. (Emphasis added.)

66. Ibid., p. 176.

67. Navnita Chadha Behera, *State, Identity & Violence: Jammu, Kashmir & Ladakh* (New Delhi: Manohar Books, 2000).

68. Ibid., p. 22.

69. Ibid., p. 27.

70. Ibid., p. 30.

71. Pakistan's Two Nation Thesis had already been severely undermined, of course, by the successful secessionist bid of Bengali-speaking, but Muslim-majority, East Pakistan in the 1971 Bangladesh war.

72. Rogers Brubaker, *Nationalism Reframed: Nationhood and the National Question in the New Europe* (Cambridge: Cambridge University Press, 1996), p. 5.

73. Ibid., p. 58. Brubaker explains the matter thusly: "External national homelands are constructed through political action, not given by the facts of ethnic demography. A state becomes an external national 'homeland' for 'its' ethnic diaspora when political or cultural elites define ethnonational kin in other states as members of one and the same nation, claim that they 'belong,' in some sense, to the state, and assert that their condition must be monitored and their interests protected and promoted by the state; and when the state actually does take action in the name of monitoring, promoting, or protecting the interests of its ethnonational kin abroad."

74. Ibid., p. 68.

75. Ibid., p. 68.

76. A.H. Suharwardy, *Tragedy in Kashmir* (Lahore: Wajidalis, 1983), p. 209.

77. See the letter from General Iskandar Mirza to Sir Olaf Caroe, written on 26

September 1968, reprinted as Appendix II in Prem Shankar Jha, *Kashmir 1947: Rival Versions of History* (Delhi: Oxford University Press, 1996), pp. 139–40.

78. Ayesha Jalal, *The State of Martial Rule: The Origins of Pakistan's Political Economy of Defence* (New York: Cambridge University Press, 1990), p. 59. (Emphasis added.)

79. Mohammad Ayub Khan, *Friends Not Masters: A Political Autobiography* (New York: Oxford University Press, 1967), p. 38.

80. Keith Callard, *Pakistan: A Political Study* (London: Allen & Unwin, 1957), fn 1, p. 279.

81. Lawrence Ziring, *The Ayub Khan Era: Politics in Pakistan, 1958–1969* (Syracuse: Syracuse University Press, 1971), p. 6; and Jalal, *The State of Martial Rule*, pp. 119–24.

82. Jalal, *The State of Martial Rule*, p. 120.

83. Herbert Feldman, *From Crisis to Crisis: Pakistan 1962–1969* (London: Oxford University Press, 1972), p. 158.

84. Ibid., fn 28, p. 158.

85. For background on Sir Owen Dixon's "regional plebiscites" proposal, see Josef Korbel, *Danger in Kashmir*, revised edition (Princeton: Princeton University Press, 1966), pp. 170–76; and Alastair Lamb, *Kashmir: A Disputed Legacy, 1846–1990* (Hertingfordbury: Roxford Books, 1991), pp. 171–75.

86. Interview, Islamabad, May 1997.

87. Interview, Lahore, May 1997.

88. Interview, Islamabad, May 1997.

89. Interview, Islamabad, May 1997.

90. Interview, Lahore, May 1997.

91. Interview, Lahore, May 1997.

92. Interview, Karachi, May 1997.

93. Interview, Lahore, May 1997.

94. Interview, Islamabad, May 1977. The Pakistan government's actual maneuvering space when it comes to Kashmir may be more limited than was implied by this respondent. Electorally speaking, any imaginable Pakistani national leader, whether military or civilian, is highly dependent on Punjab province, the most populous and prosperous of the four provinces, and it is there that his or her political fate is likely to be decided. There are strong pro-Kashmiri lobbies in that province—in the business community, the legal profession, the civil service, and military. It is politically perilous to ignore them.

95. Ibid.

96. Ibid.

97. Brubaker, *Nationalism Reframed*, p. 63.

98. Ibid., p. 63.

99. Ibid., p. 66.

100. Brubaker acknowledges that nationalization politics and processes varied widely even among the states that emerged from the disintegration of these three imperial realms. He argues, nevertheless, that the following seven "elements" were fairly common to all of those states: "

(1) the existence (more precisely the conceived or understood or 'imagined' existence) of a 'core nation' or nationality, defined in ethnocultural terms, and

sharply distinguished from the citizenry or permanent resident population of the state as a whole; (2) the idea that the core nation legitimately 'owns' the polity, that the polity exists as the polity *of* and *for* the core nation; (3) the idea that the core nation is not flourishing, that its specific interests are not adequately 'realized' or 'expressed' despite its rightful 'ownership' of the state; (4) the idea that specific action is needed in a variety of settings and domains to promote the language, cultural flourishing, demographic predominance, economic welfare, or political hegemony of the core nation; (5) the conception and justification of such action as remedial or compensatory, as needed to counterbalance and correct for previous discrimination against the nation before it had 'its own' state to safeguard and promote its interests; (6) mobilization on the basis of these ideas in a variety of settings—legislatures, electoral campaigns, the press, associations, universities, the streets—in an effort to shape the policies or practices of the state, of particular organizations, agencies, or officials within the state, or of nonstate organizations; and (7) the adoption—by the state, by particular state agencies and officials, and by nonstate organizations—of formal and informal policies and practices informed by the ideas outlined above." *Nationalism Reframed*, pp. 83–84.

101. Maya Chadda, *Ethnicity, Security, and Separatism in India* (New York: Columbia University Press, 1997).
102. Ibid., pp. 11–15.
103. Ibid., p. 12.
104. Ibid., pp. 12–13.
105. Ibid., p. 14.
106. Ibid., p. 15.
107. Ibid., p. 17.
108. Ibid., pp. 28–29.
109. Ibid., p. 70.
110. Ibid., p. 70.
111. Ibid., p. 142.
112. Ibid., p. 21.
113. Ibid., p. 143.
114. Ibid., pp. 17–18.
115. Ibid., p. 214.
116. For an unusually enterprising exhibition of research methodologies that may be employed to track identity change in situations of ethnic crisis, see David D. Laitin, *Identity in Formation: The Russian-speaking Populations in the Near Abroad* (Ithaca: Cornell University Press, 1998). Laitin's focus is language, which probably lends itself to empirical study better than religion.
117. Huntington, *The Clash of Civilizations and the Remaking of World Order*, pp. 272–91.

Chapter 4. The Problem of Conflict Resolution: The Autonomy Puzzle

1. Just how influential liberal lobbies have become in the United States is the focus of Jeffrey Berry's book *The New Liberalism: The Rising Power of Citizen*

Groups. (Washington, D.C.: Brookings Institution, 1998). For an interesting comment on this book, see Robert J. Samuelson, "Stealth Power Brokers," *Washington Post*, 8 December 1999, p. A33.

2. Words taken from one of the institute's application forms.

3. Benjamin Schwarz, "The Diversity Myth," *Atlantic Monthly* 275:5 (May 1995): 57.

4. Donald L. Horowitz, "Self-determination: Politics, Philosophy, and Law," in *Ethnicity and Group Rights*, Ian Shapiro and Will Kymlicka (eds.) (New York: New York University Press, 1997), p. 422. Among other useful discussions of self-determination, see Hurst Hannum, *Autonomy, Sovereignty, and Self-Determination*, revised edition (Philadelphia: University of Pennsylvania Press, 1990); Dov Ronen, *The Quest for Self-Determination* (New Haven: Yale University Press, 1979); Morton H. Halperin and David J. Scheffer, *Self-Determination in the New World Order* (Washington, D.C.: Carnegie Endowment for International Peace, 1992); and Margaret Moore (ed.), *National Self-Determination and Secession* (Oxford: Oxford University Press, 1998).

5. The pros and cons of secession are discussed in: Gnanapala Wellengama, *Minorities' Claims: From Autonomy to Secession—International Law and State Practice* (Aldershot: Ashgate, 2000); Allen Buchanan, *Secession: The Morality of Political Divorce from Fort Sumter to Lithuania and Quebec* (Boulder: Westview, 1991); Lee C. Buchheit, *Secession: The Legitimacy of Self-Determination* (New Haven: Yale University Press, 1978); and several essays in Moore (ed.), *National Self-Determination and Secession.*

6. For a recent survey of autonomy's application in countries around the world, see Yash Ghai (ed.), *Autonomy and Ethnicity: Negotiating Competing Claims in Multi-ethnic States* (Cambridge: Cambridge University Press, 2000). See also: Vernon Bogdanor, "Forms of Autonomy and the Protection of Minorities," *Daedalus* 126:2 (Spring 1997), pp. 65–87; and John Coakley, "Approaches to the Resolution of Ethnic Conflict: The Strategy of Non-territorial Autonomy," 15:3 (1994), pp. 297–314.

7. For legal documentation on many of them, see P.S. Datta, *Ethnic Peace Accords in India* (New Delhi: Vikas Publishers, 1995).

8. See Robert G. Wirsing, *India, Pakistan, and the Kashmir Dispute: On Regional Conflict and Its Resolution* (New York: St. Martin's Press, 1998); and Robert G. Wirsing, ed., *Kashmir: Resolving Regional Conflict* (Meerut: Kartikeya Publications, 1996). I also was a co-author of the privately published study team report, *1947–1997. The Kashmir Dispute at Fifty: Charting Paths to Peace* (New York: Kashmir Study Group, 1997).

9. Yash Ghai, "Ethnicity and Autonomy: A Framework for Analysis," in *Autonomy and Ethnicity*, Ghai (ed.), p. 8.

10. Timothy D. Sisk, *Power Sharing and International Mediation in Ethnic Conflicts* (Washington, D.C.: United States Institute of Peace, 1996), p. 5.

11. Ibid., p. 71.

12. Ruth Lapidoth, *Autonomy: Flexible Solutions to Ethnic Conflicts* (Washington, D.C.: United States Institute of Peace, 1996), p. 33. For additional commentary on ethnic autonomy and related issues, see Vernon Bogdanor, "Forms of Autonomy and the Protection of Minorities," *Daedalus* 126:2 (Spring 1997): 65–87; Hurst Hannum, *Autonomy, Sovereignty, and Self-Determination*, revised edition (Philadelphia: University of Pennsylvania Press, 1990); Ian Shapiro and Will Kymlicka (eds.), *Ethnicity and Group Rights*, Nomos XXXIX (New York: New York Univer-

sity Press, 1997); and Ted Robert Gurr, *Minorities At Risk* (Washington, D.C.: United States Institute of Peace, 1993).

13. For a sophisticated effort to classify the *cultural* rights of ethnic groups, see Jacob T. Levy, "Classifying Cultural Rights," in Shapiro and Kymlicka (eds.), *Ethnicity and Group Rights*, pp. 22–66. See also John Coakley, "Approaches to the Resolution of Ethnic Conflict: The Strategy of Non-territorial Autonomy," *International Political Science Review* 15:3 (1994): 297–314.

14. Lapidoth, *Autonomy*, pp. 49–58.

15. Ibid., p. 53.

16. Ted Robert Gurr, "Ethnic Warfare on the Wane," *Foreign Affairs* 79:3 (May/June 2000): 52–64.

17. Gurr, "Ethnic Warfare on the Wane," 53–54. Gurr's argument is more fully developed in his latest book, *Peoples Versus States: Minorities at Risk in the New Century* (Washington, D.C.: United States Institute of Peace, 2000).

18. A particularly good example of the trend is Will Kymlicka, *Multicultural Citizenship: A Liberal Theory of Minority Rights* (Oxford: Clarendon Press, 1995). See also Judith Baker (ed.), *Group Rights* (Toronto: University of Toronto Press, 1994); Donna Gomien (ed.), *Broadening the Frontiers of Human Rights: Essays in Honor of Asbjorn Eide* (Oslo: Scandinavian University Press, 1993); and Hurst Hannum, "The Limits of Sovereignty and Majority Rule: Minorities, Indigenous Peoples, and the Right to Autonomy," in Ellen L. Lutz, Hurst Hannum, and Kathryn J. Burke (eds.), *New Directions in Human Rights* (Philadelphia: University of Pennsylvania Press, 1989), pp. 3–24.

19. For a discussion of the Greenland and other post–World War II autonomy cases, see Lapidoth, *Autonomy*, pp. 99–167.

20. Sisk, *Power Sharing and International Mediation in Ethnic Conflicts*, p. 106.

21. Lapidoth, *Autonomy*, p. 12.

22. Sisk, *Power Sharing and International Mediation in Ethnic Conflicts*, p. 106.

23. Lapidoth, *Autonomy*, p. 13.

24. Autonomist models do, of course, continue to supply strategies of practical use in the less volatile circumstances that characterize many of the world's ethnonationalist conflicts. On this, see Ted Robert Gurr, "Nonviolence in Ethnopolitics: Strategies for the Attainment of Group Rights and Autonomy," *PS, Political Science & Politics* 33:2 (June 2000): 155–60.

25. Martijn van Beek, "Beyond Identity Fetishism: 'Communal' Conflict in Ladakh and the Limits of Autonomy," *Cultural Anthropology* 15:4 (November 2000): 526. Van Beek's observation echoes innumerable similar expressions of scholarly doubt about the authenticity of basic group identity. For one example, see Ronen, *The Quest for Self-Determination*, pp. 53–70.

26. For an excellent recent commentary on autonomy's limitations that is focused, like van Beek's, on the Ladakh region of Jammu and Kashmir, see Navnita Chadha Behera, "'Autonomy' in J&K: The Forgotten Identities of Ladakh," *Faultlines* 6:1 (Winter 2001): 35–59.

27. In the government of India's 1948 *White Paper on Jammu and Kashmir*, for instance, New Delhi maintained (p. 45) that

> [i]n Kashmir, as in other similar cases, the view of the Government of India has been that in the matter of disputed accession the will of the people must prevail. It was for this reason that they accepted only on a provisional basis

the offer of the Ruler to accede to India, backed though it was by the most important political organization in the State [Sheikh Abdullah's National Conference]. . . . The question of accession is to be decided finally in a free plebiscite; on this point there is no dispute. . . . The only purpose for which Indian troops are operating in Kashmir is to ensure that the vote of the people will not be subject to coercion by tribesmen and others from across the border who have no right to be in Kashmir. . . .

28. Law Kumar Mishra, "BJP Seeks Farooq's Ouster on Autonomy Report Issue," *Times of India*, 22 January 2000.

29. Balraj Puri, *J &K: Regional Autonomy* (Jammu: Jay Kay Book House, 1999). See also his essays "The Autonomy Debate," *Frontline* 17:6 (18–31 March 2000); and "Jammu On the Brink," *Hindu*, 21 August 2001.

30. *Regional Autonomy Committee Report* (Jammu: Ranbir Government Press, 13 April 1999), p. iv.

31. Ibid., p. 5.

32. For this point I am indebted to Martijn van Beek, in personal correspondence, 11 December 2001.

33. For a Jammu Hindu perspectives on the issue, see Hari Om, "The Plight of Jammu," *Hindustan Times*, 12 March 1999.

34. Navnita Chadha Behera, *State, Identity and Violence: Jammu, Kashmir & Ladakh* (New Delhi: Manohar, 2000), p. 265. Behera's enormously thoughtful and resourcefully researched book gives a detailed and revealing analysis of both the RAC and SAC reports.

35. *Report of the State Autonomy Committee* (Jammu, April 1999), p. 8.

36. Ibid., p. 77.

37. Ibid., p. 111.

38. Aijaz Ahmad, "Kashmir Conundrum: India, Pakistan, the United States, and the Question of 'Autonomy,'" *Frontline*, 17:15 (22 July–4 August 2000).

39. See "Text of Cabinet Decision on J & K Autonomy Resolution," *Hindu*, 5 July 2000.

40. Praveen Swami, "A Dangerous Game," *Frontline* 17:19 (16–29 September 2000).

41. The discussion and maps in *Kashmir—A Way Forward* (Larchmont, N.Y.: Kashmir Study Group, September 1999) draw heavily from previous work by Joseph E. Schwartzberg. See, for instance, his essay "An American Perspective—II," in *Kashmir, Resolving Regional Conflict: A Symposium*, Robert Wirsing (ed.) (Meerut, India: Kartikeya Publications, 1996), pp. 165–99.

42. *Kashmir—A Way Forward* p. 1.

43. Praveen Swami, "Partition Plans?" *Frontline* 16:21 (9–22 October 1999).

44. Praveen Swami, "A Dangerous Game," *Frontline* 17:19 (16–29 September 2000).

45. David D. Laitin, *Identity in Formation: The Russian-speaking Populations in the Near Abroad* (Ithaca: Cornell University Press, 1998), pp. 331–37.

46. See Stephen Van Evera, "Nationalism and the Causes of War," in *Nationalism and Nationalities in the New Europe*, Charles A. Kupchan (ed.) (Ithaca: Cornell University Press, 1995); and two essays by Chaim Kaufmann, "Possible and Impossible Solutions to Ethnic Civil Wars," *International Security* 20 (Spring 1996): 136–53, and "When All Else Fails," *International Security* 23 (Fall 1998): 120–56. For a recent and excellent review of the literature on partition (and a carefully drawn argu-

ment against its use to solve ethnic civil war), see Nicholas Sambanis, "Partition as a Solution to Ethnic War: An Empirical Critique of the Theoretical Literature," *World Politics* 52 (July 2000): 437–83. Finally, for an incisive critique of partition by an Indian-born writer, see Radha Kumar, "The Troubled History of Partition," *Foreign Affairs* 76:1 (January/February 1997): 22–34.

47. Stephen P. Cohen, "India Rising," *Wilson Quarterly* 24:3 (Summer 2000): 32–53. The article is much amplified in Cohen's *India: Emerging Power* (Washington, D.C.: Brookings Institution Press, 2001).

48. Cohen, "India Rising."

49. For just two of innumerable recent examples, see Sumit Ganguly, "Pakistan's Never-Ending Story: Why the October Coup Was No Surprise," *Foreign Affairs* 79:2 (March/April 2000): 2–7; and Robert D. Kaplan, "The Lawless Frontier," *Atlantic Monthly* (September 2000): 66–80.

50. "Comrades in Arms," *Times of India*, 9 October 2000.

51. For background on the Rashtriya Swayamsevak Sangh, see Walter K. Andersen and Shridhar D. Damle, *The Brotherhood in Saffron: The Rashtriya Swayamsevak Sangh and Hindu Revivalism* (Boulder: Westview Press, 1987).

52. Among other issues, General Musharraf was criticized for backtracking on a pledge to liberalize the country's blasphemy law. See Pamela Constable, "Pakistani Retreats In Battle for Reform," *Washington Post*, 5 June 2000, p. A9.

53. "Kashmir: A Taste of Peace," *South Asia Monitor* 25, Center for Strategic and International Studies (1 September 2000).

54. For a revealing commentary on the extent to which the Kashmir insurgency has been hijacked by those, on all sides of the conflict, who make a lucrative living from it, see Scott Baldauf, "In Kashmir, War Is Also Business," *Christian Science Monitor*, 13 July 2001, p. 1.

55. Task Force on America's Role in Asia, *America's Role in Asia: American Views* (San Francisco: The Asia Foundation, 2001), p. 45.

56. This relatively straight measure is urged in The Asia Foundation task force report, *America's Role in Asia*, p. 44.

57. Jessica Stern, "Pakistan's Jihad Culture," *Foreign Affairs* 79:6 (November/December 2000): 125–26.

58. Particularly comforting in the present foreign policy environment in Washington, D.C., was the observation made by Anatol Lieven, senior associate at the Carnegie Endowment for International Peace, in a recent issue of America's premier international affairs journal that to preserve the delicate domestic political balance within Pakistan "the United States will have to avoid tilting one way or the other in its relations with the subcontinent." "The Pressures on Pakistan," *Foreign Affairs* 81:1 (January–February 2002): 108.

Conclusion

1. "Pak. Concern Over Chenab Hydel Plant," *Hindu*, 2 June 2001; and "India, Pak Indus Team Likely to Meet in Delhi from May 29," *Asian Age*, 11 May 2002.

2. Admittedly, the Indus Waters Treaty is not guaranteed to withstand tensions between India and Pakistan. There have been disturbing reports in recent months, in fact, that the Indian government was considering abrogation of the treaty along with other punitive measures it was taking to force Pakistan's hand over the terrorism

issue. Celia W. Dugger, "India Calls Pakistan's Actions Against Terror Groups Cosmetic," *New York Times* Web service, 26 December 2001; and B. Muralidhar Reddy, "Indus Basin Treaty in a Limbo?" *Hindu*, 18 February 2002.

3. E. Sridharan, "Economic Cooperation and Security Spill-Overs: The Case of India and Pakistan," in *Economic Confidence-Building and Regional Security*, Michael Krepon and Chris Gagne (eds.), Report No. 36 (Washington, D.C.: The Stimson Center, October 2000), p. 79.

4. Ibid., p. 81.

5. Ibid., pp. 80–81.

6. See, for example, Colin J. Campbell and Jean H. Laherrere, "The End of Cheap Oil," *Scientific American* (March 1998): 78–83. For a recent essay that sounds the alarm for increased resource conflict, see Michael T. Klare, "The New Geography of Conflict," *Foreign Affairs* 80:3 (May/June 2001): 49–61.

7. For current and periodically updated profiles of the energy situations of India and Pakistan, see the U.S. Department of Energy (Energy Information Administration) country analysis briefings on these countries at Web site: www.eia.doe.gov.

8. "Indian LNG Projects Boom in Full Swing," *Oil & Gas Journal* 98:25 (19 June 2000).

9. Aurangzeb Z. Khan, "India and Pakistan: Bilateral Cooperation in the Energy Sector," in *Regional Cooperation in South Asia: Prospects and Problems*, Occasional Paper No. 32, Sony Devabhaktuni, ed. (Washington, D.C.: The Stimson Center, February 1997), p. 91.

10. See the two reports on this development by C. Raja Mohan, "'Peace Pipeline' on Fast Track," *Hindu*, 13 June 2001, and "Gas Pipeline: Iran May Help Overcome Pak. Concerns," *Hindu*, 14 June 2001. For two persuasive arguments that energy cooperation is the most promising route to conflict reduction between India and Pakistan, see Sridharan, "Economic Cooperation and Security Spill-Overs," especially pp. 89–94; and Shamila N. Chaudhary, *Iran to India Natural Gas Pipeline: Implications for Conflict Resolution & Regionalism in India, Iran, and Pakistan* (Web site: Trade Environment Database American University, January 2001). For additional commentary on the pipeline issue, see Gurmeet Kanwal, "Pipeline Politics: Hazards of Transporting Natural Gas to India," *Statesman*, 6 May 2001; and Shishir Gupta, "Indo-Iran Gas Project: Peace in Pipeline," *India Today*, 2 July 2001.

11. Chaudhary, *Iran to India Natural Gas Pipeline*, p. 1.

12. T.V. Parasuram, "Pakistan Urgest US Intercession on Kashmir," *Hindustan Times*, 29 June 2001.

13. Dennis C. Blair and John T. Hanley, Jr., "From Wheels to Webs: Reconstructing Asia-Pacific Security Arrangements," *Washington Quarterly* 24:1 (Winter 2001): 15–16. See also Dennis C. Blair, "Menaced by Asian Mind-Sets," *Australian* Web service, 16 November 2000.

14. In an interview with a correspondent for *Hindu* in June 2001, Deputy Secretary of State Richard Armitage was quoted as having said: "We [the Bush administration] want to have a friendly relationship with China. . . ." The relationship with India could not "be based against China . . . if it's going to be sustainable, if it's going to be credible. . . . If it were directed against China, no one in India would have confidence that it would last."

15. For an unapologetic defense of American foreign policy unilateralism, as defined by the George W. Bush administration, see Charles Krauthammer, "The New Unilateralism," *Washington Post*, 8 June 2001, p. A29.

Index

Vajpayee, Atal Bihari *(continued)*
  proposed meeting with Sharif, 31–32
  U.S. visit of, 112
Van Beek, Martijn, 202
Van Evera, Stephen, 216

W

Warikoo, K., 148
War on terrorism, 8–9, 89, 90, 229
  India-Pakistan relations and, 65–67,
    220–221
  Kashmir separatists and, 117–122

War on terrorism *(continued)*
  Pakistan's role in, 63, 64, 117, 118,
    120, 220
Washington Post, 49–50, 82, 101, 132
Wilson, Thomas, 114
World Bank, 88

Z

Zahid, Anwar, 26
Zaki, Akram, 26
Ziauddin, Lt. General, 29
Zinni, Anthony C., 30, 82

About the Author

Dr. Robert Wirsing is a South Asia regional specialist at the Asia-Pacific Center for Security Studies, Honolulu, Hawaii. He has held academic posts at a number of universities and research institutions in the United States, India, and Pakistan. Since 1965, he has made thirty research trips to the countries of South Asia. His publications include: *Pakistan's Security Under Zia, 1977–1988* (1991), *India, Pakistan, and the Kashmir Dispute* (1994), and *Kashmir: Resolving Regional Conflict* (1996).